Succession Planning and Retirement

Building a Practice of Value

Succession Planning and Retirement

Building a Practice of Value

Phil Shohet and Andrew Jenner

General Editors

145 London Road
Kingston upon Thames
Surrey
KT2 6SR
Tel: +44(0) 870 241 5719
Fax: +44(0) 870 247 1124
E-mail: info@cch.co.uk
Website: www.cch.co.uk

ISBN 1 84140 213 3

© 2002 Croner.CCH Group Ltd

All rights reserved. No part of this work covered by the publisher's copyright may be reproduced or copied in any form or by any means (graphic, electronic or mechanical, including photocopying, recording, recording taping, or other information and retrieval systems) without the written permission of the publisher.

Crown copyright legislation is reproduced under the terms of Crown Copyright Policy Guidance issued by HMSO and the Queen's printer for Scotland.

Typeset in the UK by Mac Style Ltd, Scarborough, North Yorkshire
Printed by Clays, Bungay, Suffolk

Contents

		Page
Foreword		xv
Contributing authors		xix
1	**The partnership deed – equity and salaried partners' agreements**	**1**
1.1	Introduction	1
1.2	Variations to the partnership agreement	2
1.3	The partner's duty of good faith	2
1.4	Clauses commonly included in a partnership agreement	3
1.5	Parties and definitions	4
1.6	Nature of business and duration of partnership	7
1.7	New partners – changes in the members of the firm	7
1.8	The name of the firm	8
1.9	Place of business	8
1.10	Duties of partners	9
1.11	Limits of authority	10
1.12	Insurance	12
1.13	Absence	13
	1.13.1 Holidays	13
	1.13.2 Illness and maternity leave	13
1.14	The provision of capital	15
1.15	Profits losses and liabilities	17
1.16	Account books, banking and drawings	18
1.17	Pensions	21
1.18	Management of the partnership business	22
	1.18.1 Unanimous voting	22
	1.18.2 Special majorities	22
	1.18.3 Simple majority	22
1.19	Death or retirement	23
1.20	Expulsion	24
1.21	Consequences of termination	26
1.22	Dissolution and winding-up	29
1.23	Covenants to protect goodwill	30
1.24	Salaried partners	31
1.25	Conclusion	32
2	**Equity cleansing**	**33**
2.1	Partner exit routes – setting exit routes by agreement	33
	2.1.1 Introduction	33

2.1.2	Partnership Act 1890 provisions		33
2.1.3	Winding up a partnership		33
2.1.4	Retirement by age		34
2.1.5	Selecting a retirement age		34
2.1.6	Early retirement on notice		34
2.1.7	The period of notice		34
2.1.8	The effective date of retirement		35
2.1.9	Illness		35
2.1.10	Mental illness		36
2.1.11	Timing of payments in the event of illness		36
2.1.12	Death		36
2.1.13	Timing of payments in the event of death		36
2.2	The underperforming partner		37
	2.2.1	Introduction	37
	2.2.2	Selecting suitable metrics	37
	2.2.3	Encouraging improvement	37
	2.2.4	Practical steps to improvement	38
2.3	Expulsion		38
	2.3.1	The need for expulsion provisions	38
	2.3.2	Expulsion without cause	38
2.4	Payment out		39
	2.4.1	The amount of payment	39
	2.4.2	Calculating the amount	39
	2.4.3	Goodwill	39
	2.4.4	The concept of partnership as a 'trust'	40
	2.4.5	Annuities	40
	2.4.6	Work in progress	40
	2.4.7	Partnership as an asset-accruing vehicle	41
2.5	The mechanics of payment out		41
	2.5.1	The timing of payment	41
	2.5.2	Interest	41
	2.5.3	Security	41
2.6	Post-retirement obligations		42
	2.6.1	Introduction	42
	2.6.2	Professional indemnity insurance	42
	2.6.3	Tax payments	43
2.7	Dispute resolution methods		43
	2.7.1	General	43
	2.7.2	Arbitration	43
	2.7.3	Expert determination	44
	2.7.4	Mediation	44
2.8	Conclusion		44

3	**Sources of finance**	47
3.1	Introduction	47
3.2	Sources of finance	47
	3.2.1 Partners	47
	3.2.2 The partnership bankers	48
	3.2.3 Asset finance	48
3.3	Overview of partnership finance – relative proportions	48
3.4	Partner finance	49
	3.4.1 Partner capital accounts	49
	3.4.2 Partner current accounts	51
3.5	Bank finance	52
	3.5.1 Limited liability partnerships	54
	3.5.2 Current account facilities	54
	3.5.3 Loan finance	55
3.6	Other sources of finance	55
	3.6.1 Asset finance	55
	3.6.2 Debt factoring	55
	3.6.3 Joint ventures	56
	3.6.4 Service stream finance	56
3.7	Managing growth	57
	3.7.1 Capital structure	57
3.8	Exit routes	58
4	**The future needs of clients**	**61**
4.1	Changing client requirements	61
4.2	Changing types of work	62
	4.2.1 Type 1 work	62
	4.2.2 Type 2 work	63
4.3	Changing client attitudes	63
4.4	Changing working methods	63
	4.4.1 Old versus new working methods	64
4.5	Changing practice structure	66
4.6	Networking for success	67
	4.6.1 The national firm	67
	4.6.2 The umbrella group	68
	4.6.3 Local organisations	69
	4.6.4 The individual approach	69
	4.6.5 Other professions	69
5	**Developing new skills, developing existing partners, and appointing new partners**	**71**
5.1	Introduction	71
	5.1.1 Development is everybody's responsibility	72
	5.1.2 Reviews and motivation	72

5.2		The practical issues of performance review	74
	5.2.1	Who reviews who?	74
	5.2.2	Preparation	74
	5.2.3	Questioning skills	76
	5.2.4	Listening skills	77
	5.2.5	Taking notes	78
	5.2.6	Listening techniques	78
	5.2.7	Receiving feedback	80
	5.2.8	The Johari window	80
	5.2.9	Giving feedback	80
	5.2.10	Giving feedback to partners and colleagues	82
	5.2.11	Praise and recognition	83
	5.2.12	Monitoring progress	83
5.3		Appointing new partners	84
5.4		Summary	85
6		**Networking**	**87**
6.1		Attitudes	87
6.2		How active is the firm in its marketing?	87
6.3		Awake, alive and alert	88
6.4		Fears of networking	89
6.5		The first move	90
6.6		Forgetting names	91
6.7		What to talk about	92
	6.7.1	So, what do you do?	93
	6.7.2	Small talk	94
6.8		Working the room	94
6.9		Groups	95
6.10		Your time is valuable – use it wisely	96
6.11		Giving and receiving	97
6.12		Systems and procedures	97
6.13		Critical role of the marketing personnel	98
6.14		Conclusion	99
7		**Mergers and acquisitions**	**101**
7.1		Why merge?	101
7.2		Defining the firm's objectives	102
7.3		The market place for merger, acquisition and fee disposal	103
7.4		Fee acquisition and disposal	104
	7.4.1	Buying and selling considerations	104
	7.4.2	Valuation	105
	7.4.3	Payout arrangements	106
	7.4.4	The sale agreement	106

7.5	Mergers		107
	7.5.1	Different types of merger	108
	7.5.2	Initial steps	109
7.6	Potential problems		109
	7.6.1	Goodwill	110
	7.6.2	Management structure	110
	7.6.3	Premises	110
	7.6.4	Profit-sharing arrangements	110
	7.6.5	Capital contributions	111
	7.6.6	Drawings and pension arrangements	111
	7.6.7	Working structures	111
	7.6.8	Information technology	111
	7.6.9	Professional indemnity insurance	111
	7.6.10	Professional standards	111
	7.6.11	Partner personal solvency	111
7.7	Procedures and meetings		112
	7.7.1	Initial meeting	112
	7.7.2	Exploratory stage	112
	7.7.3	Investigative stage	114
	7.7.4	Technical procedures	114
	7.7.5	Concluding stage	115
7.8	The agreement		115
7.9	Post-agreement follow-up		116
	7.9.1	Client review	117
	7.9.2	Partners and staff	118
8	**Consolidation**		**119**
8.1	Creating the right climate		119
8.2	Issues facing medium-sized practices		119
	8.2.1	Lack of investment	119
	8.2.2	Management structure	120
	8.2.3	Unlimited liability	120
	8.2.4	Retirement and retention	120
	8.2.5	Capital growth	121
	8.2.6	Succession	121
8.3	The concept		121
8.4	Perceived advantages		122
	8.4.1	The integrated approach	122
	8.4.2	National coverage	122
	8.4.3	Local knowledge with national support	123
	8.4.4	Cross-selling opportunities	123
	8.4.5	Other growth opportunities	123
	8.4.6	Single brand and culture	123

	8.4.7	Incentivised staff	123
	8.4.8	Central support functions	124
8.5	The disadvantages		124
	8.5.1	Undercapitalisation	124
	8.5.2	Market fluctuations	124
	8.5.3	Failure to achieve targets	125
	8.5.4	Initial income reductions and other considerations	125
8.6	Conclusion		125
9	**Property issues**		**127**
9.1	Introduction		127
9.2	Forms of property tenure		128
	9.2.1	Freehold	128
	9.2.2	Leasehold	129
	9.2.3	Intermission	132
9.3	Property strategies – making your property work for you		132
	9.3.1	Ownership structures	133
9.4	Leasehold strategies		137
	9.4.1	Repair/dilapidation	137
	9.4.2	Planning for growth/contraction	137
	9.4.3	Leasehold disposals	138
	9.4.4	Over-rented premises	138
	9.4.5	Short lease term	138
	9.4.6	Old fashioned building	139
	9.4.7	A declining market	139
9.5	Conclusion		139
10	**IT (internal/external)**		**141**
10.1	Information technology (IT)		141
10.2	IT practice survey		142
10.3	Technology and practice		146
10.4	Knowledge management systems		147
10.5	Learning		148
10.6	Technology assessment		149
10.7	IT staff in practice		150
10.8	Broadband and its impact in the UK		151
10.9	Security is the best policy		154
10.10	Extensible business reporting language (XBRL)		155
Appendix 1	Definitions		158
Appendix 2	The Technology Leadership Scorecard™		159
11	**Professional indemnity insurance**		**161**
11.1	Housekeeping to build your business		161
11.2	What level of cover should be taken?		163

11.3	Financial services – a way to increase the turnover of your practice and add value	163
11.4	Run-off	164
11.5	Succession planning from within	165
11.6	Examples of claims within the profession	166
	11.6.1 Complacency and bad habits	166
	11.6.2 Turning a blind eye	166
	11.6.3 Offering advice on a subject you do not specialise in	166
	11.6.4 Failure to understand a potentially complex subject	166
	11.6.5 Loss of document cover	167

12	**Financial management**	**169**
12.1	Introduction	169
12.2	Strategy and planning	169
12.3	Profitability and scope for improvement	171
12.4	Fees	173
12.5	Managing time	174
12.6	Other expenditure	177
12.7	Working capital	177
12.8	Cash management	179
12.9	Managing work in progress	180
	12.9.1 Booking time	180
	12.9.2 Monitoring and analysing work in progress	181
	12.9.3 Recognising unbillable time	181
	12.9.4 Converting work in progress into fees	181
12.10	Managing debt	182
	12.10.1 Responsibility for overall policy and control	182
	12.10.2 Risk management	183
	12.10.3 Terms of business	184
	12.10.4 Invoicing and collection	184
	12.10.5 Monitoring and recovery	185
	12.10.6 Criteria	185
12.11	Performance data	186

13	**Quality control**	**187**
13.1	Why have quality control?	187
13.2	What should quality control cover?	187
13.3	Why should a firm with competent partners and staff need quality control?	188
13.4	How can quality control help?	189
	13.4.1 Profitability	189
	13.4.2 Retaining existing clients	190
	13.4.3 Gaining new clients	190

	13.4.4	Fee negotiations	190
	13.4.5	Recruiting	191
	13.4.6	Training	192
	13.4.7	Technical skills and competence	193
	13.4.8	Standard audit documents	193
	13.4.9	Staff and job planning	194
	13.4.10	Performance appraisal	194
	13.4.11	Promotion policies	195
	13.4.12	Client relations (including responses to letters)	196
	13.4.13	Inefficient practices by partners and managers	198
	13.4.14	The structure of the firm	198
13.5	Establishing and maintaining effective quality-control procedures		199
	13.5.1	Complying with quality-control requirements where the firm is a registered auditor	199
	13.5.2	Striking the balance between standards and profitability	200
	13.5.3	Quality control beyond compliance	200
13.6	Using external quality controllers		201
	13.6.1	What are the advantages of using an external quality controller?	201
13.7	Keeping the quality-control system running		202
	13.7.1	Essential steps to maintaining effective quality control	202
13.8	Succession planning and quality control		204
Appendix 1	Questions that an effective quality-control system should be able to answer		205
Appendix 2	Qualities of an effective quality controller		208

14	**Marketing and promotion**	**211**
14.1	Introduction	211
14.2	Strategic business plan	211
14.3	Strategic tools	212
	14.3.1 Brand development	212
	14.3.2 Website	214
	14.3.3 Marketing planning	215
	14.3.4 Marketing communications	219
14.4	Conclusion	223

15	**Motivational leadership**	**225**
15.1	Introduction	225
	15.1.1 What can be changed?	226
	15.1.2 Is there a choice?	226
	15.1.3 Are leaders born or made?	226
15.2	Motivation	232

		15.2.1	Possible characteristics of motivated, demotivated and unmotivated people	232
		15.2.2	Understanding people	233
		15.2.3	Maslow's hierarchy of needs	234
		15.2.4	Macgregor's theory (the X-Y theory)	236
		15.2.5	Hertzberg's motivational theory	236
		15.2.6	Leaders/managers and motivation	237
		15.2.7	Getting the best out of people	238
	15.3	Summary		240
16	**The structure of a practice**			**241**
	16.1	Introduction		241
		16.1.1	Organisation and growth	242
		16.1.2	Organisation and clients	245
		16.1.3	Organisation charts	246
		16.1.4	Organisation of operations	249
		16.1.5	Information technology	251
		16.1.6	Alternative structures	251
17	**The managing partner – how to run a practice**			**255**
	17.1	Leadership		255
	17.2	Management		255
	17.3	Planning		257
	17.4	Coaching		259
	17.5	Anticipation		259
	17.6	Culture		260
	17.7	Approach to the markets		261
	17.8	Partner rewards		262
	17.9	Ownership		263
	17.10	Valuation		263
	17.11	Succession		264
18	**Taxation aspects of succession and retirement**			**265**
	18.1	Introduction		265
	18.2	Income tax aspects of retirement/introduction of a partner		265
		18.2.1	The current-year basis of assessment	265
		18.2.2	Withdrawal of cash basis for professions	267
		18.2.3	Work-in-progress valuation	269
	18.3	Provision for retirement		269
		18.3.1	Pension provision	269
		18.3.2	Annuities to retired partners	272
		18.3.3	Consultancy arrangement	272
	18.4	Capital gains tax (CGT)		273
		18.4.1	The basics	273

	18.4.2	Taper relief	274
	18.4.3	Disposal of a partnership asset	274
	18.4.4	Retirement and goodwill	275
	18.4.5	Payments for goodwill by incoming partner	276
	18.4.6	Change in the capital-sharing ratio	276
	18.4.7	Distribution of assets in specie	277
18.5	Inheritance tax		277
18.6	Value Added Tax (VAT)		278
18.7	Partnership mergers		278
	18.7.1	Income tax	279
	18.7.2	CGT	280
	18.7.3	VAT	281

19 HR strategy 283

19.1	Background		283
19.2	Identifying the requirements		283
19.3	Impact of technology		284
19.4	Staff planning and succession planning		285
19.5	HR strategies and solutions		285
	19.5.1	Hours of work	286
	19.5.2	Appraisal and development	286
	19.5.3	Training	287
	19.5.4	Coaching and mentoring	287
	19.5.5	Communication	287
19.6	Reward and performance payments		288
	19.6.1	Basic salaries	288
	19.6.2	Overtime payments	289
	19.6.3	Performance payments	289
19.7	Other benefits		290
	19.7.1	Recruitment	291
	19.7.2	Responsibility	291
	19.7.3	Advertising and media	292
	19.7.4	Use of website and the internet	292
	19.7.5	Use of recruitment agencies	293
	19.7.6	Networking	293
	19.7.7	Staff introductions	294
	19.7.8	Interview and assessment procedures	294
	19.7.9	Offer procedures and approval	295
	19.7.10	Referencing procedures	295
	19.7.11	Initial review of performance	296
	19.7.12	Retention	296
19.8	Support staff		297
19.9	Summary		297

Index   299

Foreword

A key issue facing independent firms of all sizes today is that of succession: how to fund the retirement of older partners whilst maintaining the profitability of the practice and making it an attractive proposition for potential incoming equity partners, merger partners or purchasers. Due to the trends and influences on the way the profession has developed in the last two decades, and because very few practices have given sufficient thought to succession, many will have to resolve major financial problems in the coming years.

To find out why this situation has arisen, we need to examine the way in which the profession has changed during the last 20 years. For the majority of practices in the 1980s the emphasis was on growth and development. This was followed by severe recession during which many firms were simply struggling to survive as best they could with no thought for expansion. Costs were cut, but partners retained. Special work all but disappeared, and many firms ceased training students. In recent years growth has again become a possibility, but global political and economic volatility mean that uncertainty is never far away. The majority of the firms that have expanded in recent years have done so through merger and not through organic growth.

We are left with the legacy of a profession with a middle-age spread; 45 per cent of partners are aged 45 or over. Most of them will be looking to retire at 60 or 65, and unless the average age of partnerships can be substantially reduced in the next few years, funding these retirements will place an enormous financial burden on any practice that has not had the foresight to develop a succession plan.

Practices with a high proportion of older partners should be looking to appoint younger replacements to fund their exit routes. However, attracting the right calibre of prospective partners is proving very difficult. There is a dearth of younger members of the profession who find the concept of partnership an attractive one. Many young accountants simply do not want to make the financial commitment or take on the responsibilities and risks associated with partnership. They are quite happy to remain as salaried employees, or to work outside of practice in a senior role. For some this is a very attractive option. Not for them no pain, no gain!

It is clear from all benchmarking surveys and available evidence that, in real terms, the financial remuneration of equity partners has changed very little in the last 10 years. There is a widening gap between high-earning firms and the remaining majority of average or below-average performers. This is undoubtedly one of the key reasons for the risk-averse attitude of prospective younger partners. Coupled with financial considerations are the major lifestyle changes that have occurred in the last 20 years (later marriage, divorce, second families, younger families and education needs), as well as the increased work-related stress caused by regulation and legislation. Quite clearly the culture and structure of the average accountancy practice will require a radical shake-up if a partnership is once again to become the career goal of most young accountants.

It is not simply in the area of Human Resources that major changes are required if practices are to achieve continuity. Partners must have a very clear idea of the range of services their clients require in both the short and the long term. They must be prepared to implement the considerable structural and cultural changes that are necessary in order to service those needs in the most efficient and profitable manner. The key question to address is: 'what do my clients need and how do I know this?'

Technical and compliance work is no longer a growth area for small and medium-sized firms and will become even less significant in the not too distant future when the audit threshold is raised to circa £5m. Practitioners must therefore develop a much greater range of business advisory skills and be prepared to diversify into new areas of corporate and personal advice if they are to maintain business growth and profitability.

Growing businesses, principally owner-managed businesses, comprise the primary target market for the profession. They look to their accountants to provide a wide range of services in addition to compliance work. Business planning, managing growth, raising finance, profit improvement, tax planning, retirement planning, pensions and investments and mergers and acquisitions are just some of the many skills the modern accountant will need to provide in order to maintain profits and fees in the practice. Partners will need to make a considerable investment in skills by either re-engineering existing personnel (including partners) or by recruiting in the desired abilities; some of the recruits possibly having a fee following whilst others may have none.

With the emphasis moving from compliance to advisory work the trend is for some practices to divisionalise. And different ownership and management structures are emerging. Essentially, this involves separating compliance and non-compliance work, retaining compliance work within the practice and creating a separate company to handle all other aspects of the firm's activities. Not only does this improve efficiency, but it creates a business with value which can provide a dividend income for the shareholders or which can be viewed as a saleable asset to create an exit route.

Some firms are adding specialist departments through merger or acquisition, but unfortunately the majority of small and medium-sized practices have given very little thought to creating a practice structure that will service the needs of the clients, improve profitability and ensure continuity through effective retirement and succession planning.

In this publication our aim has been to address the question of building a practice of value, and planning for a healthy, proactive life (including retirement). We have brought together experts in every area of practice management and development to contribute their experience. Their advice, if followed, will enable practitioners to build businesses of real value whilst creating exit routes for retiring partners that will not be detrimental financially to continuing development and profitability.

If their contributions provoke your thoughts, prick your consciences, and lead to positive action, then we can gauge our efforts a success. We wish you enjoyable reading.

Phil Shohet
Andrew Jenner
London June 2002

We would like to express our special thanks to our colleague Alice Spink at KATO Consulting for her assistance, patience and understanding in co-ordinating the contributions from the various authors, and for liaising with the team at CCH on our behalf.

Contributing authors

George Bull – Baker Tilly (Chapter 3 – Sources of Finance)
George Bull is a tax partner in the London office of Baker Tilly, Chartered Accountants. He is head of the firm's Professional Practices Group and is primarily involved in providing leading-edge business and taxation advice to professional firms. Before joining Baker Tilly he was head of the commercial services department in a law firm where he was involved in strategic decision making as well as day-to-day management. He is an approved Lexcel consultant to the Law Society and a member of the Association of Partnership Practitioners.

Jo Clarkson – The CapEx partnership (Chapter 5 – Developing new skills)
Jo Clarkson has been a director of the CapEx partnership since 1998, providing equity funding and ongoing management support to privately-owned businesses across a range of sectors. Prior to establishing CapEx, she spent 10 years with PKF, initially as a Director of Human Resources in Leeds, and from 1996 as a Director of the national consultancy practice. She combines HR experience in the accountancy profession with the wider experience of funding and developing businesses in which effective succession planning is critical to achieve commercial success. Jo Clarkson also reviewed **Chapter 15 – Motivational leadership** written by Sharon Klein of RD Associates.

Paul Druckman – Orange Consulting (Chapter 10 – IT)
A Chartered Accountant by training, Paul has primarily operated as an entrepreneur in the world of IT, and especially software, since qualification in 1979. Currently Managing Director of Orange Consulting, he has other business interests including new business ventures along with non-executive director positions. In 1999, 10 years after founding his own business, he sold his solution centre to an international IT group. He was previously a director and shareholder of the UK's leading provider of software for accountants during the 1980s.

Paul is also the Vice-President elect of the Institute of Chartered Accountants of England & Wales, and a member of the IT Faculty and of its SME Forum. He is also being an elected member of the Council for London.

Paddy Gregan – Brookstreet Des Roches (Chapter 1 – The partnership deed)
Paddy Gregan is the head of the Company Commercial Department at Brookstreet Des Roches in Oxfordshire. He advises a wide range of owner-managed businesses and professional partnerships on a range of legal issues, including agreements, practice finance, partnership disputes and property

matters. He was the advisory editor and contributor for Butterworths *The Encyclopaedia of Forms and Precedents* (Volume 30 – Partnership).

Finlay Forbes – CharterGroup (Chapter 13 – Quality Control)
Finlay Forbes is currently a practice consultant with CharterGroup specialising in technical compliance and quality control reviews. He qualified as a Chartered Accountant in Rhodesia (as it was then) in 1972. His previous roles have included being senior technical training manager for KPMG and training manager for Blick Rothenberg.

James Hewetson – Matthews & Goodman (Chapter 9 – Property Issues)
James Hewetson is a Chartered Surveyor with over 25 years' experience in practice in central London. He is a partner is Matthews & Goodman, a firm of strategic property advisors and consultants, with offices in London, Liverpool and Manchester. He is a leading partner of the valuation consultancy team and is frequently appointed as an Expert Witness.

Malcolm Hurst – Hurst (Chapter 17 – The Managing Partner)
Malcolm established Hurst & Company in 1982. From small beginnings Malcolm has led Hurst (as the firm is now called) to become a major independent in the North West. He specialises in providing strategic business, corporate finance and tax advice to private businesses.

Nigel Jones (Chapter 12 – Financial Management)
Former Council member of the ICAEW and Chairman of the Business Board, Nigel has recently retired from the TLT solicitors, after 12 years of managing and consulting in large regional legal practices. He was formerly Chief Accountant of Imperial Tobacco.

Will Kintish – Kintish (Chapter 6 – Networking)
Will Kintish is the Managing, and subsequently Senior, Partner with a 20-partner accountancy practice. He now presents and trains in the art and skills of networking. He is a member of the British Business Consultants and Trainers Academy and of the Professional Speakers Association. Information on all aspects of practice management is available from the website: www.kintish.co.uk

Chris Ladkin – SBJ Stevenson (Chapter 11 – Professional Indemnity)
Chris Ladkin is Managing Director of SBJ Professional – the specialist Professional Indemnity business within SBJ Stevenson Ltd Insurance Brokers (30 years in Insurance and the last 20 specialising in Professional Indemnity). The company arranges professional indemnity insurance for around 4,000 professional clients, 3,000 of which are accountancy practices.

Contributing authors

Andrew Mallet – Broomfield & Alexander (Chapter 18 – Taxation Aspects)
Andrew Mallet joined Broomfield & Alexander in January 2000 and is responsible for the delivery of the firm's tax advisory services.

He qualified as a Chartered Accountant in 1991 and spent five years in the corporate-tax department of an international firm, before specialising on the tax issues facing owners and their businesses. Andrew concentrates on formulating tax strategies for owner managers through their lifecycle, from the commencement of business to the ultimate disposal.

He is heavily involved in capital tax planning for business transactions, such as incorporating, acquisitions and disposals and exit and succession planning.

He is also a member of the Chartered Institute of Taxation, and is currently Chairman of the South Wales branch.

Bruce Page – Longbridge International (Chapter 19 – HR Strategy)
Bruce Page qualified as a chartered accountant and worked overseas for KPMG as an audit manager. On his return to the UK he moved into recruitment and subsequently spent five years as personnel director for Coopers & Lybrand before becoming Managing Director of a leading financial recruitment consultancy. Bruce currently works for Longbridge International where he specialises in HR work for professional firms and also executive search for the professions at senior levels.

Phil Shohet and Andrew Jenner – KATO Consultancy Ltd (Chapter 4 – The future needs of clients, Chapter 7 – Mergers and acquisitions, Chapter 8 – Consolidation, Chapter 16 – The structure of a practice)
Phil Shohet and Andrew Jenner are directors of KATO Consultancy Ltd., a specialist consultancy which provides practice development, fee acquisition and merger search and other advisory services to the accountancy profession. They are co-authors of the Institute's 1997 publication *Accountancy Practice Mergers and Fee Acquisitions*. Phil Shohet is a previous Commercial Director of the ICAEW and Andrew Jenner a previous Director of the Practice Advisory Service.

Simon Young – LawGroup UK (Chapter 2 – Equity cleansing)
Simon Young qualified as a solicitor in 1977. He was appointed partner with Veitch Penny in 1980 and was managing partner from 1980 onwards. He has an MBA in legal practice management and is a member of both the Council and the Standards Board of the Law Society. Simon is author of Limited Liability Partnerships (Tolleys) and writes a regular column on management issues for the New York Journal. He also lectures in a range of practice management topics.

Jim Yuill – CharterGroup (Chapter 14 – Marketing and Promotion)
Jim Yuill is director of marketing at CharterGroup, a leading UK network of accountancy firms. He has over 20 years' management experience in the manufacturing sector, including running his own business for 12 years. Before joining CharterGroup in January 2001, he was engaged in a consultancy for a marketing communications company involving analysis, strategic and creative marketing.

1 The partnership deed – equity and salaried partners' agreements

1.1 Introduction

Most partners say that they never look at their partnership agreement once it has been drawn up. It is a point of some debate as to whether some even read it before it is signed. For some other partners, actually reading the document can cause its own problems.

It should not be forgotten that because of the statutory definition of a partnership contained in s1 Partnership Act 1890 (PA 1890) the mere action of carrying on business in common with a view to profit will create partnership. The terms which may then apply might be left to oral evidence as to the intentions and dealings between the partners, but any remaining terms which are not clear will be implied by the statute.

Strictly speaking, a written agreement is not necessary but even where there is written evidence it can be, for example, as simple as an exchange of letters setting out the parties' intentions, the nature of the partnership business to be conducted and the date of commencement.

Having a formal partnership deed or agreement offers a number of advantages but also some disadvantages.

The main advantages are certainty and control of the business. Certainty is obtained because you can cover matters that would otherwise be the subject of some doubt or statutory implication. The document can be used to specifically answer any questions that may have arisen during the negotiation process and all partners can be clear about the nature and extent of their relationship with each other. Because the implied provisions of the PA 1890 do not usually suit the particular needs of a partnership, agreed controls can be ensured through the terms and conditions of a partnership agreement. For instance, in relation to profit shares, the PA 1890 assumes and implies equality, and in relation to termination the PA 1890 requires nothing but the most informal giving of notice to bring the partnership to an end.

In terms of disadvantages the complexity of settling an agreement and the costs of that exercise are usually given as reasons against having a formal written agreement. Perhaps an informal and successful business relationship which has worked well struggles with the formality or complexity of having to codify terms and conditions.

Experience demonstrates that relatively informal agreements are preferable with smaller working partnerships. It is true that drafting and negotiating the terms and conditions of a formal agreement can be a time-consuming process. However, a formal partnership agreement is able to deal with potential issues that may have been foreseen, so that if disputes arise there can be a common point of reference around which a matter can be resolved with certainty. Additionally the terms contained in a formal partnership agreement can be adapted to suit the type of profession being carried on to balance professional requirements and individual requirements.

1.2 Variations to the partnership agreement

As partners can reach agreement to overcome the limitations of the PA 1890, so they can by mutual consent vary the terms set out in a partnership agreement. Indeed, this right is expressly covered by s19 PA 1890, which provides that:

> 'the mutual rights and duties of partners whether ascertained by agreement or defined by the Act may be varied by the consent of all the partners, and such consent may be either expressed or inferred from a course of dealing.'

Sometimes variations can arise informally and through a course of conduct or dealing, but in other circumstances a supplemental agreement or deed of variation may be created to record the change.

1.3 The partner's duty of good faith

The purpose behind a partnership agreement is the creation or continuance of the firm as a unit, thus any powers conferred on the partners as individuals are intended to benefit the firm and not simply the individual partner alone. As such, those powers must be exercised in good faith and for the benefit of the firm as a whole. This means that a partnership agreement will generally be construed in such a way as to prevent one partner being able to use it to defraud another. Thus, any partner seeking to exercise power conferred by the partnership agreement in an attempt to conceal or hide fraud will be overturned by a court as ineffective. As a further consequence of this the courts will prevent one partner using the partnership agreement as a means to exploit power or obtain unfair advantage where this is inconsistent with mutual trust and confidence and working relationships at the heart of the partnership.

1.4 Clauses commonly included in a partnership agreement

There is no such thing as a standard partnership agreement, which is one of its strengths because it is adaptable and can meet the particular needs of a business or the parties joining together. However, there are some clauses that can be commonly found in a partnership agreement, including the following:

1. the parties, definitions and interpretation;
2. the nature of the business and duration of the partnership;
3. new partners;
4. the name of the firm;
5. the place of business;
6. duties of partners;
7. limits of authority;
8. insurance;
9. absence – holidays;
10. absence – illness and maternity leave;
11. the provision of capital;
12. profits, losses and liabilities;
13. accounts, books, banking and drawings;
14. pension;
15. management;
16. death or retirement;
17. expulsion or compulsory retirement;
18. consequences of termination;
19. dissolution and winding-up;
20. covenants to protect goodwill;
21. arbitration.

Although the application of the PA 1890 has been referred to, partners are unlikely to be conversant with the detail of that Act and so it is better and more usual practice to include express terms, even if to some degree they repeat aspects of the PA 1890.

1.5 Parties and definitions

Each of the parties to the agreement should be clearly identified and distinguished where relevant from each other. Care will need to be taken if the firm comprises chartered and certified accountants or unqualified partners, in the event of a multi-disciplinary practice. Particular reference needs to be made to the requirements of the Institute or Association (as the case may be) for rules on designation and in respect of audit work and investment business. In the case of larger and more complex modern practices with a multitude of partners, it may be preferable to create schedules of the names and addresses of each category of partner.

In the specimen clause below there is also an extract of a definitions section of a partnership agreement. The expressions are used later in this section.

THIS DEED is made the day of 200

BETWEEN the parties whose names and addresses are set out in the First Schedule

WHEREAS

(1) The parties to this Deed wish to carry on in partnership the business and profession of [chartered or certified] accountants from the Premises referred to below

(2) The said parties wish [their partnership to commence with effect from or to record that their partnership commenced from] (date) in continuation of the Former Partnership referred to below

THIS DEED WITNESSETH as follows:

1. DEFINITIONS AND INTERPRETATION

1.1 In this Deed and the schedules to it the following terms shall unless the context otherwise requires have (whether with or without the definite article) the following meanings:

Parties and definitions

'the Accountants'	(name of accountants) or any other firm of chartered accountants approved by the Partners to be appointed as accountants to the Firm
'the Association'	the Chartered Association of Certified Accountants
'Audited Accountants'	the accounts of the Partnership prepared and audited in accordance with clause [17]
'Commencement Date'	(date)
'Continuing Partners'	those Partners (or where the context admits only one remaining Partner that Partner) who were members of the Partnership immediately prior to the Succession Date and are not the Outgoing Partners
'this Deed'	this partnership deed as the same may be amended or supplemented from time to time
'Financial Year'	the period from (date) in one year to (date) in the next year (inclusive) or such other period as the Partners may agree from time to time
'Firm'	the Partnership firm
'Firm Name'	the name mentioned in clause [4.1] or such other name as may be chosen as the Firm Name under that clause from time to time
'Former Partnership'	the partnership carried on by (names) prior to the Commencement Date under [the Firm Name or (name)]
'ICTA'	the Income and Corporation Taxes Act 1988
'the Institute'	the Institute of Chartered Accountants in England and Wales
'Maximum'	the maximum percentage of the Net Relevant Earnings derived by a Partner from the Partnership for a Financial Year and which is for the time being eligible for relief under Chapter IV of Part XIV of ICTA
'Net Relevant Earnings'	the same meaning as in Section 646 of ICTA
'Outgoing Partner'	a Partner who ceases to be a member of the Partnership by his death or as a result of his retirement or expulsion in accordance with any provision of this Deed and including (where the context admits) the personal representatives trustee in bankruptcy or receiver of any such Partner

'Partners'	the parties to this Deed and such other persons as may be admitted to the Partnership including (where such have been appointed) their respective personal representatives trustees in bankruptcy receivers and administrators
'Partnership'	the partnership carried on under this Deed
'Partnership Bank'	(name of bank) or such other bank as the Partners may choose from time to time
'Partnership Interest Rate'	the base lending rate of the Partnership Bank plus [2%] or such other rate as the Partners may from time to time agree
'Premises'	(describe premises) and in addition to or in substitution for such premises such other property as the Partners shall agree
'Profits'	the distributable profits of the Firm in any Financial Year as shown in the Audited Accounts
'Succession Date'	in respect of an Outgoing Partner the date of his death retirement or expulsion (as the case may be)
'Tax'	income tax capital gains tax value added tax national insurance contributions (whether employer's employee's or self-employed) business rates (where levied in respect of premises) and all interest or penalties levied or leviable thereon as well as all other governmental levies or imposts in the nature of tax and all interest and penalties thereon in every case where leviable on the Partners by reference to the Partnership in respect of the Partnership business

1.2 In this Deed:

    1.2.1 reference to any statutory provision shall include any statutory provision which amends or replaces it and any subordinate legislation made under it

    1.2.2 the masculine includes the feminine

FIRST SCHEDULE

The Partners

(Equity Partners)

Name   Address

1.6 Nature of business and duration of partnership

The nature of the business needs to be clearly stated. The first and most important reason is that this then identifies the business that the partners have agreed to carry on and following on from that establishes the agency relationship which each partner agrees to, thus allowing individual partners to bind the partnership. As the business carried on is fundamental to the operation of the partnership it would be usual that only a unanimous decision of the partners could change the basic objectives.

The agreement will usually contain provisions identifying the date on which the business is to commence and its likely duration. So that one can identify when each partner acquires the authority to bind co-partners and from which time a partner is bound with his co-partners with unlimited liability for the debts and obligations of the firm, it is essential that the commencement date is certain.

It is possible for a date in the future to be specified if a business has yet to commence. To avoid any arguments or misunderstandings the actual date of commencement should always be shown, but if no commencement date is shown in the partnership agreement then it will generally be construed as beginning from the execution of the deed.

2. NATURE OF BUSINESS AND DURATION

2.1 *The Partners shall [with effect] from the Commencement Date carry on the business of the business and profession of [chartered or certified] accountants in partnership [and in continuation of the Former Partnership.] The termination of the Partnership with regard to a Partner shall not terminate the Partnership with regard to the remaining Partner*

2.2 *The nature of the Partnership business may be changed only by the unanimous vote of the Partners*

1.7 New partners – changes in the members of the firm

A partnership is a personal relationship between business people and the commitment of hard work in pursuit of a common vision has often been compared to marriage. As such, to admit a new member to the relationship should require the approval of all of the existing partners. Sometimes partnership agreements can provide that a simple or particular majority of the partners can determine the introduction of a new partner. In admitting a new partner either a new partnership deed or a deed of accession should be executed by all of the existing partners and the new partner to bind all of the partners to the terms and conditions of the partnership agreement.

3. NEW PARTNERS

If a new Partner is admitted to the Partnership that event shall be evidenced by a deed supplementary to this Deed executed by such new Partner and by all the other Partners so that the terms of this Deed shall after such change continue to govern the Partnership notwithstanding such change

1.8 The name of the firm

As the firm name is the principal means by which the business is identified it has clear importance and the identity can also go to the value of the goodwill of the business. In more recent times the firm name is often categorised as the 'brand' of the partnership. Often in the case of a small business the partners will simply choose their own names to describe the business, but in large partnerships this is impracticable and there may be some other name that the partners wish to choose. The name chosen must not cause confusion in the minds of the public with some other established business. The risk is that another business may successfully bring an action for passing off. Once chosen the name and identity of the partnership needs to be included on all documents, letterheads, nameplates and elsewhere in connection with the operation of the business.

4. FIRM NAME

4.1 *The Firm Name of the Partnership shall be (name) and the Partnership shall be known by and contract in the name of and conduct its business using only the Firm Name from time to time. Each of the Partners acknowledges that all proprietary and other rights in the Firm Name are vested exclusively in the Firm*

4.2 *The Firm Name shall be changed only by unanimous vote of the Partners*

4.3 *The Partners shall comply with the provisions of the Business Names Act 1985 and any regulations of orders from time to time made thereunder*

1.9 Place of business

The place of business is likely to be of significance and importance to the partners and possibly to the general success of the business itself. Usually the place of business is where the partnership books are kept. With larger national and regional and even international businesses, there may be more than one office.

Where premises are owned by one or more of the partners care will need to be taken to ensure that the partnership has adequate rights of occupation to protect the firm's commercial needs.

In some instances individual partners may have ownership of some property, but there is not necessarily an implied right that the partnership has rights of occupation if none have been expressly granted.

It is beyond the scope of this book to go into the many and various ways in which the ownership of premises for a partnership can begin, or how they can be recorded, but a range of ownership possibilities include:

(a) a lease being held as partnership property;
(b) a freehold or leasehold interest being licensed from an existing partner to the partnership;
(c) an existing freehold or leasehold interest held by an individual partner who grants the partnership a periodic tenancy or lease;
(d) an individual partner holding a freehold interest who agrees to convey that interest to a partnership on terms, either absolutely or subject to some sort of option;
(e) an existing lease which is held by one partner but held on trust for the benefit of the partnership and possibly pending assignment;
(f) an existing lease which is held by some of the partners in trust for the partnership as a whole;
(g) the grant of a new lease to all of the partners which is to be held as partnership property.

5. PLACE OF BUSINESS

The Partnership business shall be carried on at the Premises which at all times shall be Partnership property

1.10 Duties of partners

As mentioned above, the partnership agreement should be used to set out the details of the duties between the partners expressly, rather than rely on any which are implied from the Act. There will be a wide variation of partners' duties from firm to firm but they could commonly cover the following areas:

6. PARTNERS' DUTIES

Each Partner shall:

6.1 be just and faithful to the other Partners and at all times give to the other Partners full information and explanations of all matters relating to the affairs of the Partnership

6.2 devote his full time and attention to the Partnership (except when absent as provided in clauses 10 or 11) and diligently and faithfully employ himself in the Partnership business and use his best skills and endeavours to carry on that business for the benefit of the Partnership

6.3 punctually pay his separate debts and indemnify and keep indemnified the other Partners from and against all losses damages actions proceedings and costs that they may suffer or incur arising directly or indirectly from his failure so to do

6.4 (except where the Partners otherwise resolve) bring into the general account for each Financial Year all fees emoluments and commissions received by him from any office employment or position which he now holds or may in future hold while a Partner (and whether the same is held by virtue of his being a member of the Partnership or otherwise) [or which he may receive in any way in his capacity as (state capacity)]

6.5 observe the professional rules of practice and conduct of the [Institute or Association]

1.11 Limits of authority

As a result of the agency principal, which allows each partner to bind his co-partners to contractual obligations (s5 PA 1890), it is appropriate to impose sensible limits so that no partner has authority to exceed such limitations. Indeed, if a partner exceeds such authority that breach may also be the subject of an express indemnity requiring the defaulting partner to compensate his co-partners. Additionally, and more significantly, therecould be a material breach of duties which may lead to expulsion.

7. LIMITS OF AUTHORITY

7.1 Except where otherwise provided below no Partner shall without the consent of all of the others:

Limits of authority

7.1.1 either directly or indirectly and whether on his own account or otherwise engage in any other business profession or occupation or hold any office or employment while remaining a Partner

7.1.2 take any person into executive employment or grant any person a training contract or appoint any person as an agent of the Partnership

7.1.3 terminate the employment of any employee or agent of the Partnership except where in the circumstances instant dismissal is appropriate

7.1.4 lend any of the money of the Partnership to any person or persons or use the name or any other property of the Partnership other than for the purposes of the Partnership business

7.1.5 give any security or promise for the payment of money on account of the Partnership or enter into any guarantee for the indebtedness of the Partnership other than in the ordinary course of business or with the approval of the other Partners

7.1.6 enter into any bond or bail or become guarantor for any person

7.1.7 knowingly cause or suffer to be done or omitted to be done anything whereby the Partnership may be prejudiced

7.1.8 draw accept or indorse any cheque or other bill of exchange or promissory note on account of the Partnership unless authorised in accordance with the then current mandate of the Partnership Bank account

7.1.9 compromise compound or release any debt due to the Partnership except in the ordinary course of business for any single transaction up to a limit of [£   ]

7.1.10 assign mortgage or charge the Profits or Partnership assets or any part of them or his interest in the Partnership or any part of it

7.1.11 use to the detriment or prejudice of the Partnership or except within his authority as a Partner divulge to any person any trade secret or any other confidential information concerning the business investments or affairs of the Partnership or any of its clients which may come to his knowledge while he is a Partner and which shall not have become public knowledge (otherwise than through his default)

7.1.12 take responsibility for the conduct of any audit on behalf of a client of the Partnership when he is not for the time being authorised so to do pursuant to the Institute's Audit Regulations OR the Chartered Certified Accountants' Practising Regulations 1998

7.1.13 conduct any investment business otherwise than

(a) in accordance with the category of authorisation granted to the Partnership pursuant to the Institute's Investment Business Regulations OR the Chartered Certified Accountants' Investment Business Regulations 1996 or

(b) where so required by the said Regulations under the supervision of Partner or other person who is competent OR qualified to conduct such business thereunder

7.2 Any Partner committing a breach of any of the above provisions of this clause 7 shall indemnify and keep the other Partners indemnified from and against all losses damages actions proceedings costs and expenses arising directly or indirectly out of such breach without prejudice to any power of expulsion vested in the Partners by this Deed or otherwise

1.12 Insurance

These days professional partnerships must carry adequate professional indemnity insurance cover. It is likely that professional regulators also have requirements for cover.

In addition the practice is also likely to have assets of value which need to be insured and with regard to individual partners care needs to be taken as to the impact of sickness and possibly carrying adequate health cover. Insuring life and health and possibly the consequences of economic failure will carry significant premiums and provision should be made for the maintenance of such policies.

8. THIRD PARTY ASSURANCE

8.1 Should the Partnership Bank or any other person require one or more of the Partners to guarantee the Partnership's indebtedness (present future actual or contingent) or require one or more of the Partners to stand as surety for any such indebtedness the decision to accede to such a request shall require the consent of the Partners

8.2 Following a decision to give a third party assurance:

8.2.1 as between the Partners at the date it is given any liability actually incurred from the giving of the third party assurance or which may arise in the future under such assurance shall regardless of who formally gives the same be borne between those Partners in the proportions in which they are at such date entitled to share in the Profits

8.2.2 an Outgoing Partner shall be released from liability under this clause with effect from his Succession Date and in the event that he is one of the persons who formally give the third party assurance the Continuing Partners shall use their best endeavours to procure that he is formally released from it. Pending such release the Continuing Partners shall indemnify the Outgoing Partner and keep him indemnified from *and against all losses damages claims proceedings costs and expenses which he (or his estate) suffers as a result of delay in obtaining or failure to such release*

8.2.3 *on the admission of a person as a new Partner unless he agrees to the contrary he shall not share in any liability whether past present or future arising under clause 8.2.2 in relation to any third party assurance given before he became a Partner]*

1.13 Absence

1.13.1 Holidays

It is a quirk of the PA 1890 that the obligation on a partner to devote his full time and attention to the business of the firm does not, as a result, allow for holidays or absence. The ridiculous situation, therefore, arises that taking a holiday could be a breach of a partner's obligations in the absence of express provisions covering absences.

Nowadays partnership agreements not only cover absence due to holidays but also study leave and sabbaticals.

Some agreements go on to cover details as to how periods of absence may also require cover by a locum. In the case of extended absences or sabbaticals there may be some impact on a partner's rights and entitlements to share in profits.

10. HOLIDAYS

10.1 Each Partner shall be entitled to take in each calendar year in addition to public and religious holidays such annual holidays not exceeding [5] weeks in the aggregate [of which not more than [3] weeks may be taken consecutively] as shall be individually agreed with the other Partners from time to time and may with their consent carry forward into the next calendar year up to [one-half] of his entitlement.

10.2 A Partner may take as additional annual holidays under clause 10.1 a further period not exceeding [3] weeks for the purpose of caring for his family during or immediately after the adoption or birth of any new child or children of the family.

1.13.2 Illness and maternity leave

The absence or illness of a partner can often impose great strains on a practice. In particular if the absence is for a lengthy period then the other members of the firm will be left to carry out work that would have normally been undertaken by the absent partner. However, the absent partner will also need some security as to his financial arrangements. In drafting a partnership agreement, consideration needs to be given to a partner's incapacity due to illness and it should be agreed for how long the absent partner should continue to receive his share of profits. Are the other partners to have any power to expel an absent partner from the partnership and if so what are the precise circumstances? As previously mentioned, insurance may also be required or available to cover sickness.

It is now usual for modern partnership agreements to include provisions covering pregnancy and maternity leave. Although female partners are not entitled to the same statutory maternity rights as employees, it is generally accepted common practice that provisions similar to the statutory maternity rules are a sensible starting point when drafting maternity leave provisions in the partnership agreement.

11. ILLNESS OR PREGNANCY

11.1 A Partner who is incapacitated by reason of illness accident or other cause (exclusive pregnancy) from carrying out his or her duties under this Deed shall produce such evidence as [the management committee or the senior Partner] may reasonably require of his or her incapacity

11.2 A Partner who becomes pregnant shall be entitled to up to [6] months' leave of absence. Up to [11] weeks may be taken prior to the expected date of confinement but the period of leave may commence earlier if her doctor certifies that it should. Such absence shall not affect the rights of the Partner to leave of absence under any other provision of this Deed and shall not be counted for the purpose of clause 11.6

11.3 A Partner who becomes pregnant shall give to the other Partners as much notice as is reasonable in the circumstances of:

  11.3.1 her expected date of confinement
  11.3.2 the date on which she expects to leave work
  11.3.3 the date on which she expects to return to work

11.4 If a Partner is incapacitated as described in clause 11.1 or is on leave of absence under clause 11.2 then:

  11.4.1 for the first [3] months of absence the Partner shall continue to be entitled to his or her full share of Profits
  11.4.2 for the next [3] months the Partner shall be entitled to one-half of his or her full share of Profits
  11.4.3 for any further period of absence the Partner shall not be entitled to any further share of Profits

11.5 In calculating apportionments of a share of Profits under clause 11.4:

    11.5.1 calculations of absence shall be made on a daily basis out of 365 days allocated if necessary to the Financial Years in which the days of absence occurred

    11.5.2 repeated absences for any cause mentioned in this clause 11 which occur with less than [1] week's interval between them shall be counted as one continuous period of absence

11.6 If a Partner shall be incapacitated as described in clause 11.1 for an aggregate of [210] days in any period of 365 days the other Partners may during the continuation of the incapacity or within [2] months following the end of such period give to the incapacitated Partner not less than [4] weeks' notice in writing of their intention to terminate the Partnership as to the incapacitated Partner and at the expiration of such notice the Partnership shall be terminated but only as to such incapacitated Partner

11.7 Any Partner shall if so required by the other Partners on reasonable notice in writing allow himself to be medically examined by a medical practitioner nominated by the other Partners. The Partner so required shall authorise his own medical adviser to supply and the other Partners shall authorise the examining practitioner to supply each to the other such information and records about the health of the Partner concerned as shall reasonably be requested. The other Partners shall supply to the Partner concerned a copy of the report of the examining practitioner but only with the consent of the examining practitioner

1.14 The provision of capital

Every business needs to consider its capital requirement and for a partnership it is the partners who contribute that capital. Explicit provision needs to be included to cover these arrangements. Usually the proportions in which capital is to be contributed are stated in monetary terms, even if in some instances a contribution is made in kind. Quite often capital may be contributed unequally, but regardless of that fact clear provisions should indicate how much capital each partner is expected to provide and what entitlement a partner has for the return of capital upon a termination or dissolution or winding-up of the partnership.

Care needs to be taken regarding the basis on which any further capital may be required in the future. It may be that sums are required to be advanced by a partner in excess of the general contribution to capital but these may be regarded as loans and attract a preferential rate of interest.

The Partnership Deed – Equity and Salaried Partners' Agreements

---

Care should also be taken in the event of accepting a capital contribution in kind to avoid any misunderstanding. For example, if a partner allows the use of some asset, e.g., premises, that partner may assume that the provision of the premises is in some way a contribution to partnership capital and assets. However, if that is a mere concession then it should be clearly stated to be so.

When considering partnership capital it is also worth understanding what the capital goes to in terms of property, including land and buildings, intellectual property and other assets, equipment and know-how as well as the goodwill of the partnership.

12. CAPITAL AND PARTNERSHIP PROPERTY

12.1 All Partnership assets including goodwill and the premises in which the Partnership business shall from time to time be carried on shall be Partnership property and shall (unless otherwise agreed) belong to the Partners jointly or shall (if vested in any individual Partner) be held by him in trust for all of the Partners and the other Partners shall indemnify such Partner against all liability which may arise whether directly or indirectly out of such ownership.

12.2 Within [2] months following approval of the Audited Accounts in each year the Partners shall on the advice of the Accountants estimate the total amount of capital required for the Partnership in the then current Financial Year. Any excess of the amount so estimated over the existing capital shall be contributed by the Partners in the same proportions as those in which they are entitled to share in Profits for the Financial Year in question and their capital accounts shall be adjusted accordingly (such adjustment to take effect as at the commencement of the Financial Year in respect of which such contributions are made) and in order to give effect to such adjustments contributions or withdrawals shall be made by the Partners in accordance with the principles set out in this clause.

12.3 Where additional capital of more than £& is required from a Partner under clause 12.2 he may at his option either pay such sum to the Partnership or allow it to be withheld from his drawings under clause 14.1 and in either case so as to provide the total sum required in equal instalments over not more than [2] years.

12.4 Where under clause 12.2 the capital contributed by a Partner is in excess of the amount required from him then:

    12.4.1 the Firm shall pay him such amount (if more than £   ) in equal instalments over not more than [2] years from the end of the Financial Year just ended or in any other case within [3] months of the approval of the Audited Accounts for such Financial Year

12.4.2 amounts due to a Partner under clause 12.4.1 shall bear interest until payment at the Partnership Interest Rate

12.5 In all other cases in which additional capital is required from a Partner he shall pay such sum to the Partnership within [3] months after the other Partners shall have requested him in writing to do so

12.6 On a Partner's first joining the Firm the Partners shall by applying the principles set out in clause 12.2 estimate the amount of capital to be contributed by him as at the date of his joining and he shall pay such sum to the Partnership immediately

12.7 Except as provided in clause 12.4.2 no interest shall be payable upon the capital of any Partner

12.8 Except as provided in this clause 12 or with the agreement of all the other Partners no Partner may withdraw capital from the Firm

12.9 Any profits or losses or liabilities of a capital nature shall belong to or be borne by the Partners [in the same proportions as those in which they are or would have been entitled to share in the profits for the Financial Year during which such profits losses or liabilities arise or in the proportions set out in the third schedule] and shall be carried to the capital account of the Firm and treated as adjustments to capital on the basis set out in clause 12.2.

1.15 Profits losses and liabilities

Some consider that this is the most important clause in any partnership agreement. Profits are important to any business providing the reward and living to the partners, but also helping to meet the costs of administration of the business and the salaries of the employees. Thus, the partnership agreement needs to clearly provide how the net profits are going to be divided amongst the partners and in what proportions.

The basic principle under the PA 1890 is that, in the absence of agreement to the contrary, the net profits of a partnership in any year will be split equally regardless of what work was done and how the particular income was obtained.

The general example below merely sets out a simple approach to profit sharing, but there are now very well-established mechanisms for determining profit share by reference to fixed equity division, sometimes referred to as 'lock-step', which perhaps starts at a low level for a junior equity partner and rises to some sort of parity with seniority. Other profit arrangements are performance related, being linked to fee earning and sometimes referred to as 'eat what you kill'. Some formulae link performance-related profit sharing with systems of appraisal, others value a partner's performance not only in fee earning but in terms of management input, and others in terms of the ability to generate new work, introduce new clients, or develop new practice opportunities.

13. PROFITS, LOSSES AND LIABILITIES

13.1 The Profits of an income nature for each Financial Year shall belong to the Partners in such proportions as are set out in the second schedule or as shall otherwise be agreed by all of the Partners from time to time

13.2 All losses and liabilities of an income nature of the Firm shall unless otherwise agreed by all of the Partners be borne by the Partners in the same proportions as those in which they would have been entitled to share in the Profits for the Financial Year during which such losses or liabilities are incurred

SECOND SCHEDULE

Division of Profits

The Profits shall be divided between the Partners as follows:

Name of Partner	Percentage of Profits

1.16 Account books, banking and drawings

Money is the fuel on which the business runs and so controlling the flow of funds into and out of the business and also measuring and recording that is vitally important for all of the partners.

The partnership agreement will usually specify the partnership bank and identify how cheques and money received by the firm should be handled and paid into the partnership bank account. Reference should be made in the relevant clause to the rules of the Institute or Association covering the handling of clients' money, and can act as a reminder to comply with those policies. Further provisions can deal with the making of payments and cheque signatories. With the advent of electronic banking, internal authorities and regimes may be required to supplement bank mandates and authorities. For electronic banking sometimes all that is needed is the relevant password or pin code.

In addition, the partnership will need each year to produce a set of accounts in order to confirm the firm's profits and losses for the financial period.

It may also be agreed that the partnership will retain such sums as are required for partners' personal tax liabilities, but this is not now as important as it used to be following the Finance Act 1994 after which each partner is assessed individually on his or her share of profits with no joint and several liability for the firm.

14. DRAWINGS

14.1 Each Partner may draw [out of the Partnership Bank account] on account of his entitlement to his share of the Profits on the first day of each month such monthly sum and such additional drawings as may be agreed in advance by the Partners

14.2 Share of Profits shall not be drawn out unless and until there is a surplus available after providing for:

14.2.1 (except to the extent that all of the Partners otherwise agree) all anticipated future liabilities (including liabilities for Tax) of and claims against the Partnership

14.2.2 any sums which the Partners have agreed shall be left undrawn by a Partner in order to provide for the payment of premiums for life or pension policies taken out or to be taken out by him

14.2.3 any sums which the Partners have agreed shall be left undrawn by a Partner to recoup sums owed by him to the Partnership

14.3 If the total of the sums drawn out by any Partner in any one Financial Year together with other items debited against his current account for that year shall be found to exceed his entitlement for that year he shall repay the excess to the Partnership either:

14.3.1 immediately on the adoption of the Audited Accounts for that year to the extent that the amount of such excess put his current account into debit or

14.3.2 in all other cases within [28] days of his being requested so to do by the other Partners

15. BOOKS OF ACCOUNT

Proper books of account shall be kept by the Partners showing all receipts and payments on behalf of the Firm and all such other matters transactions and things as are usually written and entered into similar books of account. Such books of account shall not be removed from the Partnership Premises. Each Partner shall by himself or by his duly authorised representative have free access to such records and shall be entitled to take copies of them for the period during which he is a Partner and for [2] years after his Succession Date and the Partners shall at all times (and without prejudice to the generality of the foregoing requirements) comply with the requirements of the Institute or Association for the maintenance of books and records.

16. BANKING

All money and securities belonging to the Partnership shall be paid into the Partnership Bank account at or deposited for safe custody with the Partnership Bank. All cheques on the Partnership Bank account shall be drawn in the name of the Partnership [Any special rules for cheque signing or electronic banking.]

17. ANNUAL ACCOUNTS

17.1 As at the last day of each Financial Year the Partnership shall instruct the Accountants to take an account of the assets and liabilities of the Firm and of all dealings and transactions of the Firm during the Financial Year and of all matters and things usually contained in account of a like nature taken by persons engaged in a like business including without limitation due provision for Tax for which the Partnership is liable to account and in taking such account a fair and reasonable valuation shall be made of all items requiring valuation. In the preparation of such accounts there shall be brought into account the increase or decrease in value of all work-in-progress and money earned during the Financial Year to which they relate (whether or not such money shall have been actually received during that period) and proper provision shall be made for all bad and doubtful debts. No account shall be taken of goodwill. Such accounts shall be prepared for approval by all of the Partners within [6] months of the end of the Financial Year to which they relate [and shall be certified by the Accountants as giving a true and fair view of the Firm's affairs and profit and loss in the Financial Year]

17.2 The balance sheet shall be signed by all of the Partners and the Audited Accounts shall then become binding on each of them except that any Partner may require the rectification of any manifest error discovered in any of the accounts within [6] months of the date when the balance sheet was signed by all of the Partners

17.3 In the event that draft accounts are not approved by all of the Partners within [2] months of being submitted to them the Partners shall refer any point of dispute for resolution by such member of the Institute of Chartered Accountants in England and Wales as shall be nominated for this purpose by the President of such Institute and the ruling of such member on the point of dispute shall be final and binding on all Partners. In considering any such point of dispute such member shall be acting as an expert and not as an arbitrator

18. TAX

Each of the Partners (including a retired or Outgoing Partner) who is or was a Partner in any Financial Year shall (except as otherwise provided in this Deed) indemnify the other Partners Jointly and severally for his proportion of any Tax paid by the Partnership in respect of that Financial Year]

1.17 Pensions

Most firms now insist that partners make adequate provision for their retirement through a personal pension. Although it is often argued that this is not an area that other partners should interfere with and that it is a matter for personal financial planning for each individual partner, this agreement has an inherent flaw and weakness. In some cases considerable pressure (emotional and financial) can be put upon partners when a partner approaching retirement age suddenly indicates that no adequate provision has been made and the partner cannot afford to retire. This can in turn cause considerable problems for succession and redistribution of profit shares.

For all of these reasons a provision that requires partners to contribute to some form of personal pension scheme is essential and indeed remains a tax effective form of investment for the self-employed.

19. PENSION PREMIUMS

Each Partner over the age of [39] shall if appropriate continue to pay premiums in respect of retirement annuities and shall contribute to personal pension schemes approved for the purposes of Chapter IV or Part XIV of ICTA and shall (unless agreed by the Partners) pay by way of premiums in respect of each Financial Year an amount equal in aggregate to the percentage of his Net Relevant Earnings set out below:

Age of Partner at the end of the Financial Year	Percentage of Net Relevant Earnings to be the lesser of
40 to 44	the Maximum and 10%
44 to 49	the Maximum and 15%
50 and over	the Maximum only

1.18 Management of the partnership business

In the absence of any provision to the contrary the PA 1890 entitles each partner to participate in the management of the business. Depending on a number of factors this may or may not meet the needs of the particular firm. Careful consideration will need to be given as to whether some or all of the partners are to participate in the management of the business and to identify what partners' management rights and responsibilities may be.

It is usual to provide that decisions will be taken by a majority vote among the partners. However, for certain matters of business, a special voting majority may be required. Just like companies it is prudent to consider whether a certain minimum number of partners should be present at a partners' meeting in order to constitute a quorum to ensure that the decisions taken are valid and bind the other partners.

It is also usually sensible to consider a provision requiring regular partners' meetings to be held, say, on a monthly or quarterly basis. Nowadays and in larger and more complicated practices the day-to-day responsibilities for management can be delegated either to management committees of partners or to professional managers or Chief Executives who undertake the work in accordance with policy guidelines that may be mandated for them. It may also be the case that decisions are made so that the senior partner is formally appointed and then presides rather like a chairman at partners' meetings.

Some examples of different voting majorities are indicated below.

1.18.1 Unanimous voting

Changing profit shares, fixing partnership capital, dissolving the partnership or varying the provisions of the partnership agreement.

1.18.2 Special majorities

This includes changing partnership premises, altering pension provisions, changing insurance requirements or waiving restrictive covenants, and may possibly extend to appointing salaried partners.

1.18.3 Simple majority

This could cover decisions such as changing the firm name, altering holiday entitlement, deciding not to act for a particular client, changing the partnership accountants, or electing a senior or managing partner.

These lists can of course be extended to cover just about any foreseeable management decision to suit the particular partnership.

20. MANAGEMENT

20.1 Except where otherwise provided all matters relating to the management and conduct of the affairs of the Partnership and any agreement decision or approval required by this Deed to be made or given by the Partners shall be decided by votes taken at a meeting of the Partners. At such meetings each Partner shall be entitled to one vote and resolutions shall be passed by a simple majority vote except as provided in clause 20.2. Meetings of Partners shall be convened on not less than [14] days' notice given to each of the Partners [wherever he may then be]. The necessary quorum for such a meeting shall be not less than [two-thirds] in number of the Partners at that time present in person or by proxy (who shall be another Partner appointed by a written instrument signed by the absent Partner and presented to the meeting) [It shall not be necessary to give notice of a meeting to any Partner for the time being absent for the United Kingdom]

20.2 At a Partners' meeting those matters for which under this Deed the approval or decision of all of the Partners is required shall be resolved only by a unanimous vote of all those Partners present or voting by proxy

20.3 At a meeting of Partners at which a resolution for the expulsion of any Partner is sought the Partner in question shall be entitled to be advised a reasonable time beforehand of the grounds in support of his proposed expulsion. For such a resolution to be effective all of the Partners other than the Partner [or Partners as the case may be] whose expulsion is sought must vote in favour of the resolution whether attending the meeting or voting by proxy

1.19 Death or retirement

Failure to include specific provisions to cover the retirement or death of a partner can, under the provisions of the PA 1890, lead directly to dissolution for all of the partners.

A well-established business with considerable goodwill would not wish technical dissolution to arise time and again as partners leave, or indeed as new partners join. Continuity and stability are needed to build and maintain value in the goodwill of the firm.

Thus, the basic clause can provide for the period of notice that is needed and can deal with conflicts when two notices of retirement are served at the same time, or perhaps where a partner dies during someone else's notice period.

Subsequent clauses will deal with the financial provisions and the taking of appropriate accounts and valuations of a deceased partner or retiring partner's share of the assets.

21. RETIREMENT

21.1 Any Partner may retire from the Partnership on giving not less than [6] months' previous notice in writing to the [other Partners or the senior Partner for the time being] expiring on the last day of any Financial Year and the date of expiration of such notice shall be his Succession Date but without prejudice to any provision in this Deed entitling the other Partners to terminate the Partnership in respect of him or to expel him during the currency of the notice

21.2 If a Partner who has given a notice under clause 21.1 dies during the currency of the notice then the notice shall become void

21.3 If two or more Partners give notice under clause 21.2 expiring on the same date the notice of the [older Partner or Partner first in seniority] shall alone be effective and that of the other or others shall be void

21.4 A Partner shall retire at the end of the Financial Year during which he reaches the age of [65] years as if he had given notice under clause 21.2 to that effect

21.5 Following service of a notice under clause 21.1 the other Partners may at any time thereafter suspend such Partner from the Partnership upon such terms as they in their absolute discretion may decide and which terms shall be notified in writing to all Partners

1.20 Expulsion

It is desirable for the prudent management of a partnership that there should be an express provision permitting the expulsion of an individual partner when some material breach of the partnership terms and conditions occurs, or some specified event happens. Such a provision then enables 'problem' individuals to be removed from the partnership without affecting the continuity for the other partners. Any expulsion clause should give certainty and state in clear terms what breach may give rise to the right to expel and, in the circumstances, what terms of notice are to be given and what type of majority of partners' decision is required.

It is appropriate for a firm to consider including powers of suspension, garden leave and also procedures to be adopted as part of any expulsion procedure.

It should be noted that if procedures (e.g., for hearings or appeals) are established to deal with expulsion matters, they do need to be followed carefully and failure to follow the correct procedure could give the 'problem' partner a defence and possible claim against the partners if their powers are exercised unfairly or arbitrarily.

22. EXPULSION

22.1 If any Partner shall:

    22.1.1 commit a serious breach of any of the provisions in this Deed which is calculated to result in the Partnership's suffering a material disadvantage and which (if capable of being remedied) is not remedied within [14] days of a request from the other Partners for him so to do or

    22.1.2 cease to be properly registered as a member of the [Institute or Association] or be suspended for any period or otherwise be penalised by the [Institute or Association] as a result of any act or omission whatsoever and howsoever arising

    22.1.3 be guilty (to the reasonable satisfaction of the other Partners) of any deliberate or persistent breach or other continuing material breach of the professional or ethical standards of the [Institute or Association] or of any conduct which harms or may tend to cause damage to or injure the reputation and good name of the Partnership and its practice

    22.1.4 fail to hold a current practising certificate

    22.1.5 be guilty of any conduct likely to give rise to the suspension withdrawal or imposition of any conditions on his practising certificate or insolvency licence

    22.1.6 be guilty of any conduct likely to give rise to the suspension withdrawal or imposition of any conditions on the auditing certificate issued to the Partnership by the Institute OR the Association

    22.1.7 be guilty of any conduct likely to give rise to the suspension withdrawal or imposition of any conditions on the investment business certificate issued to the Partnership by the Institute OR the Association

    22.1.8 fail to account for money received by him in respect of any Partnership transaction or

    22.1.9 fail to pay to the Partnership within [30] days of being requested in writing to do so any sum owed by him to the Partnership or

    22.1.10 act in any other respect contrary to the good faith which ought to be observed by all Partners or act in such a way as to be in the opinion of all of the other Partners materially detrimental to the Partnership as a whole or

    22.1.11 have no reasonable prospect of paying or be unable to pay his debts the amount or aggregate amount of which equals or exceeds the bankruptcy level (within the meaning of s267 of the Insolvency Act 1986) or enter into a compromise for the benefit of his creditors generally or

22.1.12 be convicted of any criminal offence [other than a minor motoring offence] or

22.1.13 become a patient within the meaning of [s94(2) or s145(1)] of the Mental Health Act 1983 or

22.1.14 do or suffer any act which would be ground for dissolution of the Partnership by the court then the other Partners (but only if they are more than one) may convene a Partners' meeting which shall be conducted in accordance with the provisions of clause 20.3 and having so resolved may at any time within [3] months after becoming aware of such breach by notice in writing given to the Partner concerned expel him from the Partnership and the date of service of such notice shall be his Succession Date

22.2 Any question concerning the power to expel or the expulsion or purported expulsion of a Partner under this clause may be referred to arbitration under clause 27 and if it is found in any consequent proceedings that such Partner was unlawfully expelled then within [30] days after the final determination of such dispute the expelled Partner may by notice in writing resign from the Partnership with immediate effect

1.21 Consequences of termination

As already mentioned, the partnership agreement should set out provisions that deal with the consequences of termination of the partnership in the event of one or more partners leaving or being expelled. It is obviously desirable that there should be some sort of mechanism for the valuation of a partner's share. Accounts will need to be drawn up and details such as the withdrawal of capital and the payment of undrawn profits will need to be included.

Even when these sums are ascertained, careful thought needs to be given to the terms of payment of such sums, particularly if it is necessary to make payment by instalments.

23. CONSEQUENCES OF TERMINATION

At the Succession Date the Outgoing Partner's share in the capital and assets of the Partnership including goodwill (if any) shall immediately transfer to and vest in the Continuing Partners proportionately to their respective shares in the capital and assets of the Partnership immediately prior to the Succession Date and subject to the following conditions:

23.1 On the Succession Date the Partnership shall be terminated but only as to the Outgoing Partner and it shall continue as between the Continuing Partners

23.2 The Outgoing Partner shall be entitled to his share of the Profits for the Financial Year during which the Succession Date occurs apportioned on a daily basis for the period from the commencement of such Financial Year to the Succession Date

23.3 The Partnership shall instruct the Accountants to prepare as quickly as is reasonably practicable a balance sheet as at the Succession Date and a profit and loss account for the period from the date of the last Audited Accounts (or from the commencement of the Partnership if no Audited Accounts have been adopted) to the Succession Date and the costs of doing so shall be a debt due from the Partnership as constituted immediately prior to the Succession Date in question. Such balance sheet shall be prepared on the same basis as has been adopted in the Partnership Accounts and in particular shall take account of debts owed by or to the Outgoing Partner and the items mentioned in clause 14.2

23.4 Any undrawn balance of the Outgoing Partner's share of the Profits to the Succession Date shall be paid to him not later than [12] months from the Succession Date together with interest from the Succession Date at the Partnership Interest Rate

23.5 The Continuing Partners shall within [24] months after the Succession Date pay to the Outgoing Partner a sum equal to the balance then standing to the credit of the Outgoing Partner's capital account together with interest from the Succession Date at the Partnership Interest Rate but excluding any value attached to goodwill as at the Succession Date. The Outgoing Partner shall not be entitled to any further capital payment in connection with his ceasing to be a Partner

23.6 The liability of the Continuing Partners to make payments to the Outgoing Partner under clauses 23.4 and 23.5 and under the indemnities provided for in clause 8.2.2 shall be joint and several but as between themselves every such payment and any such liabilities arising under such indemnities shall be born by them in the proportions mentioned in clause 13.2

23.7 If the Outgoing Partner shall cease to be a Partner otherwise than by reason of death due notice of the fact that he has ceased to be a Partner shall be given by the Continuing Partners in the London Gazette and in a newspaper circulating in the locality of the Partnership Premises

23.8 The Continuing Partners shall pay and discharge all debts and liabilities of the Partnership at the Succession Date except any debt or liability in respect of income tax attributable to the Outgoing Partner's share of the

Profits and except any debt or liability in respect of any claim arising from any negligent or wrongful act or omission of a Partner to the extent that such claim is not covered by insurance and shall keep the Outgoing Partner indemnified from and against such debts and liabilities except as aforesaid and all actions proceedings costs claims and demands in that respect provided that nothing in this Deed shall be construed so as to remove any lien that the Outgoing Partner may at any time have over the Partnership assets

23.9 *The Outgoing Partner shall on or before his Succession Date deliver up to the Continuing Partners lists of clients' correspondence and all other documents papers and records (in whatever form these may be stored) which may have been prepared by him or have come into his possession while he was a Partner and he shall not retain copies of them. Title and copyright of all such documents shall vest in the Partnership*

23.10 *The Outgoing Partner shall use his best endeavours to ensure that all work of a professional nature including appointments directorships public offices or other duties or positions is transferred to the Continuing Partners or as they may direct*

23.11 *During the period of [24] months following the Succession Date the Outgoing Partner or his duly authorised agent shall be permitted by appointment to inspect the books of account records letters and other documents of the Partnership during normal business hours so far as they relate to any period preceding the Succession Date and all information which the Outgoing Partner or his duly authorised agent shall thereby obtain shall be kept strictly confidential by the Outgoing Partner and by such duly authorised agent and the Outgoing Partner shall indemnify and keep the Continuing Partners indemnified from and against all losses damages and costs which they may suffer arising directly or indirectly out of a failure to comply with this restriction*

23.12 *The Outgoing Partner shall sign execute and do all such documents deeds acts and things as the Continuing Partners may reasonably request for the purpose of enabling the Continuing Partners to recover and get in the book debts and other assets of the Partnership or for the purpose of appointing a new trustee of any of the Partnership property or for the purpose of conveying assigning or transferring to the Continuing Partners any of the Partnership property which immediately prior to the Succession Date is vested in the Outgoing Partner as one of the Partners or in trust for the Partnership*

23.13 *In consideration of the covenants by the other Partners contained in this Deed each of them the Outgoing Partner and the Continuing Partners irrevocably appoints each and any of the other Outgoing and Continuing*

Partners his attorney for the purpose of signing executing and doing all notices documents deeds acts and things at any time required to be signed executed or done by him

1.22 Dissolution and winding-up

It may be that a firm comes to the end of its existence either naturally or because a majority of partners wish to dissolve the practice. The partners should discuss this possibility and include a clause which provides established rules to be applied in the event of dissolution or winding-up. Once again the PA 1890 does have a statutory framework which could be applied on the dissolution or winding-up of a partnership but these provisions may not be appropriate to a modern accountancy practice and in the circumstances, appropriate and up-to-date provisions should be expressly included in the agreement.

The specimen clause which follows refers to s44 PA 1890. It provides for the order of settling losses and distributing assets as follows:

'in settling accounts between the partners after a dissolution of the partnership, the following rules shall, subject to any agreement, be observed:

(a) losses, including losses and deficiencies of capital shall be paid first out of profits, next out of capital, and lastly, if necessary, by the partners individually and in proportion to which they were entitled to share profits;

(b) the assets of the firm including the sums, if any, contributed by the partners to make up losses or deficiencies of capital, shall be applied in the following manner and order;

- in paying the debts and liabilities of the firm to persons who are not partners therein;
- in paying to each partner rateably what is due from the firm to him for advances as distinguished from capital;
- in paying to each partner rateably what is due from the firm to him in respect of capital;
- the ultimate residue, if any, shall be divided among the partners in the proportion in which profits are divisible.'

24. DISSOLUTION AND WINDING-UP

24.1 *The Partnership may be dissolved by not less than [three-quarters] of the Partners at any time giving at least [3] months' notice in writing to the other Partner, or Partner of their intent and upon the expiry of such notice the dissolution shall take effect*

24.2 Upon the expiry of a notice under clause 24.1 or if the Partnership shall otherwise be dissolved the winding up of the business and undertaking of the Partnership shall be administered in accordance with s44 PA 1890

1.23 Covenants to protect goodwill

Covenants to protect goodwill are provisions which are often referred to as 'restrictive covenants'. Inevitably when a partner leaves for reasons other than death it may be that those who continue wish to protect their customers' goodwill. Clearly for some firms it could be very damaging if a leaving partner was allowed to set up and compete with the business, particularly if the leaver had received a payment in respect of the goodwill of the business. Thus, you normally include a restrictive covenant within a partnership agreement to prevent a former partner from competing with the business. In principle such a provision is perfectly acceptable provided it does not constitute an unreasonable restraint of trade. If the scope of the restriction, whether in terms of duration or the matters covered, is deemed to be unreasonable because it is too wide or lasts for too long a period, then it will be struck down. The restriction may also extend to obligations not to poach other members of the partnership or other employees of the firm.

25. COVENANTS

25.1 Each Partner covenants with all the other Partners that:

25.1.1 (except when the Partnership is dissolved) he will not within a period of [2] years from his Succession Date either on his own account or for or jointly or in conjunction with or on behalf of any other person firm or company whether directly or indirectly solicit business entice clients or interfere with the relationship between the Partnership and its clients or any of them where such persons are clients of the Partnership at his Succession Date or have been so at any time during the period of [12] months prior to his Succession Date [provided that his covenant shall not extend to clients who it is agreed between the Outgoing Partner and the Continuing Partners were introduced to the Partnership by the Outgoing Partner while he was a Partner]

25.1.2 (except when the Partnership is dissolved) he will not within a period of [2] years from his Succession Date in competition with the Partnership either on his own account or for or jointly or in conjunction with or on behalf of any other person firm or company whether directly or indirectly deal with advise or otherwise act for any person firm or company who is at his Succession Date or shall have been at any time during the period of [12] months prior to his Succession Date a client of the Partnership

25.1.3 (except when the Partnership is dissolved) he will not within a period of [2] years from his Succession Date either on his own account or for or jointly or in conjunction with or on behalf of any other person firm or company whether directly or indirectly solicit or endeavour to entice away offer employment or partnership to or enter into partnership with or employ any person who was at any time during the [2] years prior to such Succession Date a Partner in or employed by the Partnership

25.2 Each Partner covenants with all the other Partners that:

25.2.1 (except when the Partnership is dissolved) he will not after his Succession Date either for himself or for or jointly or in conjunction with or on behalf of any other person firm or company represent himself as Partner in an employee of or a consultant to the Partnership or that he is in any way connected with or has authority to bind the Partnership

25.2.2 (except when the Partnership is dissolved) he will not after his Succession Date either for himself or for or jointly or in conjunction with or on behalf of any other person firm or company use the Firm Name or any name which may in any way (whether visually audibly or otherwise) be confused with the Firm Name

25.3 Each of clauses 25.1.1, 25.1.2, 25.1.3, 25.2.1 and 25.2.2 constitutes an entirely separate and independent restriction on each Partner so that if one or more are held to be invalid for any reason whatever then the remaining covenants shall be valid to the extent that they are not held to be invalid

1.24 Salaried partners

It is quite often the case that when someone is called a 'salaried partner' in reality they are not a partner at all but are in fact an employee. As such, the salaried partner takes no part in decision taking or risk and invests no capital in the firm. There are arrangements which partnerships operate to give certain junior partners 'guaranteed' profit share. They are treated as self employed and suffer tax under Schedule D. However, what does tend to happen is that the salaried partner is 'held out' on notepaper or in the list of partners at the principal business address as a member of the partnership. Being 'held out' means that a salaried partner may be able to bind his co-partners in contractual matters, and be bound in to contracts made by other partners.

In either case a salaried partner should always seek a full indemnity from the equity partners so that, in the event of there being any personal liability or claim on the salaried partner, he can look to the equity partners for cover. As for the equity partners they may be content to provide the indemnity but may wish to make an exception in the event of any fraud or wilful neglect on the part of the salaried partner. This sort of exception can be the subject of considerable and difficult debate. A specimen form of indemnity clause could be as follows:

> *[the Equity Partner] jointly and severally covenant to indemnify and keep indemnified [the Salaried Partner] [and his personal representatives, estate and effects against all liabilities for all or any losses, debts, actions, proceedings, costs, claims and other obligations of the Partnership except liability arising from fraudulent or malicious act or default on the part of [the Salaried Partner] provided that such exception shall not include any liabilities which may be covered by professional indemnity insurance or other commercial insurance or such other commercial insurance as the partnership shall maintain from time to time and including so far as may be applicable any liabilities that would be so covered by the said insurance but for any excess or deduction required under the terms of any policy for such insurance.*
>
> *The Equity Partners further undertake that they shall obtain a joint and several covenant and indemnity in favour of the salaried partner in the same terms as herein provided from all or any further Equity Partner joining the partnership.*
>
> *[Any such indemnity clause should ultimately be part of the document executed as a deed so there is no question as to the presence of any consideration for the indemnity or its enforceability].*

1.25 Conclusion

Readers should be aware that this chapter provides general guidance and that, in connection with any specific partnership issues, professional advice may need to be taken.

2 Equity cleansing

2.1 Partner exit routes – Setting exit routes by agreement

2.1.1 Introduction

The previous chapter dealt with the partnership deed in respect of various aspects. It cannot be stressed too highly that, in order to do what you can to protect the value that is to be built up within the business, it is essential to have in place a properly documented partnership constitution, in the shape of such a deed or agreement. The first part of this chapter focuses on one especially vital part of such documentation which is, sadly, the most likely to be contentious and to have needed the most careful of drafting, namely what happens when one or more partners leave the firm.

2.1.2 Partnership Act 1890 provisions

The reason that it is so essential to have correct documentation in place, and for that paperwork to deal fully with this situation, is that the alternative is simply too horrible to contemplate! The Partnership Act 1890 (PA 1890), which still deals with the framework which operates in default, i.e., if there is no agreement to govern the position, gives no right for any partner simply to leave the partnership by means of a unilaterally given notice. If, therefore, any partner wishes to leave such a partnership (which is known as a partnership at will) he has no option but to serve notice to terminate the partnership, which is effective immediately.

2.1.3 Winding up a partnership

If such a notice is served or if the partnership is otherwise terminated (i.e., by the death of a partner or by the inclusion of another partner) then the partnership is to be wound up (unless there is contrary agreement), with its assets being liquidated and its liabilities discharged. The fact that this is in most cases the last course of action which actually suits anyone is recognised in the Law Commissions' Consultation Paper 'Partnership Law' (no.159), published in 2001, which advocates removing the right to terminate the overall partnership unilaterally, and giving the right for one partner to withdraw on notice. Until that happens, it is for the draftsman of the agreement to cover the options.

2.1.4 Retirement by age

Most agreements will still provide for the retirement of all partners upon their attaining a certain age. Some, especially where the firm has been founded by a strong character who is determined to be able to soldier on if he so wishes, do not. This should be avoided if possible, as it is likely to lead to arguments in future years, when others will feel the founder is not making a sufficient contribution, but he still considers it to be 'his' firm. Better by far to have a normal retirement age, even if there is then an option by agreement to extend that age.

2.1.5 Selecting a retirement age

There has been a trend in recent years for retirement ages in agreements to be reduced, so that 60 or even 55 has become common, rather than the 65 that used to be the norm. That may now be considered to pose a problem, however, as in many cases the pension funds which partners have been building up, in the hope that they would yield a decent income from the chosen age onwards, are proving to be seriously inadequate as a result of the poor performance of their underlying investments and the low rate of return from compulsory gilt-linked annuities in a low-interest and low-inflation age. It may therefore be appropriate to build in a mechanism for the review of the standard age, for the potential benefit of all.

2.1.6 Early retirement on notice

Almost all agreements will provide for a partner to be able to retire from the partnership upon the expiry of a period of notice to be given by him, which he is at liberty to serve at any time. It is possible for a minimum age to be stipulated before such a notice can be effected, but this is seldom advisable as, if there is discontent, it simply has the result of locking in dissent. If early retirement is perceived as a potential problem, e.g., because of restricted availability of capital to pay out the retiring partner, then it is better to allow that partner physically to leave on normal notice but on terms that postpone his ability to commence withdrawal of his capital.

2.1.7 The period of notice

The question arises as to what the suitable period is for such a notice. It is impossible to offer universally applicable guidance. Indeed, when introducing the legislation that provided for the members of a Limited Liability Partnership ('LLP') to be able to give such a notice, the Government expressly refused to legislate for what would constitute 'reasonable' notice as they said the variety of circumstances which could affect firms precluded this. It is in effect a juggling act, between the firm's wish to retain the services of the outgoing partner in order to manage a smooth transition to a successor who might take a considerable time to appoint; and the outgoing partner's wish to be gone. If too short a period is adopted then there may be insufficient allowance for time to adjust to the need to recruit, and the period for such recruitment, including the need for a new appointee to give notice. If too long a period is chosen however, then the outgoing partner may grow bored and disillusioned, and become a negative force in contacts with staff and clients. (It should be borne in mind that, unless expressly provided for, there will be no right for the remaining partners to compel their retiring partner to take 'garden leave'.) Further, it may impel him towards a breach of whatever the agreement says, since it may become in practice impossible for him to find other employment without being willing to break the agreement, as few prospective employers will be willing to wait for more than a few months. It is better perhaps to have a relatively short period which is unlikely to be broken and which does offer an opportunity to manage the situation.

2.1.8 The effective date of retirement

The other point to bear in mind is whether any such retirement can only be effective as from a normal year end date. In practice, if it is, then that places restrictions on the prospective leaver (as mentioned in the last paragraph). It is probably fairer to allow retirement at any time of the year unless there are special factors which make the year end abnormally important for the firm. This may, however, result in extra cost to the firm in providing cessation accounts, though it may be possible to avoid this by providing for the time apportionment of the normal year's accounts, for the purpose of calculating the entitlement of the departing partner. If cessation accounts are needed, it may be fair to pass all or some of the cost of producing them on to the departing partner.

2.1.9 Illness

The agreement will also need to provide for what happens in the event that a partner is rendered unable to perform his duties illness. This may be a single, prolonged, illness or a cumulative series of absences. Normally an overall period of absence of, say, a year would be allowed for before the ability was conferred upon the other partners to require their sick colleague to leave. One area which may cause problems is if the ill partner wishes to return on a part-time basis. Does this stop the clock running, or is he still to be regarded as absent for the purpose of calculating the total period?

2.1.10 Mental illness

The nature of the illness which causes the absence may be physical, or of course it could be mental. In an age when 'stress' seems increasingly to be the first word that leaps to many an uncertain doctor's lips, then such absences are bound to be more frequent. Care should therefore be taken to differentiate between absence through troubling but not threatening illness (for which the normal period as above will be appropriate) and the onset of insanity, where the other partners will wish to have the right to remove their sick colleague immediately, in order to protect their position.

2.1.11 Timing of payments in the event of illness

If the partnership provides insurance, for its own benefit and/or for that of the individual partners, which yields either income or capital payouts after a set period of illness related absence, then the agreement should tie into this as far as timing is concerned.

2.1.12 Death

The position under the PA 1890 is that the death of a partner terminates the partnership, whatever the wishes of the surviving partners, if it has not previously been agreed that this shall not be so. The agreement should therefore be clear that the partnership itself continues regardless. The other matter of principle which needs to be addressed is whether the heirs of the deceased partner can actually take over his share in the business and become partners or whether they are simply entitled to be paid out the value of his interest. For businesses which wish for continuity and for maximised value, the latter is the more appropriate.

2.1.13 Timing of payments in the event of death

As to the timing of such a payout, again any insurance provision may need to be taken account of. For instance, an agreement might provide that a partner who simply retired was only able to withdraw his capital over a three-year period by instalments; but that the estate of a deceased partner should be paid out within a month of receipt of the payment of an insurance payout sufficient to cover the debt. There may also be a wish to provide that certain payments on account can be made within the period immediately after death, to cover current family obligations, even if probate has not yet been granted.

2.2 The underperforming partner

2.2.1 Introduction

One of the most sensitive issues which afflicts partnerships is that of the partner who is perceived as underperforming. The personal nature of partnership is such that there will almost inevitably be different performances required of partners, in the sense of their fulfilling different roles both externally, in terms of the work they do in the provision of the goods or services which the firm sells, and internally, in relation to the management and administrative tasks within the firm. The problem which that throws up is that, to get a fair measure of the input of each partner, a number of different metrics will need to be considered. That is not always easy for partners to realise, especially if the culture of the firm is one which focuses on one aspect only.

2.2.2 Selecting suitable metrics

In a professional service firm, attention is commonly focused billing. What mental allowance then needs to be made, by the high-billing partners for the fact that one of their colleagues may be operating in an area susceptible to cyclical variation which is currently in a slump, so that he is denied by the market the chance to bill highly; or for another who may have spent most of the last few months overseeing a major IT procurement and installation programme? The leaders of the firm need to ensure that a suitable range of measures is chosen, and accepted, by all partners, which recognises contributions of any nature.

2.2.3 Encouraging improvement

Even then, there may still be those who are seen as underperforming against that backdrop of a range of factors. How then should they be handled? The first task for the firm is to recognise that its efforts, at least in the first instance, should be focused on trying to return the partner – who, after all, would presumably not have attained partnership had considerable potential not been shown – to full performance. Discussions should centre around what the causes of the difficulties are, whether they are personal or professional. It needs to be clear what the partner is expected to do, and he must be fully aware of his place in the strategic business planning of the firm. It is not unknown for partners to be criticised for failing to achieve goals they had not accepted or did not know had been set for them.

2.2.4 Practical steps to improvement

Once all concerned are clear as to what the mutual expectations are, then practical steps towards improvement need reviewing. Are there, for instance, additional human or IT resources which need to be deployed? Is any retraining required? May changes in work patterns or personal time-management skills, be required? After any such changes have been agreed upon, then a reasonable period of time needs to be given for the problem partner to achieve the potential which has been identified, in the knowledge that performance is being monitored. All other partners need to accept that this period has to be gone through, for nothing is likely to render the exercise ineffective quicker than continual sniping from the partnership back benches.

2.3 Expulsion

2.3.1 The need for expulsion provisions

However hard partners try to get an underperforming colleague back up to scratch, the point may come when it becomes apparent that that is not going to work, and that he has to go. In many cases the partnership agreement will not provide for expulsion in the absence of any tangible wrongdoing, i.e., mere ineffectiveness itself does not give an entitlement to expel. In such cases the other partners have very restricted rights. They can of course try to persuade their errant partner that it is in his interests to go elsewhere, but if that does not work they may themselves have to contemplate leaving, or even (if the agreement permits) terminating the partnership.

2.3.2 Expulsion without cause

The only effective way to avoid this is to give the power for expulsion without cause, even if it is called something else, such as a right to require a partner to retire. This will need safeguards built in, in terms of requiring either all other partners to concur (known sometimes as an 'all bar one' policy), or a significant majority. Some large partnerships delegate this power to the management board, etc., but that would be rare for a small to medium size firm. It would in theory be possible to provide that the power only arose in certain circumstances, e.g., if certain thresholds were not reached, for instance as to chargeable hours recorded or bills rendered, but in practice those are likely to lead to argument as to interpretation, and will serve only to prolong the agony. If things have come to such a pass, it is suggested that it will be better all round for action to be relatively swift and certain. Apart from the partners' own relationships, staff morale and client confidence are likely to suffer if there are protracted arguments, as the reality is that it is rarely possible for these to be fully hidden from the view of others.

2.4 Payment out

2.4.1 The amount of payment

In most cases, the partnership agreement will have, as at least the starting point for the amount of any payout, the balance(s) shown to the credit of the outgoing partner in the firm's books. This will apply whatever label the partners have chosen to give to such accounts, i.e., whether they are simply shown as partners' funds or are split into capital accounts/current accounts/loan accounts, etc.

2.4.2 Calculating the amount

The agreement may, for calculation purposes, refer back to the balances shown in the last accounts. Alternatively it may require cessation accounts to be prepared, or treat the cessation as occurring at a year end, whatever its actual date. It may provide for time apportionment of profits and drawings over the period since the last accounts. Whatever the approach, it needs to be amply clear which option has been provided for. It also needs to be clear as to whether the accounts themselves will need any adjustment. The classic example is the valuation to be accorded to any properties shown in the accounts, which are likely to be included at historic cost, with no adjustment having been made to their ostensible value since their purchase. Should they be revalued for the purposes of calculating the outgoing partner's share? In most cases, unless the firm has actively followed a policy of frequent revaluation, the fair answer is yes. That is now presumed by law in the absence of direction to the contrary within the agreement (*Gadd* v *Gadd* 2002) 8 EG 160).

2.4.3 Goodwill

Perhaps the biggest difference between the expectations of entrepreneurs in company and partnership scenarios respectively is with regard to goodwill. In the company context, the value of shares is (at least before any minority discount is applied) a reflection of the overall market worth of the business, which is as likely to be measured as a multiple of turnover or profit as it is to be related to the value of underlying assets. In the partnership world, however, the only way for this to be reflected is in the nebulous and increasingly rare concept of 'goodwill'. Fewer partnerships than before provide for this at all. If it is to be reflected at all, the need is for it to be precisely defined.

2.4.4 The concept of partnership as a 'trust'

The theory that underpins this concept is that a partnership is almost a living thing, and that the partners at any time hold it as some sort of sacred trust for partners yet to come. To encourage those partners, less and less is made of any requirement that they contribute any incoming capital. The result is that, particularly in professional service firms where the requirement for capital to fund the business has grown hugely in the era of all-pervasive IT, the working capital needs of the business, insofar as they are sourced internally, have to be met from that capital which was originally contributed by the more senior partners, and by retained profit contributed by all. This in turn puts more burden on continuing partners when their senior colleagues, with relatively high account balances, come to retire. To complete the circularity of the argument, the junior partners thus contend that they should not be subject to the burden of having to fund any goodwill payments as well as capital repayments.

2.4.5 Annuities

Much the same applies to another method of extracting value from a partnership after leaving it, which is again less popular than it used to be, namely annuities. Here, the theory was that, to match the concept that partners held the firm in trust for their successors, so equally those successors had a responsibility to their former colleagues, which would be discharged by the payment to them or their widows of an annuity. Now, the counter-argument is that, since profits reflect the input of the current partners, it is wrong for them to be obliged to pay any part of those profits to those who are no longer contributing. This is bolstered by the fact that, if the firm at any time wishes to convert to an LLP, any annuity obligation would be a powerful disincentive since the accounting standards applicable will require the full capitalisation of annuity obligation which (even if profit linked) will require annual professional valuation with its attendant costs. At least one major firm is believed to have shed its annuity obligations in advance of conversion, just to avoid this problem.

2.4.6 Work in progress

The other intangible asset which is unlikely to be fully valued in the balance sheet, particularly in the sphere of professional service firms, is work in progress. True, the work in progress of staff does now require to be fully shown for tax reasons. The work in progress of equity partners (often the highest-billing participants) still does not, however, since it is not considered as a 'cost' to the firm. Therefore, unless the partnership agreement provides for some extra payment to be made in lieu of the outgoing partner's share of this asset (and few do) then he will have no way of recouping this.

2.4.7 Partnership as an asset-accruing vehicle

All of these factors, with regard to goodwill, annuities and work in progress, mean in the writer's view that partnership is, in reality, a singularly unattractive vehicle for the accruing of extricable capital value. Rather, efforts should be made throughout the partner's working life to make it a vehicle for income and cash generation, with as little as possible being left in as working capital, and with the income being used to generate an investment portfolio to take the place of any expectation of major capital contribution from the firm.

2.5 The mechanics of payment out

2.5.1 The timing of payment

It is comparatively unlikely that there will be a 'one size fits all' arrangement for the timing of payments out. The event that gives rise to the entitlement is likely to govern this. Thus, in the event of death, partners may well have all wished to protect their families, and will thus require a relatively swift payment out, backed by insurance to be prudent. Equally, if expulsion takes effect, it would often be seen as inequitable to kick a partner out and yet hold on to his capital, so again fairly rapid payment would be provided for. On the other hand, retirement would only give rise to entitlement to payment over a period of years by instalments. Further, in the event of early retirement (unless the firm wished to encourage this) there might be a minimum age which has to be attained before any payments become due.

2.5.2 Interest

Where payment is to be deferred, it would normally be appropriate for interest to be payable on the then outstanding balance. Generally, this would be at a rate linked to that of the partnership's bank rather than an absolute rate.

2.5.3 Security

A potential problem is that the entitlement to payment is likely to be entirely unsecured. (The same applies to other post-departure obligations of the remaining partners, such as the indemnity normally given against partnership debts, or the requirement for the provision of continuing professional indemnity insurance cover.) In practice there is little that a departing partner can do about this, and he is thus dependent for his peace of mind on the continued prosperity of the business and its partners. (This is one area where LLPs may be perceived by an outgoing member as undesirable, for amongst the liabilities which members' personal estates will be protected against will presumably be the obligations of the LLP, as an incorporated body, to its former members.)

2.6 Post-retirement obligations

2.6.1 Introduction

There are a number of potential post-retirement obligations, in both directions, which it is also prudent to have provision for. First and foremost is the need for an indemnity to be given to the outgoing partner for the continuing debts of the partnership. Where possible, this should extend to his release from any specifically identifiable obligations, e.g., banking covenants, finance agreements, leases, etc. The likelihood is, however, that this will not always be feasible, perhaps because third-party consents may not be forthcoming, and so there will be a heavy degree of reliance upon the future financial performance of the firm. The indemnity will normally apply to everything except the individual's own wrongdoing.

2.6.2 Professional indemnity insurance

It should, however, extend to an individual's negligence, since the agreement should place an obligation upon the partners to continue to provide a suitable level of cover. Further, since the amount of the uninsured excess element of any such cover will be entirely in their control, it should not provide for the continuing partners to be able to recoup from their former colleague merely because the actual payment will have to come from their pockets rather than the insurers by reason of its being below the uninsured limit. The obligation should extend to the provision of run-off cover in the event that the firm should be wound up without a successor practice, though it might be fair in such circumstances to expect all, including a retired partner, to contribute to the potentially high cost of such cover (subject to his being protected against any escalation of cost resulting from a poor claims record in the years since he left).

2.6.3 Tax payments

Although partnerships are no longer obliged, as a matter of law, to pay the income tax bills of the constituent partners, nonetheless many firms have in practice continued to do so, operating on the theory that it is safer that way, since they know the tax is paid and they will not be adversely affected by default on the partners' behalf. In that event, the agreement needs to be clear as to what payments should be made from the outgoing partner's capital or current account after his departure, and how that should be treated in terms of adjustments to provisions already made.

2.7 Dispute resolution methods

2.7.1 General

There is an old saying that, if it comes to the stage where the partnership agreement has to be taken out of the safe, it is too late anyway since the damage has already been done. There is no doubt that partnerships can lead to dispute and, just as with a marriage, the often intensely personal relationships generated by partnerships can in turn lead to some extremely bitter battles. Better by far, therefore, to have some form of provision for a method of dispute resolution provided for in the agreement.

2.7.2 Arbitration

Historically, the most commonly found provision has been a clause requiring any dispute to go to arbitration in accordance with the current statutory provisions, and with a process for the agreement or nomination of a suitable arbitrator. The object of arbitration, i.e., a process where a binding decision can be made by a third party which parties are obliged to follow and which can be enforced by court order, is to avoid the costs and delays seen as attendant upon litigation through the courts. This may, however, be more of an illusion than a reality, especially since the Civil Justice reforms of the late 1990s. Arbitration is still an adversarial process, requiring detailed documentary submissions and often advocacy skills, just as litigation is. Arbitrators are under wide statutory duties and find themselves forced to adopt litigation-like procedures so that neither side can claim that an unfair advantage has been given to the other. Further, unlike judges, arbitrators require to be paid by those whose disputes they are required to settle. Whilst, therefore, arbitration is likely to be provided for in many agreements, thought should be given as to whether it is an appropriate mechanism.

2.7.3 Expert determination

An alternative is that a decision can be made, again to bind the parties, not by an arbitrator determining matters in judicial manner by weighing the evidence presented to him, but by an expert, using his own knowledge of a professional field, to come to a decision on the facts as presented to him. Here, it may even be provided that, apart from strictly factual submissions, the parties do not even have the opportunity to make their case to the expert. This form of determination is likely to be best suited to technical professional problems, such as what the accounting treatment of a matter ought to be. The partnership agreement may wish to provide for arbitration on some matters, and expert determination on others.

2.7.4 Mediation

Another increasingly popular option is that of mediation. This is, however, very difficult to provide for in an agreement entered into many years before the dispute arises, since the very different nature of the mediation process means that its likelihood of success is dependent upon there being a genuine resolve on the parties' behalf to come to a mutually concessionary settlement. If the parties are simply at loggerheads, and see their problems in terms of yes/no questions, then mediation will not succeed. There has to be a willingness to give ground. The mediator functions in an entirely different manner from a judge, an arbitrator or an expert. He decides nothing. His role is simply to be an informed but impartial go-between, suggesting possible settlement options, giving an opinion (privately) to each of the parties of the points they are strong or weak on, and running between the parties as messenger to try to bring them to common ground and agreement. It is a very difficult task which may not succeed. In other words, mediation may not result in a disposal of a dispute and may leave other methods, such as litigation, to follow on. It is, however, an option which is being much encouraged, and indeed observations of the judiciary are leading to the idea that parties may be penalised in costs if they do not at some stage, whether before or after the issue of proceedings, at least attempt formal mediation if informal negotiations are unsuccessful.

2.8 Conclusion

It is essential, for the preservation and maximisation of value within the context of a partnership, to have a properly drawn document to govern the workings of the partnership, and for the process which produces that document to focus clearly on at least the following matters, namely:

- dealing with the circumstances in which individual partners may cease to be partners, so that –
    - the opportunity for instant unilateral determination is avoided; and
    - attention is given to –
        - both normal and early retirement;
        - both physical and mental illness;
        - death;
- agreed upon measures for partners' performance are clearly known, so that –
    - encouragement can be given to underperforming partners;
    - a process for expulsion exists which is fair, but clear and decisive;
- clear provisions exist for determining the amount of payout to partners, which specify whether and, if so, how –
    - goodwill is to be payable;
    - annuities are to be payable;
    - partners' work in progress is to be valued;
    - assets are to be revalued;
- the mechanics of payment out are provided for, with the differentiations necessary to cope with different causes of cessation;
- post-retirement obligations are considered;
- suitable provision is made for the process by which disputes, of different potential sorts, are to be resolved.

3 Sources of finance

3.1 Introduction

Cash is the lifeblood of professional practices, just as it is for every business. Professional practices which conduct themselves through the medium of partnerships are, however, unable to raise finance through the issue of shares or debt-based instruments.

Most professional practices have the facility to select the choice of business medium: general partnership; limited liability partnership (LLP); limited company or plc; or, occasionally, limited partnership. However, certain professional bodies prohibit or limit the extent to which their members may share profits with individuals who are not regulated by the same body. This precludes or limits the extent to which external equity finance may be obtained by those practices. An example of such a regulatory body is the Law Society in respect of solicitors.

This chapter concentrates primarily on the sources of finance available to businesses practising through the medium of partnership.

3.2 Sources of finance

Three sources of finance are available to the typical professional practice.

3.2.1 Partners

Partners finance their practice in two principal ways. First, through fixed capital. For some firms, fixed capital may simply represent the amounts which partners have chosen to introduce from time to time to meet particular needs of the business, or which they have left as undrawn profits after drawings have been extracted from the business and provision has been made for tax liabilities. In other firms, required capital contributions may be prescribed as part of the firm's profit-sharing structure. In either case, partners who have not been able to accumulate capital from undrawn profits may introduce capital from personal sources or may borrow it, typically from a bank.

Second, current accounts representing the balance of undrawn profits available to each partner.

3.2.2 The partnership bankers

In addition to providing capital loans to partners, the firm's bankers will typically provide three types of finance:

- current account/overdraft;
- short-/medium-term loans;
- long-term loans.

At a time when interest rates are low firms may wish to control the cost of future finance by increasing the level of practice finance which is obtained through fixed rate or capped term loans.

3.2.3 Asset finance

Increasingly, firms make use of leasing arrangements or term loans to finance asset purchases or improvements. However, relatively few professional firms make use of debt factoring as a means of financing the practice.

3.3 Overview of partnership finance – relative proportions

Because partnerships are not obliged to publish their accounts, it is particularly difficult to obtain a clear picture of the financing arrangements of professional firms. However, past experience coupled with published figures and the various benchmarking surveys suggest that the typical medium–large legal, accounting or property professional firm may be financed as follows.

Table 3.1 Partnership finance for a medium–large firm

	%
Partners	
Fixed capital	35
Current accounts	30
Banks	
Overdraft/current account	20
Short-/medium-term loans	5
Long-term	5
Other	
Leasing, asset finance and debt factoring	5
	100

When reviewing these figures, it should be recognised that they are averages drawn from the professional services sector. They are not necessarily typical of any particular firm and are certainly not 'model' figures which might be applied to any firm.

Subject to these limitations, the figures are nevertheless instructive. They show that almost two-thirds of firms' financing is derived from the partners. However, it should be recognised that, particularly among younger partners, a significant proportion of their fixed capital may also have been borrowed from a bank. Overall, it appears that more than half of all partners borrow to fund their capital accounts.

Among the medium–large professional firms, the average partner capital account balance is in the region of £90,000, but this figure is subject to wide variations between firms and may frequently be less than £40,000 or more than £150,000.

In addition to partner capital loans, banks provide approximately 30 per cent of practices' finance.

Each firm must decide on its own capital requirements which will vary according to the needs of the particular business and the position in the growth cycle of the firm.

The diversity within the professional service sector is almost as great as that to be found within corporate businesses. Smaller and start-up practices will typically be financed by a combination of private capital, borrowed partner capital and overdraft. The firm's bankers will generally require personal guarantees together with appropriate security. By contrast, some of the largest professional practices are very substantial businesses with strong brands. The proven track record of these businesses, together with the strength of the covenant which they offer, simultaneously offers them access to a greater diversity of finance types and sources, while reducing or eliminating the need for personal guarantees.

3.4 Partner finance

As noted above, partners' accounts represent the dominant source of finance in a typical professional practice.

3.4.1 Partner capital accounts

In smaller and traditional firms, the balances on partner capital accounts are often allowed to build up as a response to the cumulative financing requirements of the business. This may result in a situation where a few senior partners effectively provide the greater part of the capital account finance of the firm. While attractive at the time, this may be undesirable for two reasons. First, a significant proportion of the assets of those individuals may be put at risk within the partnership. Second, other partners may feel that the arrangement gives those partners undue influence in the control and direction of the practice. Most firms, therefore, specify a required capital contribution for partners which:

(a) provides adequate levels of partner capital as part of the financial structure of the practice;

(b) specifies clearly the amount of an individual partner's capital contribution and the date by which it must be made available to the firm;

(c) may link partner capital requirements to a broader profit-sharing structure. The linkage is customarily made to a partner's 'points', 'shares' or position in the firm's 'lockstep';

(d) lays down clear provisions regarding the payment by the partnership of interest on capital account balances. Typically, interest will be paid at a rate slightly in excess of the rate which would be paid on borrowed capital;

(e) if the firm wishes to discourage excessive capital balances, may provide that no interest is paid on amounts in excess of the required capital contribution; and

(f) provides for the repayment of excessive capital balances to partners.

In these arrangements, interest paid on capital account balances will generally be treated as a first call on the partnership's profits which are available for distribution.

Funding

With more than half of all partners facing the need to borrow funds to finance their capital contributions, partnerships will generally arrange a suitable loan facility with a bank. These arrangements offer considerable administrative simplification to all parties while eliminating the need for individual partners to disclose confidential partner information to other banks.

The question is often raised as to whether partner capital loans should be sourced from the practice's principal bankers. Conventional wisdom is that, where circumstances permit, there may be merit in using a separate bank for this purpose.

Such loans are made to partners subject to an undertaking from the partnership that no capital will be returned to the partner personally until the outstanding balance of the bank loan has been repaid. Often, arrangements are made for the partnership to pay interest on the capital loan direct to the bank. Interest payments are debited to the partner's current account with the firm. In the past, banks have generally been prepared to leave these loans outstanding for so long as an individual was a partner in the firm. If the capital requirement increased as the individual progressed within the partnership, it was possible to obtain further loan finance to fund that increase. More recently, banks have been reluctant to provide further loan finance for the foreseeable progress of a partner within the firm. Instead, banks increasingly expect to see such additional capital requirements financed out of personal sources or retained profit shares.

At the same time, banks are encouraging a debate with partnerships with a view to arranging for initial partner capital loans to be replaced by capital built up out of retained profit shares over a period of, say, five years. While this may have clear attractions in terms of reducing the bank's exposure to a particular professional practice, it presents obvious difficulties to new partners who may not only have to build up new capital but also support a family, pay school fees, etc.

Tax relief for interest paid

Partners in a general partnership or LLP are able to obtain tax relief on interest paid in respect of loans used to finance their partner capital accounts. Specifically, tax relief can be obtained in respect of interest paid on loans taken out to:

- purchase a share in a partnership; or
- contribute capital to a partnership or to lend money to a partnership, provided the money is used wholly for the purposes of the partnership business; or
- to pay off another loan where relief would have been available under either of the above criteria.

Provided the partner has not recovered any capital from the partnership, tax relief is available in respect of interest paid during the period when the partner was a member of the partnership. Interest relief ceases to be available once the partner retires, regardless of the fact that he may be unable to withdraw his capital for some time thereafter.

3.4.2 Partner current accounts

Partnerships frequently operate a policy whereby partners may draw a fixed amount per month on account of the current year's expected profit share. This is intended to enable partners to meet living costs. In computing the amount of the monthly drawing, larger partnerships often adopt a conservative approach. Those firms which set aside tax reserves for their partners will deduct appropriate amounts when computing the monthly drawing.

Once the partnership accounts for the year have been adopted, profit shares will be credited to partner current accounts whereupon it might be thought that those profit shares could be withdrawn from the practice. This would represent a significant drain on the finances of the practice. Many larger partnerships therefore impose conditions on the arrangements for drawing the profits of the previous year. For those firms, those profits might be drawn in three or four tranches according to whether the individual partner, the office or the firm as a whole has met its current year targets in working capital management. If the total value of unbilled work in progress and uncollected cash (generally known as 'lockup' and expressed as a number of weeks' turnover) does not meet the firm's targets, then the distribution of profit shares will be deferred. This has the effect of incentivising partners in working capital management while reducing the need to increase a firm's overdraft. While this approach is less usual among smaller firms, many would benefit from adapting this to their own requirements.

Cash management

These factors effectively smooth the fluctuations in partner current account balances at any time. Those firms which retain tax reserves on behalf of their partners will also benefit from the availability of these funds during extended periods of the year. However, the tax payments which fall due on 31 January and 31 July each year may place a significant strain on practice finances. Tax payments, payments of rent and payments of VAT should therefore be staggered where possible. Inevitably, though, the cumulative effect of these must be taken into account when considering the extent to which practice finance requirements will be met by the firm's bankers.

3.5 Bank finance

Before considering the practice's bank, or banks, as a source of finance it is instructive to reflect on the way in which the attitude of banks to the professional services sector has evolved.

Traditionally, banks have regarded professional firms as reliable and secure customers. A number of partnership failures together with growing sophistication in evaluating banking propositions has led banks to recognise the enormous diversity within the professional services firms and hence to realise the importance of assessing each lending proposition on its own merits. In particular, banks are now much more likely to be prescriptive when communicating their views on:

- the maintenance of partner capital levels;
- the ratio of borrowed to self-funded partner capital;
- working capital management;
- the rate at which profits are distributed to partners.

When evaluating its position with regard to a particular professional practice, a bank will consider a wide range of factors including:

- the profitability and cash flow of the business;
- the management structure and effectiveness;
- retention and development of key people;
- liquidity and key performance ratios.

In addition to being provided with copies of the partnership's annual accounts, the bank will generally wish to see monthly or quarterly management accounts together with the forward-looking business plan.

Whether lending to a partner to fund his capital contribution or to the partnership itself, a bank will review its total exposure to the practice without particular regard to whether funds are being advanced to an individual partner or to the partnership as a whole.

All partners in a general partnership will be contractually bound in respect of the obligations regarding the partnership current account or overdraft facilities and loans. Incoming partners are, as a matter of course, required to accept a similar liability to the firm's bankers. To the extent that personal guarantees are required, partners will wish to negotiate terms whereby they may be released from these guarantees on their retirement from the practice.

When reviewing profit-sharing arrangements, a partnership may feel it appropriate to change the capital contributions of partners. Typically, this may involve the repayment of excess capital balances when measured against the revised requirements, while giving time for partners with increased capital requirements to make up the new balances. The strains which this imposes on the partnership's finances should not be overlooked. Cash flow planning should be undertaken to ensure that no unintended cash flow shortfalls occur. The need to allow extended periods of time for partners to introduce new capital can of course be overcome if the rate of interest paid to partners on their capital balances exceeds the rate charged by the bank on partner capital loans.

3.5.1 Limited liability partnerships

At this point, it is appropriate to mention the position of limited liability partnerships (LLPs). Introduced with effect from 6 April 2001 and available throughout Great Britain (but not Northern Ireland), GB LLPs are bodies corporate whose members are taxed in a similar fashion to partners in an unlimited partnership. Members of the LLP benefit, in theory at least, from limited liability. However, unlike other partnerships, LLPs are required to file accounts with the Registrar of Companies. These accounts, which must be audited unless audit exemptions apply, are prepared on the true and fair basis.

During the consultation phase which led to the enactment of the Limited Liability Partnership Act 2000, many banks expressed caution that lending to LLPs would leave them more exposed. As a result, the issue of personal guarantees for members of LLPs was debated. These guarantees would, of course, reduce the effectiveness of the limitation of liability.

Many bankers seem to draw confidence from the application of true and fair accounting to LLPs. Banks welcome the fact that a professional practice which conducts business through the medium of an LLP will produce accounts in a similar format to the typical corporate customer of the bank. This enables the bank to understand the business proposition more readily. Whether this enables banks to dispense with personal guarantees from members of most LLPs remains to be seen.

Banks may also draw some comfort from the fact that an LLP can give security in the same way as a company. The bank's perception of the quality of that security will very much depend upon the profile of the professional firm. For example, the size or nature of the professional firm may be such that, in difficult financial times, the partners might disagree among themselves or leave with their clients. In such circumstances, there is a risk that the value of both work in progress and debtors would be damaged. This would make any security considerably less attractive to a bank.

3.5.2 Current account facilities

Every professional practice requires a current account and most make use of an overdraft facility at some time during the year.

Each firm therefore must determine and agree with its bankers the level of its overdraft facility. For this purpose, the most important consideration will be the pattern of overdraft finance required by the business, as disclosed by the annual budgeting process. This will help the firm identify the annual fluctuation in finance requirements which may most readily be addressed through overdraft finance. It will also help quantify core finance requirements which may be effected through short-, medium- or long-term loan arrangements. By using interest rate management mechanisms such as fixed rates, capped rates or collars, future finance costs may be quantified with reasonable certainty and kept to a realistic minimum. All this may come at a price in terms of flexibility if the loan agreement contains penalties for early redemption. Equally, even at the outset of a new loan arrangement, thought ought to be given to the issues which might arise on refinancing at the end of the loan should interest rates have moved sharply upwards in the intervening period.

The range of services offered by banks under the general heading of 'current account' reflects the diversity in the professional services sector. At one end of the spectrum, a traditional branch-based current account may be sufficient. For large firms, particularly those with significant volumes of transactions, on-line banking will be required. Solicitors, accountants and others handling client money will also require client account arrangements which may be the subject of a separate audit.

3.5.3 Loan finance

This has already been touched upon. When considering loan finance, practices may wish to consider sources other than their customary bankers. Other banks and financial institutions may have an interest in developing a relationship with the firm and may offer more competitive terms as a result.

3.6 Other sources of finance

3.6.1 Asset finance

Term loans, leasing arrangements or, occasionally, hire purchase may be used to finance specific areas of expenditure such as new computer systems, building improvements or motor cars.

3.6.2 Debt factoring

While generally available to professional practices other than solicitors, most firms have been reluctant to make use of debt factoring because of a perception that this may impair client relationships. Furthermore, the costs of debt factoring have to be set against the improved cash flow which may result.

3.6.3 Joint ventures

In areas as diverse as financial services and property, professional firms may enter into joint ventures. Under the terms of these joint ventures, the professional firm will typically bring its skills while the other party may bring opportunities and finance. The profits are then shared according to the terms of the joint venture agreement. Firms should be aware of these possibilities and the related financing issues, which are somewhat outside the scope of this chapter.

3.6.4 Service stream finance

Banks and other financial institutions may offer types of finance geared to particular service streams. For example, solicitors may require finance in respect of personal injury work. Following changes in civil litigation proceedings brought about by the Access to Justice Act 1999 and the withdrawal of Legal Aid, insurance companies now provide a range of policies to meet claimants' legal costs where there is an unfavourable outcome.

Following these changes, certain banks now provide solicitors with funding products for personal injury cases, financing both disbursements recoverable in a successful action and work in progress. Such products may allow solicitors to finance more cases and regulate their cash flow.

An example of how finance may be provided for a motor accident case is as follows.

Table 3.2 Financing the cost of a motor accident case

	£
Initial investigation fee	250
Fee for obtaining medical notes and records and hospitals	40
Police report (1 in 4 cases at £50)	15
Work in progress	300
Insurance policy to cover all of the above in the event that the case does not proceed or is lost	65
	670

The financing cost of such facilities will depend upon the number of cases, the source of such cases and the perceived risk of non-settlement.

3.7 Managing growth

While the growth and development of the practice will be accompanied by changing financial needs, the need for close management of working capital, particularly the billing of work in progress and the collection of debts, is a constant theme for all firms. Banks will wish to see regular management accounts for the practice and will be quick to point out any perceived loss of control of working capital. It is not unknown for banks which are concerned about a practice's working capital management to require a restriction or moratorium on drawings until the working capital position has been remedied. Strong financial management within the practice and a close relationship with the firm's bankers are important if both parties are to be spared unpleasant surprises. While medium–large firms have in the main embodied these approaches in their day-to-day management, smaller firms could often apply the same principles of cash management to their own advantage.

3.7.1 Capital structure

An important element of the management of the growth of a practice is the admission of new partners. These may come from within the firm or may be recruited from elsewhere. Whatever the source, the existing partners must have a clear policy on the equity structure of the firm. In the broadest terms, should they tend to restrict equity to a limited number of partners, or should the equity base be broadened? Each school of thought has its advocates. In addition, trends change over time. From the mid 1980s to the late 1990s a balance of commercial and taxation considerations led many practices to broaden the equity base. The admission of new equity partners was felt to strengthen the firm by diversifying the skills available at partner level and so attracting new forms of work to the practice.

Recent years, however, have seen a return to a more traditional type of thinking which finds many practices drawing a distinction between proprietorial and operational issues. Motivated in part perhaps by the increasing possibility of securing a capital sum on exit (or by a recognition that not all partners are equal), many small–medium firms are reinforcing two-tier partnership structures with 'full equity' and 'fixed share equity' partners.

Whichever of these routes is followed, sophisticated partner remuneration systems are increasingly being implemented to incentivise personal performance, encourage team behaviour and provide a secure foundation for the finance of the practice.

3.8 Exit routes

Exit routes, by which may loosely be meant the realisation of an opportunity to transfer an interest in the business to a third party in a way which releases funds to the existing partners, may take a variety of forms:

- the admission of a new partner;
- the admission to partnership of a team of partners from another firm;
- merger with a smaller firm;
- merger with a larger firm,
- sale of proprietorial interests to a corporate vehicle such as a 'consolidator' or financial institution;
- incorporation of the practice followed by the issue of shares or loan notes to a third party investor, or by flotation on a Stock Exchange.

In broad terms, the admission of a new partner to a well-run small practice may provide additional capital to the firm, so allowing the capital contributions of the existing partners to be reduced. Similar comments may apply to admission of a team of partners although in the latter case the increased capital is likely to be required to fund growth within the business. As the size of a unit added increases, so the quality of the financing of the practice becomes more important if the firm is to be an attractive 'home' for its new members.

Finally, on the scale of partner-driven exits, a merger with a large firm will require an attractive 'target' firm. Finance is only one factor to be taken into account in a merger. On a merger with a larger firm, the overdraft of the acquired firm may simply be taken over and be replaced by the practice finance arrangements of the acquiror firm. Alternatively, depending on the terms of the merger, the old overdraft and the debtors of the old practice may be left with the old partners who will arrange for debts to be collected and the overdraft repaid out of the proceeds.

Figure 3.1 Growth and exit routes

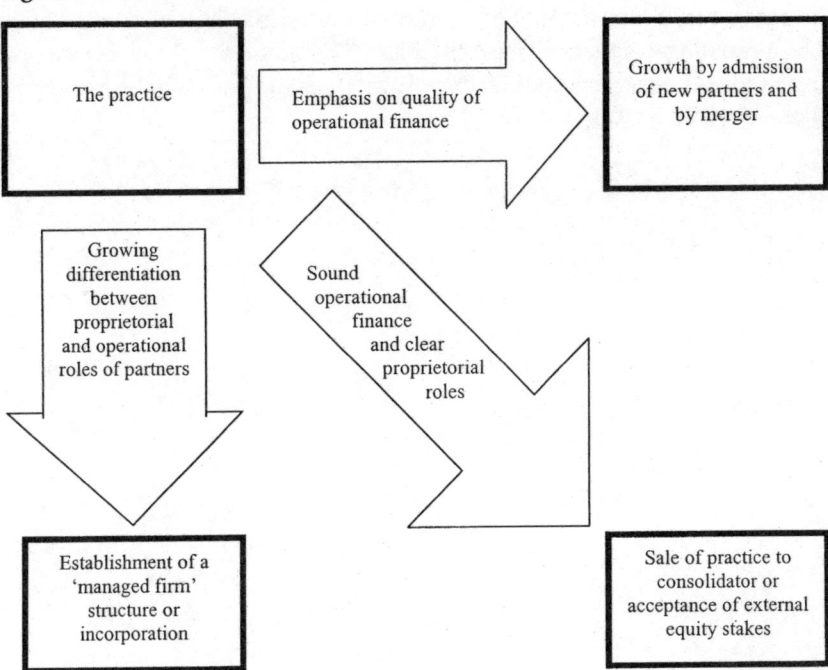

Exits achieved in this way place increasing emphasis on the quality of the finance arrangements of the practice:

This illustration also demonstrates the importance of differentiating between the proprietorial and operational roles of partners. This point is fundamental to an exit route via the admission of external equity where the equity providers will not be operational partners in the business. These issues are, of course, also encountered as a traditional practice moves to the model of a 'managed firm'. This process of transition, and indeed the simple process of incorporating a professional practice without the immediate possibility of an external body requiring an equity stake, can be an extremely important and useful discipline in the development of a firm.

In these circumstances, the exit process will typically be characterised by partners receiving an equity stake, loan note or other debt instrument in the acquiror, broadly in consideration for their giving up their proprietorial interest in the existing firm. By widening the equity-holder base, the nature of the equity return will become clearer as dividends and/or interest are paid. However, those partners who retain operational roles within the practice may well find that their annual earnings from the business have been reduced. In

Sources of finance

considering the total return from their business activities, they therefore need to compare the total amount of dividends, interest and earnings received with the preceding partnership's profit share. The amount of any capital sum received and the prospect of further growth in value must also be included in the reckoning.

4 The future needs of clients

4.1 Changing client requirements

The needs of the owner managed businesses (OMBs) and small companies (SMEs) that make up the majority of both the existing and target markets for independent practices have changed substantially in recent years and will continue to do so in the foreseeable future. They now expect far more from their accountants than simply compliance work. Although audits will continue to be required by companies that do not fall beneath the threshold, these clients expect their accountants to be business advisers in the true sense and are looking for a wide range of added-value consultancy services.

Clients are also more demanding; they want more for their money and they want to pay less, so firms need to ensure not only that they are providing the services their clients need, but also that all the work – whether compliance or consultancy – is produced in an extremely cost-effective manner.

Firms should also bear in mind, if they have not realised it already, that client loyalty has all but disappeared. Gone are the days when clients would seldom consider switching to a different accountant. Today they know it is a buyers' market and will not hesitate to take their business elsewhere if they think they can pay less for the same service or get a wider range of services.

It has been clearly demonstrated in several surveys that the modern business sees the provision of audit and tax compliance work as the least of their requirements from an accountant. Their expectations, in order of perceived importance are:

- business planning;
- profit improvement;
- wealth protection;
- tax mitigation;
- raising finance;
- shareholder/proprietor issues (e.g., disputes or personal financial planning);
- family business dynamics;
- acquisitions, mergers and disposals;

The future needs of clients

- retirement;
- compliance (audit and tax).

Business owners will almost always turn first to their accountants for advice on all aspects of business management and development. However, if firms want to retain the growth companies that are the key to their own continued success they cannot afford to wait for clients to ask for advice. They need to be proactive in identifying clients' requirements and offering the services that fit those requirements.

Independent practices are essentially OMBs themselves. With few exceptions, the added-value services that they should be offering to their clients are the ones they need also and which, in theory, they should therefore be well-equipped to provide.

4.2 Changing types of work

Few independent practices have the resources to offer all of the services listed above and later in this chapter we will examine the various options that will enable them to broaden the range of services they can provide. In the first instance, however, there needs to be a review of attitudes and working practices within the firm with regard to the different types of work undertaken.

4.2.1 Type 1 work

Type 1 work is cost driven and includes:

- audit;
- accounts preparation;
- simple tax returns;
- bureau services;
- bookkeeping services.

This is work that clients need, but will buy purely on cost, and the cheaper the better. Therefore, firms need to ensure that their practices are geared up to provide it. Basically, this type of work is simply factory processing and should be treated as such. Expensive partner time must be reduced to a minimum and systems put in place to ensure that this type of work – although produced to a high standard in terms of quality – is extremely cost effective.

For firms that do not have the capability – or the desire – to expand into added-value services, compliance work can still be extremely profitable provided it is approached in this fashion.

4.2.2 Type 2 work

Type 2 work is benefit driven and includes all the added-value services listed above. This is work that clients value and which, because it has a perceived value in terms of the contribution it can make to the growth and prosperity of their businesses, they are both ready and willing to pay for. For the vast majority of independent firms this is where their potential for growth lies and where they must concentrate their efforts to develop or buy in the skills that are required to ensure that clients' needs are met.

4.3 Changing client attitudes

The fact that clients these days seldom feel a sense of loyalty to their accountants means that they are much more likely to shop around for the advice they need. Unless firms are extremely proactive in identifying and satisfying those needs before the client has had a chance to consider the alternatives, they may well find that the client has either decided to move on without consulting them, or thrown them into a competitive pitch situation with several other practices. Indeed, some companies review their arrangements with professional advisers on a regular basis and, no matter how much they may value the service being provided, will automatically seek assurance that they are getting the best deal by putting their contract out to tender.

Surveys have shown that the three most commonly stated reasons for going to tender are, in order of importance, cost, range of services and quality. Also seen as important are industry sector experience and international connections. At the bottom of the list are geographic convenience and the number of offices that the firm has in the UK. Thanks to modern communications, having advisers on the doorstep is no longer a priority, and size is seen as relatively unimportant provided the firm can offer the breadth of services required.

4.4 Changing working methods

As we have seen, if firms are to maximise profits from compliance work they are going to have to streamline their working methods in this area. However, changes in client requirements and attitudes also means that a radical rethink of working methods throughout the practice will be required if growth and profitability are to be maintained.

4.4.1 Old versus new working methods

The organisation of the practice

Unfortunately many practitioners still take the view that a professional practice is not the same as a commercial business. They also do not see any reason why the working practices that they have used for compliance work should not be applied to any of the added-value services that they are now called upon to provide. Not only will this have an extremely negative effect upon practice management efficiency, it will also reduce profitability and prevent the firm from achieving its growth potential.

GPs and specialists

Although there are some highly specialised niche practices, historically the majority of medium-sized independent firms could be described as GPs with certain individual partners having specialist skills that they could call upon as required. There was no structured approach to the provision of specialist services. The changing needs of clients mean that this type of structure is no longer appropriate.

Firms need to be organised into specialist departments with dedicated partners and staff. Although there can be some interdepartmental movement of staff, either for training purposes or to cope with sudden influxes of work, each should be viewed as a separate profit centre with its own budget for Human Resources and marketing and production purposes.

Looking forward

Under the old working methods firms mainly operated on the basis of historical data supplied to them by the client from which they produced reports/accounts/tax returns, etc. The modern firm needs to be looking in the opposite direction. If practitioners are to provide real added value to their clients they must look at what is likely to happen in the future, relying on trends and projections to spot business opportunities – for themselves as well as for their clients.

As well as being forward-thinking, the new working methods require practitioners to have a much greater knowledge and understanding of their clients' businesses, aims and aspirations. The objective should be for the client to consider the firm as a crucial element in their business development and success.

This can only be achieved if the advice given is based on a real understanding on the part of the firm.

Elsewhere in this book we look at how a modern practice should be structured, but in terms of identifying and satisfying the future needs of clients' firms need to consider the following before attempting to design a workable practice plan:

1. What is our business?
2. What is our market?
3. What resources (financial and human) do we need to penetrate that market?
4. What is our organisation now?
5. What are the external factors we need to consider?
6. How does our existing structure work, and how is it meant to work?
7. Does the structure meet operating requirements, and what changes are necessary to increase effectiveness?
8. What management is needed for the future?
9. Is staffing sufficient in various departments?
10. Is there a need to recruit expertise?
11. Does the structure provide performance recognition?
12. How big do we want the firm to be?
13. Where will the necessary capital and income come from?
14. Have you analysed current clients' industry practices and market potential? What are the trends? What is the profit potential. Who are our primary competitors?

Charging for services

Partners must realise that they are running a commercial organisation and think of themselves as businessmen. The old working methods simply do not apply to the modern provider of business services (which is how accountants should be positioning themselves). In the past fees were earned on the basis of time spent, and many clients were charged annually. Today, even though compliance clients are still charged time-based fees, they should expect to make interim payments – usually by standing order – throughout the year.

For business services clients the picture should be very different. Fees should be earned on the basis of value for money as seen from the client's perspective. Provided they believe they are getting the best quality service and advice that is making a real contribution to the success of their organisation they will be prepared to pay a premium. In general, fees will be project based and partners must accept that – although recording time input may be useful – they should not charge on the old basis of time spent by the firm, but on value received by the client.

Regulation and risk

Although some firms – particularly those that have fallen foul of them – chafe at the ever-increasing regulations that surround compliance work, the ICAEW, other accountancy institutes and the regulatory bodies are there as much to protect the members' interests as those of their clients. With the exception of financial services, the unregulated areas which now form the only real business growth area do not have that protection – either for firm or client. Although the rewards are greater there are attendant risks and firms need to ensure a high level of skill and expertise in every added-value service they offer and instigate a system of checks and balances that will enable them to maintain quality standards.

Competition

The competition for compliance work is confined almost exclusively to other accountancy firms, but clients have a much wider choice of providers when it comes to the business advisory services that fall into the 'added value' category. For example, banks, insurance companies and IFAs are all rivals and firms need to invest a considerable amount of time and effort in promoting themselves as the preferred alternative if they are to compete effectively.

4.5 Changing practice structure

A great many firms are beginning to find that that the traditional structure of an accountancy practice is not the most efficient vehicle in which to drive the business forward and meet the changing needs of clients. The partnership structure – as well as exposing the partners to risk – frequently mitigates against the implementation of change on a timely basis. Where no individual has overall control and the business is run effectively by committee it can prove impossible to obtain a consensus of opinion on the way forward, effectively stopping practice development in its tracks.

This is just one of the reasons that firms are increasingly looking to incorporation as a means of providing a better vehicle for growing and adding value to their practices. The benefits will include, inter alia:

- a management structure that can react quickly to the changing needs of firm, clients and marketplace;
- no personal liability risk – makes partnership/directorship a more attractive proposition, enabling the firm to recruit high-calibre personnel;
- separating out the non-compliance work – creates a saleable asset (or assets) which can be realised at any time;
- greater ability to raise capital.

Adapting the practice structure to conform to the commercial realities of the marketplace will help to create a business of real value. Increases in efficiency and profitability will, of course, impact directly on the incomes of the partners and on their succession plans. Firms that are planning to solve succession issues through sale or merger will find themselves in an extremely strong position when negotiating with potential purchasers or merger partners, whilst those planning on retaining their independence will have no problems funding exit routes or attracting the right replacements.

4.6 Networking for success

No matter how much restructuring takes place or how efficiently the practice is run, the fact remains that the resources to create and staff enough added-value service areas to satisfy the needs of every client are beyond the means of the majority of independent firms. In **Chapter 8** we have examined the merits of a judicious merger, both as a means of extending the firm's range of services and to fund exit routes and/or further practice development.

There is, however, an alternative for those firms that recognise the necessity of branching out into new areas in order to improve profitability and ensure practice growth, but do not wish to go down the Mergers and Acquisitions route. Networking with other firms will allow them to bolt on a range of services to their existing portfolio and, through the exchange of information, may even help them to develop faster as they are able to learn from the mistakes (and the successes) of others.

There are a number of networking opportunities available to the independent practice as follows.

4.6.1 The national firm

Some of the larger national practices offer an 'almost a merger' situation which, whilst allowing individual practices to retain their independence, offers a broad range of specialist, management and training skills from their central bank which the members of their network or associated firms can call upon on an ad hoc basis.

A pre-eminent example is Horwath Clark Whitehill. The firm has a central core of profit-sharing offices and a group of associates. These are all independent firms that pay a membership fee for which they receive certain benefits, and obtain other support services on a 'pay as you go' basis. Common to the core firm and the associates is a quality-control arrangement. This is in contrast to firms such as Grant Thornton and Baker Tilly, which are national partnerships with centralised profit sharing. However, before entering into arrangements with national practices it is important to bear in mind that, although they may be able to offer a full range of services, there may well be a substantial loss of independence.

4.6.2 The umbrella group

The objective of the umbrella group is to help its member firms – generally small and medium-sized practices – to compete effectively with much larger rivals. CharterGroup is a good example of the groups that are currently active. Each member pays an annual subscription and must have an annual quality-control review. Best practice forums, industry groups and technical groups are a strong feature which brings together the members to discuss, innovate and refer as appropriate around the network. Knowledge is shared and can be used for the general good, but in a situation where the firms are (through membership) in a non-competitive situation. In some cases firms are encouraged to group together in order to compete for work (national audits for example) which, on an individual basis, they could not hope to win. Thus, although retaining full independence, they can act as a national practice and derive these benefits.

As well as networking opportunities with other member firms, these organisations generally offer a variety of centralised services from interfirm comparisons and professional training to personalised publications, and in some cases can use the collective buying power of the organisation to obtain discounts on major items of expenditure such as computer hardware and software, professional indemnity insurance, marketing, publications, etc.

These organisations pose no threat to a firm's independence, but can offer a very effective means of broadening its range of skills. Membership can also help to prevent the insularity that can occur if firms rely solely on promotion to partner from within; they expose firms to the ideas and experiences of the other members and give them a wider perspective on management and development issues.

4.6.3 Local organisations

Firms in many parts of the country have set up local self-help groups to offer assistance to each other. With no central organisation the onus is very much on the individual practices to seek each other out and organise their own reciprocal arrangements for client services or the exchange of information and ideas. For some this is an extremely successful method of having a skill base available without investing in additional staff. However, there is a risk of client poaching or defection, particularly if a larger firm has access to a small firm's clients. It is therefore important for individual firms to ensure that restrictive covenants are enforced.

4.6.4 The individual approach

Rather than join an organisation or group, some firms prefer to seek out their own contacts. An increasing number of small practices have decided that, rather than compete in the general practitioner market, they will turn themselves into 'boutiques' specialising either in one particular discipline or one type of client. Examples include corporate finance, tax planning, insolvency and IT consultancy. Using such specialists has many advantages for the smaller firm; in particular the fact that there is little scope for client poaching and the practitioner can be confident that the specialist he uses for, say Mergers and Acquisitions work or corporate recovery is not interested in his client per se. Thanks to modern technology-finding such specialists is not only comparatively easy, but, for the same reason, there does not necessarily have to be close geographical proximity between client and specialist so firms can use a much wider net to trawl for the services they need to buy in.

4.6.5 Other professions

In larger firms non-accountant partners have now become the rule rather than the exception. Smaller practices should not overlook the advantages of networking with members of other professions who, as well as providing advisory services to clients, can be an extremely valuable source of referred work. Financial services is one area in particular where smaller firms are increasingly taking advantage of the opportunities for joint working, either through a joint venture, or by referral. For those reluctant to set up their own financial services operation, networking with independent financial advisers is the best introduction to this lucrative area.

Networking with bankers, IT consultants and other professionals can also make a very real difference to a firm's bottom line as well as the level of client satisfaction.

Small and medium-sized firms

For small and medium-sized firms, networking should be a formal part of their development strategy, whether or not they need it to develop client services. Without it they risk stagnation and, ultimately, a very real threat to their continuing independence.

Each option may help the firm to organise itself profitably by providing access to specialist areas for developing new business, creating added value and the opportunity to recruit or 'buy in' new or potential partners. Opportunities for merger, or (for the smaller firm) sale will also present themselves with network members providing real but comfortable alternatives for practice succession.

5 Developing new skills, developing existing partners, and appointing new partners

5.1 Introduction

Today's most forward-thinking organisations are becoming 'learning organisations'. They appreciate the need to create a learning environment, to get everybody to 'think learning' at every opportunity.

If a practice is to have sufficient competent people in the future, it needs to embrace this philosophy now. This applies to all of the different groups within the practice, partners and staff, and the same principles apply to ensure you get the best out of all these groups. Knowing which skills need to be developed relies on you having a clear vision and plan for the future of your practice. Ensuring your people develop the skills you need means having an effective system of performance reviews.

Too often in businesses, there is one 'rule' for the staff and another for the bosses when it comes to performance management and carrying out reviews of performance. However, it is arguably even more 'mission critical' to have an effective review process for the most senior individuals in the business, as they will be most influential in shaping the business and creating success for the future. For that reason we will concentrate on performance management as the framework for developing new skills, and existing partners, and as a tool for identifying the need for 'new blood' in the practice.

The process of identifying the need for new skills is therefore the same for all of the groups of people in your organisation, and needs to link effectively to your business planning process to ensure that you are identifying both the skills that you need to deliver the business results you want, and the people who either have those skills or the potential to develop them. If you do that effectively you will also identify where you need to bring new talent into the practice, including new partners. With an effective performance-management system you will be in control of the future – without it, success may well be in the lap of the gods!

Points to identify:

- Who will be the practice's 'stars' of the future?
- How are they being prepared?
- Who makes sure that they get the training they need?
- How often do they receive constructive feedback?
- Do they know what they need to do to reach the next rung on the ladder?
- How can the practice widen their breadth of experience?
- Does the practice address their weaknesses as well as 'pat them on the back' for their strengths?

5.1.1 Development is everybody's responsibility

To a degree, everybody has some responsibility for their own development. Without doubt, everybody who has even just one person reporting to them is responsible for *their* development too. Balancing this responsibility with everyday targets and job roles can be difficult, but if the time is taken, the practice will be repaid several times over from the extra motivation and skills gained by the staff and partners.

All organisations need a framework within which they can undertake regular assessment of an individual's performance, their future potential and their training and development needs. A performance review system does this by looking back over the recent past to assess what has been achieved, but more importantly to agree what could be achieved in the future. The formal review can be carried out every 12 months, to fit in with the practice's business planning and review cycle, with regular updates to monitor progress and make adjustments to keep on track.

It provides an opportunity to see how an individual's talents can be developed to the benefit of the practice, and having an effective performance review system is key to successfully developing new skills for staff and partners, and ensuring that an individual's performance is not being adversely affected by a whole range of factors.

5.1.2 Reviews and motivation

Employees who feel that their employer values their contribution tend to work better than those who just feel like 'another number on the payroll'. Reviews are a prime opportunity to stimulate renewed commitment from employees by reinforcing to them how vital their role is to the practice.

It is also a rare chance for the individual to take time out of their ordinary routine and to raise any issue which may have been causing concern and affecting their performance at work. If the right environment is created by the reviewer, issues which it would be difficult to raise during the normal working relationship can often be discussed openly, with a positive outcome for the individual and the practice.

There are of course no golden rules for motivating all individuals. Though pay is important for most people, it is rarely the real motivator. Some people thrive on praise and recognition, others love to keep learning, some enjoy helping others and the business, some like working for a boss who takes a genuine interest in them as a person, and their home life too. Some individuals are very ambitious, and want to see a possible career path mapped out for them, others just want to do a good job and go home on time each night. In reality, both staff and partners will fall into these categories. It is essential to get the best possible performance out of them all, to ensure that as partners they are delivering the results the business needs, and that the staff who will be the partners and other key individuals in the future, are being identified and their skills developed.

Performance in a job can be split into three key areas, and each should be addressed in a performance review:

- what the individual does – the tasks and responsibilities which form the core of their role;
- how they behave – the way they go about doing their job, the way they relate to colleagues, their style of working;
- what they contribute to the business – what they actually achieve in helping the business to meet its business objectives and targets.

Performance reviews can also help towards each of the following:

1 a chance to clear up misunderstandings;
2 a chance to sort out problem areas in the individual's job;
3 an opportunity to stimulate staff and partners by praise and encouragement;
4 an opportunity to make sure the individual is aware of your opinion of their work;
5 a time to identify training and development needs;
6 a chance to consider the individual's future;
7 an opportunity to assess an individual's value and their remuneration;

8 a chance to listen to an individual's problems and worries;

9 an opportunity to get an individual to recognise their weaknesses and agree to address them.

The ultimate objective, however, *has* to be to improve the firm's performance!

There is no single 'right' way to carry out performance reviews, however there are a number of factors which influence how effective they are. The key is to devise a system which works well in your particular practice, which will mean taking into account the following fundamental requirements.

5.2 The practical issues of performance review

5.2.1 Who reviews who?

In reality, who will carry out the reviews will depend on the practice's internal structure, and how many people there are in the practice. Many organisations simply follow their line management structure, but sometimes it is better to have the reviews carried out by someone who will do it well, in conjunction with the line manager, to make sure the practice gets the best value out of the process. What is not desirable for the practice is people going through the motions of the process with no real benefits. An organisation needs to work out what is right for them. The key is that it needs to be done for everyone – particularly partners!

5.2.2 Preparation

The best review meetings require preparation by *both* the reviewer and reviewee. For the reviewee, a process of self review prior to the meeting has a number of benefits:

- the reviewee takes a degree of ownership for the review and feels that their contribution is valid;
- reviewees often identify weaknesses for themselves making them much easier to address jointly without defensiveness;
- reviewees tend to be harder on themselves than their reviewer and hence it often provides an opportunity to praise the individual;
- the whole performance review becomes more of a meeting for discussion than an interview where the reviewer dominates the proceedings.

It may seem obvious, but the more effort that goes into the preparation for the review by the reviewer the more benefit is likely to be derived by both parties. Part of the preparation is in the mechanics of the meeting – getting the environment right for a positive exchange of views with an equally positive outcome.

Paperwork

The paperwork for a review process does not need to be complicated. Many organisations simply use a blank sheet of paper with headings on it to make sure that all the areas above are thought about in advance, discussed at the meeting and any action points are noted and copies kept by both parties to make sure they happen. It is important to use a style of paperwork which fits the 'culture' of your practice – and one that will not put people off or detract from the real purpose of the meeting. It is equally important to make sure that all of the individuals involved in the process understand how it works, and the paperwork, before getting started.

Time

Arrange a time convenient to both reviewer and reviewee in advance. This should be approached realistically. It would be best to schedule at least 1? hours so that proceedings do not feel rushed, but longer may be needed depending on the issues and the individual.

Place

Hold the meeting somewhere where there will be no interruptions. Ensure other people know not to interrupt you except in an emergency. (The reviewee needs to know that their review is being treated as a priority activity.)

Mental preparation

Apart from completing the appropriate paperwork and making arrangements with the reviewee, the reviewer will also need to take some time out to consider the areas that need to be discussed and plan how to raise any difficult issues. The reviewer should be familiar with the individual's areas of responsibility – there is nothing worse that sitting down with someone and discovering how little you actually know about their job and how they are performing.

Written preparation

It is also useful for the reviewer to note down examples of specific situations that illustrate the points s/he hopes to discuss during the review.

It is a good idea for the reviewer to actually write down some of the open questions that could be asked to get the reviewee talking. A tip would be to write these in big bold letters, perhaps even highlighted in colour so that they can be read quickly and naturally and do not interrupt the flow of the proceedings.

It may also be useful for the reviewer to make a brief summary of the key points that he hopes to cover, again in big easy-to-read letters so that the list can be easily checked through before concluding the meeting.

5.2.3 Questioning skills

If the reviewee is to talk for a high proportion of the time, the reviewer has to be very skilled in asking the right questions. Questions can basically be divided into two types, as follows:

Closed questions

These are questions that the person can only respond to with a 'yes' or 'no' answer. For example, 'Do you think you have done all you can to maximise fee income for your department?' These kinds of questions are useful when the reviewer wants to get the reviewee to agree about an issue, but will be no use in getting the person to talk. If care is not taken, they can also turn into leading questions, forcing the other person into a corner, 'So you do not want to change roles then?' This can result in the reviewer putting words into the individual's mouth without them having a chance to say what they really want to say.

Open questions

Particularly at the outset of the meeting, these questions will be most useful to the reviewer. They get the reviewee to open up and therefore will help the reviewer to understand more about how they are thinking, their views on their performance and how they feel they can change.

For example, 'How do you feel you've been doing since you've taken over your new role?' or, 'What would be the best way to arrange that then, Jack?'

Care should be taken to ask only one question at a time. Overlap should be avoided, e.g., 'Where did you first discover this, why didn't you report it and how have things changed since then?' The reviewee will forget certain parts, avoid parts and most importantly will probably feel rather intimidated.

Table 5.1 Key words for asking questions

Open	Closed
How	Did
Why	Can
When	Have
Who	Do
What	Will
Where	Is
	Would

Care should also be taken with 'Why' questions as they can sound judgmental, as if the reviewer is accusing the other person. For example, 'What is your reasoning behind that?' can elicit the same answer as 'Why did you do that?' in a more pleasant way.

Other good questions to get the reviewee to open up are the 'Tell me about' kind, e.g. 'Tell me more about your ideas for a new service in the Tax Department' or 'Tell me why you felt that was the best part of the job'.

5.2.4 Listening skills

Within the meeting, the reviewee should talk more than the reviewer. In order to make this happen the reviewer will need to use good questioning techniques (as already described), but the reviewer will also need to ensure that he is a good listener.

The British in general are *not* good listeners. Because we can think much faster than we can talk, we tend to use up the spare capacity created while another person is talking by thinking about other things, e.g., what we are going to say next, or who our next meeting is with. Then when it comes to our turn to talk again, we are not able to build on what the reviewee has just said because we were not listening properly.

A reviewer should:

- always be prepared to sit out those awkward silences. A few seconds feels like a long time when nothing is said but may cause the reviewer to 'jump in' and not let the reviewee say what is really on their mind, having plucked up the courage to do so. Give the reviewee time to find the right words;
- always provide encouragement to open up if necessary. The reviewee may need convincing that the reviewer really does want to hear what they have got to say;

- never assume you know what the reviewee is going to say. A reviewer may often be wrong and 'put words in their mouth';
- always remember that silence and shyness do not necessarily indicate lack of ambition. An attempt to draw the reviewee out of themselves should be made. An opportunity should be taken to find out what every individual wants to do now and in the future – there may be some surprises!
- keep clarifying and summarising what the reviewee is saying to show concern and to check that you really do understand them;
- always beware of hearing only the good, and filtering out the things you really do not want to hear!

5.2.5 Taking notes

Watching you write down what they are saying may well help the reviewee to feel that you are taking them seriously, but:

- the reviewer should tell the reviewee that this will be done at the outset;
- the reviewer should ensure that taking notes does not keep them so preoccupied that the result is that the reviewer is no longer listening to the reviewee;
- the reviewer should remember to look up and establish eye contact with the reviewee as often as possible.

5.2.6 Listening techniques

The seven most important listening techniques are listed below. Note the purpose of each and the examples given.

Table 5.2 Seven most important listening techniques

	Techniques	Purpose	Example
1	Restatement (paraphrasing, reflecting content).	To check meaning and interpretation with the other person. To show you are listening and that you understand what is being said. To encourage the speaker to analyse other aspects of the matter and to discuss it with you.	'As I understand it, your plan is …' 'This is what you have decided to do and the reasons are …' 'You didn't get the new job …'
2	Clarifying questions.	To get additional facts. To help the person explore all sides of a problem.	'Can you clarify this?' 'Do you mean this …?' 'Is this the problem as you see it now?'
3	Neutral responses (minimal encouragers).	To convey that you are interested and listening. To encourage the person to continue talking.	'I see.' 'Uh-huh.' 'That's very interesting.' 'I understand.' Nod your head. Smile.
4	Summarising.	To bring all the discussion into focus to highlight the main themes. To serve as a springboard for further discussion on a new aspect or problem.	'These are the key ideas you have expressed …' 'If I understand how you feel about the situation …'
5	Reflecting meanings (feeling and content).	To show that you understand how the person feels about what he is saying. To help the person to evaluate and temper his own feeling as expressed by someone else.	'You're confused about the situation.' 'It was a shocking thing as you saw it.' 'You felt you didn't get a fair share.'
6	Reflecting feelings.	To become more aware of the individual's feelings. To help the person focus on the emotional aspect of the issue.	'You look angry.' 'You seem disappointed.'
7	Silence (pause).	Silence is often effectively used following a question to allow the sender time to think and respond.	

5.2.7 Receiving feedback

A reviewer needs to be prepared to receive feedback as well as give it. The following may be a useful guide:

- make sure you really listen;
- say 'thank you' for any praise you are given;
- control the urge to justify/defend yourself against criticism;
- take time to absorb what has been said;
- ask for further clarification and suggestions as to how you could act differently.

5.2.8 The Johari window

The Johari window is a useful way of examining feedback – feedback about a blindspot is particularly useful but often the hardest to receive and accept.

Table 5.3 Johari window

	You know	You do not know
Others know	ARENA	BLIND SPOT
Others do not know	FAÇADE	UNKNOWN

5.2.9 Giving feedback

Feedback is the sharing of information that points to an area where performance has been particularly effective or to an area where current behaviour could be changed in order to improve performance.

Negative feedback

This is when the reviewer merely replays when something went wrong – it is essentially destructive and is only used by accident or to terminate relationships! It describes a perceived negative behaviour, without proposing a solution, e.g., 'You are always complaining'.

Constructive feedback

This highlights how the person could do better next time. It needs to be delivered sensibly. It focuses on specific observable facts: e.g., 'Last week you could have helped to complete the assignment if you had gone out of your way to review the files by Friday'.

Giving any form of criticism is always difficult, but should not be avoided as it is often the key element in changing a person's behaviour. What is critical, however, is how the criticism is given.

Ten golden rules for constructive feedback

(1) Ensure the reviewee appreciates that this is the basis for learning, not punishment – if well explained, and conveyed in a sensitive manner the reviewee should be made to feel that the criticism is a starting point for learning and may well feel relieved that it is 'out in the open'.

(2) Give help about how to improve – e.g., 'Yes, I do think the quality of your files have been getting better but you do not seem to be completing them as quickly as we would like. What effect do you think this could have on the business?'

(3) Be specific about the area of which you are being critical – give examples and don't generalise. People are rarely totally awful in every aspect of their performance, e.g., talk about the specific paperwork that they tend to be late in returning, rather than all administrative duties.

(4) Encourage the reviewee to share their views on their performance with you, rather than you giving specific advice – this will be achieved by asking open questions relating to your areas of concern *first*, rather than giving an opinion.

(5) Provide balanced feedback – do not just dismiss strengths or areas where performance is acceptable. Make sure the individual recognises why they are valuable to the company.

(6) When giving criticism, soften the tone but not the message – views should be stated thoughtfully. The reviewer should show concern for the reviewee's feelings but not water down the message.

(7) Avoid exaggeration – if the reviewee can give a specific example to prove the reviewer has exaggerated, it will immediately shatter the value of the whole meeting.

(8) Do not give any surprises – if there are areas of major concern, they should not have been left until the performance review to bring up. If the reviewer has been managing that employee well, they should have already discussed these points at previous meetings.

(9) Turn negatives into positives – e.g., 'I'm always grateful for the speed at which you produce your reports, but I wonder if your thoroughness could not be improved a bit. What do you think?'

(10) Focus on the behaviour and its effects rather than the person/personality – it is important to refer to what the person does rather than how

they are viewed as an individual, e.g., 'When you talked a lot at the meeting, it did not give everyone a chance to speak' rather than, 'You are a bit of a loud mouthed so and so!'

5.2.10 Giving feedback to partners and colleagues

A 'manager' will be required to give both technical and interpersonal feedback to a range of individuals on an ongoing basis. A manager should apply the same feedback model and technique when giving feedback to peers, as well as staff.

The following guidelines will help a manager present their feedback and increases the value of what they say (the most important thing to remember is to give feedback on the behaviour and not on the person).

Table 5.4 Feedback guidelines

Sequence	Explanation
1 'When you …'	Start with a 'when you …' statement that describes the *behaviour* without judgement, exaggeration, labelling, attribution or motives.
2 'I feel …'	Tell how their *behaviour* affects you.
3 'Because I …'	Now say why you are affected that way.
4 Pause for discussion	Let the other person respond. Be prepared to discuss the situation, and together analyse the problem, generate solutions and set goals. It is vital for the receiver of feedback to take ownership of the feedback and be part of the problem-solving. Only if it is absolutely necessary, do you propose your own solution (Steps 5, 6 and 7).
The next three steps (5, 6 and 7) are a very good way of presenting expectations to the other person.	
5 'I would like …'	… describe the change you want the other person to consider …
6 'Because …'	… and why you think the change will alleviate the problem.
7 'What do you think?'	Listen to the other person's response. Be prepared to discuss options and compromise on the solution.

5.2.11 Praise and recognition

Research shows that there is a link between recognition, self esteem and effective performance. People who feel good about themselves produce good results. We tend to suffer from a lack of praise and recognition at work because few people know how to give and receive it very well.

The Americans often refer to the concept of 'strokes' – things that are said or done that have an impact on other people's esteem.

- *Positive strokes* – may include commenting on the excellent figures that week, or just giving somebody a bit of time and attention. These are likely to have a positive impact on esteem.
- *Negative strokes* – such as destructive criticism, sarcasm or being rude or abrupt can lead to a loss of self esteem and should be avoided at all costs when looking at ways to develop others. The praise offered should be genuine. Do not hold back from offering it due to embarrassment and try to reinforce praise even further if the recipient shrugs it off as not being of any great consequence.

5.2.12 Monitoring progress

The single most common reason for the failure of performance reviews to deliver results, is the failure of both parties to monitor progress against the actions that have been agreed. A meeting with a client to review the services delivered, and agree how he could be serviced more effectively in future, would be a waste of time if the actions agreed were not implemented and this may result in a worsening of the relationship rather than an improvement. The same is true of a performance review with an employee or partner. If both parties do not work together to ensure all the action points are addressed, then the benefits will be lost and the impact will be negative.

Training and development needs, identified in the review, of course need to be addressed, and this may involve coaching and mentoring, new work experiences and independent learning as well as the more traditional formal training courses. The best way to develop the skill may not be the most obvious and some individuals respond better to informal 'on the job' training than formal training events.

Regular follow-ups need not be time consuming and once a routine is established they will become just part of the normal process of management in the practice. If the action plan gathers dust for 12 months and is not regarded as an important part of the overall plan to achieve the wider objectives of the business then it really was a waste of time. The most successful performance reviews are followed up every month to ensure that progress is being made, and that the outcomes are being achieved – and nothing is allowed to slip.

5.3 Appointing new partners

Even with the most effective performance review system, linking in to a focused business plan, new people will still need to be brought into the practice at all levels, including partners. The benefit of having the above processes is that it enables a practice to be clear as to what exactly they are looking for to meet the business's needs and compliment the capabilities of the other individuals.

There is a tendency when considering new partners to fall for the 'clone syndrome' – either the 'standard clone' who fits the traditional mould (age 32, trained with a 'good' firm, etc.,) – or the 'mirror clone' who is essentially like us (but perhaps a bit younger)!

The key is to be objective about what the practice really needs, getting some outside help to decide if necessary, and then setting about finding someone who meets the need. On the basis that the performance review process will have identified whether or not there are any internal candidates, this chapter will concentrate on recruiting from outside.

The process is not 'rocket science', but a few commonsense guidelines.

- When it is clear what is being looked for, it is a good idea to ask around – other professionals (lawyers, bankers and other contacts) who will come into contact with potential partners on a regular basis are a good source of possible candidates.

- A full picture of what is needed should be given, and all suggestions should be reviewed. The net can be cast as wide as possible – it should be remembered that these are only suggestions and the more there are, the more that can be applied to the selection criteria.

- Leopards do not change their spots! Whilst people can be trained and developed to give them additional skills and confidence, fundamentally, individuals do not change their whole persona as a result of undertaking a new role. If practice development is needed ('sales' in other words!) an individual who has shown no aptitude for bringing in new business in their previous roles is unlikely to change as a result of joining the practice. The best indicator of future performance is past performance, and an objective assessment is needed to decide whether an individual meets the specification.

- The practice network should be used to find out what the general view is of the candidates favoured – the practice should listen to what people say, not what they want to hear!
- Take time – if the gut feeling is that someone is not right, do not argue with it. But do not apply the same rules if the gut feeling says that they are right – if they are, they will survive the 'objective' tests and the practice will be sure.
- Partnership is like marriage – it needs to work for both parties, so time should be spent finding out what really makes the individuals tick, and making sure that the practice is comfortable that this individual can meet their needs. One of the biggest causes of failure in bringing new people into an organisation is the 'expectation gap' – everyone should be clear so there are no surprises.
- For the individual that is brought into the practice, the induction process should be planned carefully – it is a good idea to return to the principles of the performance review and ensure that the individual is clear about the practice's expectations of them in terms of their role and responsibilities, their behaviour and their contribution to the firm.
- Their performance should be reviewed regularly so they get positive feedback and any issues are dealt with quickly so they do not turn into problems.
- If the situation is not working, act quickly – if the performance review process is being used correctly it will be clear whether problems are solvable or not, and if not, the sooner the practice parts company with the individual the better. Having the wrong person in a senior position can have a significant effect on the rest of the organisation.

5.4 Summary

Creating the environment in which all of the individuals in a practice can develop and improve their performance in line with business objectives is one of the major challenges of effective management, particularly in an increasingly competitive environment. Competition for business will always be matched by competition for high-quality people at all levels of the organisation, and the most successful practices will be those that regard performance management of people as one of the most important aspects of practice management. None of this happens by accident but by the systematic use of a 'people management' framework which continually pushes people to achieve, and an objective process of bringing new people into the organisation to meet changing needs and priorities.

6 Networking

6.1 Attitudes

There is nothing quite so comfortable and secure for the accountant as sitting all day in their place of work and waiting for business to come in. It is a way of life for many – after all, it is considerably easier than hitting the road in search of new business, or cultivating existing clients.

The modern development of the profession is no different from all other businesses. It is now no longer enough to be just a technician if you wish to continue to be accepted as wholly successful. Marketing, selling and promotion are expected to be a major part of a practice's duties in today's world, and as time goes on that 'part' will get bigger.

If you want to grow your practice, there is no other choice than to increase networking activities. It cannot be done immediately, but a practice must start by taking small steps in the right direction. This may feel uncomfortable at first, but like anything, consistent practice builds permanent skills.

Practitioners usually say that they are far too busy, and that the effort outweighs the rewards. Why bother to hunt, they argue, if plenty of good referrals are coming in?

6.2 How active is the firm in its marketing?

Referrals are, of course, the lifeblood, even the oxygen that fuel fee growth in any professional practice. They come from existing clients and professional contacts because:

- of the reputable name that the firm has built;
- the firm and its people are implicitly trusted;
- the firm gives an excellent service;
- the firm recommends clients to other professionals.

However, this *activity* can be fraught with danger. The practice becomes dependent on the goodwill of these people, hoping that these introductions will continue to flow through constantly and consistently.

What happens when introductions fail to flow through constantly and consistently? Acquiring new business through referrals is a cornerstone of any firm's future. Working via referrals is the reactive approach. Gaining new business by networking is the only proactive approach. In the forward-thinking and growth-orientated practices, networking should be *a*, if not *the*, cornerstone of marketing.

Each day, clients and professional contacts decrease. They die, they retire, they sell or merge, and they change their alliances and allegiances. If a practice wants to expand and flourish, it needs a constant transfusion of new business as its lifeblood. With referrals, a practice waits on the actions of others; with networking it is the practice that makes things happen. It is a case of proactive versus reactive.

Practices that are successful and fulfilled often do not appreciate the need to come out of their safe work environment. However, if the practice can cope with more business, there is no excuse not to join the hunt.

Hunting – now called networking – is the fashionable and successful way to find new business. The dictionary definition of networking is: 'The activity of a group of people who exchange information, contacts, and experiences for professional or social purposes' (source: *Readers' Digest Complete Word Finder*).

If this all sounds rather dull, then it should be remembered that this is *real* hunting. Spot your quarry, thrill to the chase and develop a killer instinct. 'Too busy' or 'too time consuming' to join the hunt often translates as 'lack of confidence' – the root cause of cave dwelling.

However, if a practice accepts the need to market, sell and promote, then look at the alternatives to networking. Advertising and PR are a scattergun approach and are often expensive – direct mail is a disappointing one to seven per cent uptake and cold calling is too time consuming and soul destroying.

6.3 Awake, alive and alert

In any case, in a vibrant professional partnership there should never be a need for cold calling. Most practices will know hundreds of people – existing clients, other professional contacts, friends, family, people at the sports or social club, committee members – and this is just for starters. If the practice pools resources with all the other key people in the office, it will have a big and valuable database. When one of the partners is out of the office, that partner may not want to gain business from the people they meet, but it may be appropriate to ask 'Who do you know who may be interested in ...?'

Every invitation to any social function should be seen as a business opportunity, a chance to meet new contacts, to reinforce existing ones and increase fees. 'Working' a room enthusiastically will help to build the partner's confidence and raise his profile thus helping to generate new business..

A large mystique has built up over the term 'networking'. During the 1980s, networking simply used to be called talking. Asking the right questions and, most importantly, listening to the answers creates business opportunities which is the successful result of talking (or, networking). This should happen on holiday, at a social function, on the train, or even in a queue at the takeaway!

6.4 Fears of networking

Working the room requires the courage of a lion and nerves of steel. Most people feel nervous and hesitant and only the most accomplished and regular networker will feel at ease. An recent article on peoples' fears placed arachnophobia (the fear of spiders) at number one, and meeting groups of people at number two, so these fears are commonplace.

The main fears are as follows:

- fear of being trapped by an uninteresting person;
- fear of feeling foolish;
- fear of the unknown;
- feeling of not belonging;
- fear of rejection – at *every* presentation, fear of rejection is cited as being one of the main fears, but this is largely unfounded – when have you ever been rejected, as an adult, in a business or even social environment? The answer is almost invariably, *never*;
- embarrassment;
- uncertainty;
- being judged and found wanting;
- saying the wrong thing;
- feeling out of the comfort zone;

- being ignored;
- drying up;
- how others will react;
- feeling out of place;
- breaking in;
- no common ground;
- moving on;
- not knowing what to say;
- not feeling welcomed;
- not enough technical knowledge;
- not knowing who to talk to;
- not being taken seriously;
- saying the wrong thing.

This chapter will now examine practical *how to* tips and techniques to overcome all these fears, worries and uncertainties; all that is needed is practice.

6.5 The first move

When entering a social or business gathering there will always be people standing on their own. The reason they stand there is because of some, if not all, of the fears already mentioned. They are feeling somewhere between extremely nervous and petrified, otherwise why would they be on their own?

These people should be approached slowly, with a smile, and good eye contact. Asking to join them is the next step, followed by introductions – ask their name (see later for more about names). They will welcome you with open arms and make you their friend for life – well, at least for the evening. You already have at least four things in common before the conversation starts:

- you are fellow guests;
- you have been invited by the same people;
- you are in the same building;
- you have travelled to be there.

Some good questions to ask: 'Have you travelled far to get here?', 'How do you know John and Jean?', 'This is a magnificent reception room, don't you think?', and so on. Within moments you will find you have something in common.

6.6 Forgetting names

One of the worries accountants have when working the room is remembering names – or to be more accurate – forgetting names. The subject of names is generally nothing to do with one's memory. It is simply down to one's attitude. In social terms generally, and networking specifically, remembering and using people's names is a powerful tool in building and maintaining strong business and personal relationships. This area of personal development will bring many rewards. When you introduce yourself for the first time to someone, as suggested above, why not simply give your first name? The chances are they will follow suit and will also give their first name. Some say that it takes them less than three seconds before they forget their new found acquaintance's name, although often, they have not forgotten the name, they never heard it in the first place. The issue here is that both parties tend to mumble their names and not say them clearly. One way around this problem is to say: 'I'm sorry, I didn't catch your name' and the listener will merely repeat it. This is all part the three-step process in building all relationships:

1 know;

2 like;

3 trust.

When asking someone to repeat their name it shows interest and is simply part of the knowing, liking and trusting process. It is often worthwhile trying to repeat their name twice, and if more time is likely to be spent with that person, pictures or word associations can be a useful memory tool. If it feels more comfortable to give both your first and last name, then say it clearly and slowly, putting a pause in the middle. For example, 'My name is Will (pause) Kintish'. Making some comment about your name can help the listener to remember you, e.g., 'Hello, I'm Eric Gates, no relationship to Bill unfortunately', 'Hi, my name is Reena, like Tina but with an R', and so on. If they have an unusual name it is useful to ask where it came from, or how to spell it – this is all part of the building relationship process.

If meeting people you have met before, you should not be embarrassed to say, e.g., 'Please forgive me, I do remember we met at Mary's place but I have forgotten your name'. The chances are that the person is likely to say, 'Yes, I have

Networking

a problem with names also'. It is better to have seven seconds of embarrassment at this point than spend the next 15 minutes thinking: 'I wish I could remember this person's name', or 'I'm feeling so uncomfortable here, I hope no one comes up to me as I am not going to be able to introduce this person'.

Two other tips for remembering names are as follows:

1 When you are with a person whose name you know and a third party comes up to you both – if you do not know this person but it is obvious that your acquaintance does but does not introduce you, it could be that your acquaintance has forgotten the third party's name. Make it easy for your acquaintance and introduce you, the third party will introduce herself and the problem is resolved.

2 Name badges should be worn on the righthand lapel. Why? When meeting people for the first time a lot of activities take place to create that memorable and positive first impression. Hopefully, there will have been a smile and a handshake, good eye contact, and you will have introduced yourself clearly. Now is the time to worry about what this person's name is. Yes, there it is on the badge sitting a long way from your eye on their lefthand side. It is natural for you and everyone else to spend these early seconds seeking out that name. Wearing your badge on your right hand side will make it very easy for your new acquaintance to see your name immediately as you are shaking hands. It is in front of them – right at the end of your extended arm.

6.7 What to talk about

When meeting new groups of people, not knowing what to say is a cause for concern – 'What shall I talk about?', 'there is likely to be no common ground', 'I am not good at the small talk', 'I am going to dry up', 'I may say the wrong thing', are just some of these concerns.

The answer to all these fears is quite simple. It is far more important to be interested than interesting. Interested introverts will create much better impressions than interesting extroverts. In other words, it is better to be a good listener and encourage others to talk about themselves. People love talking about themselves ... let them. It is not necessary to do too much talking because the two key proficiencies, which should be employed in the networking arena, are the skill to ask open questions and to listen attentively and actively. We are all given two ears and one mouth and if we use them in that proportion then the chances are all doubts and concerns will disappear. Nothing is learnt by talking, but everything is learnt by listening. As already discussed, there are at least four subjects in common, even when meeting people for the first time.

By using these four common areas there will already be questions to ask after the initial introduction has been made.

6.7.1 So, what do you do?

After these first few questions, at a seminar, business or social event, one of the most common questions to ask is: 'So, what do you do for a living?' It is usual at this point that people tell you what they are rather than what they do. 'I'm an accountant', 'I'm a solicitor', 'I'm an environmental consultant'. This is an important moment in networking; remember at the end of the day networking is simply word-of-mouth marketing. If all the guidelines have been followed to date and the right impression has been created, now is the time to move gently from the small talk to the potential business opportunity. When asked the question, 'So, what do you do?' let your listener understand how your clients' benefit from the services you offer, rather than telling them what you are. Experience says that when you tell someone you are an accountant, their thought processes go like this:

1 they think you must be boring;

2 they take two mental steps back;

3 they begin to consider how they can get away as soon as possible!

What is happening here is that an impression has been created for them just by saying that you are an accountant.

There are many different classifications, characterizations and philosophies of marketing, but five worth remembering are:

- positioning – knowing what and to whom you are selling;
- packaging – putting your positioning ideas into verbal and written words;
- promotion – becoming visible and credible (remember: know, like, trust);
- persuasion – focusing on the needs of actual and potential clients by careful listening and then acting;
- performing – doing what you say you will do when you say you will do it.

The words used define how well you package yourself. Using myself as an example: 'Will, what do you do for a living?' I say ,–'I help my clients to attract more business.' Nine times out of 10 the listener will say to me: 'How do you do that?' At this point I often go into my elevator speech (elevator as in lift). Imagine someone asks you what you do and you have 15 seconds to impress them going down from the 23rd floor to the ground. I would answer something like this: 'You know how many professionals have a fear of networking and as a consequence do not get as many new clients as they would like? Well, what I do is give them tips techniques and ideas which, when they practise, will eliminate all those worries resulting in them building more confidence to go out seeking new business.'

The objective is to create an impression that the listener will take away having met you. With passion and enthusiasm, saying something like: 'I help my clients to become more successful or financially secure' (or whatever you will feel comfortable with) will mean that your *packaging* will be effective, as you will have created for your listener an impression of an appealing and interesting person. What a difference a few words will make!

6.7.2 Small talk

At this juncture it is absolutely imperative that it is understood that networking is *not* selling. Networking is simply the building of relationships with a view, possibly, in the future, to doing some business to your mutual benefit. It is not possible to walk into the room, have a 10-minute conversation, tell people what you do and expect them to want to use your services. Unfortunately, life just is not like that! 'How long have you been in business?', 'What do you see as your biggest challenge in the next few months?' and 'How many people work with you?', are always good questions to see how big a business someone is in.

Other topics of discussion include: sport; interests and hobbies; travel and holidays; current events; and family. Care should be taken when discussing the last topic – this should left until the other person is known a little better.

In summary, big business cannot be done until the all-important small talk has been carried out.

6.8 Working the room

This section will examine an area of working the room with which professionals often struggle – the actual moving around the room, disengaging and breaking into groups. The problem comes when you wish to extricate yourself from someone you have had the courage to approach, but do not know how to go about it.

If you are both fellow guests at a function, you do not owe it to this person to spend the rest of the evening with them. Think about it for a moment, the chances are that this person wishes to move on as much as you do but like you they simply do not wish to offend or cause any embarrassment.

One of three of things can be done:

1. After you have finished speaking you can simply say, 'Well, Jo, it's been great meeting you, enjoy the rest of the evening. Please excuse me as I promised to go and talk to Gerry over there.'
2. You could say: 'I'm going to get another drink, would you like to come?'
3. The coward's way out is: 'Please excuse me, I need to go to the loo!', and then make sure you move well away from the person.

Whichever you use, it should be done with respect, integrity and politeness. Good manners are good business; bad manners bring no business.

The important aspect here is to move with or without your new-found friend. Using the second idea of moving to the bar is an opportunity to leave the person with someone else, or for them to leave you. It is rare both of you will be at an event where you do not know anyone so moving to the bar usually has the desired effect. When you do bump into someone you know, even though you are a guest at an event, act as a host. Do not just say: 'Hi Lou, this is Jo' and leave it there. Play host something like this: 'Lou let me introduce you to Jo who I've just met this evening. He has a fascinating business selling sand to Middle Eastern Companies and, Jo, Lou here and I have been friends for years. He runs a business helping growing exporters raise finance from people who are looking for high-risk high-return opportunities.'

These introductions are designed to get the two people talking quickly and with ease and reassurance. Who knows what may happen – you just might have created some potential for both? This of course makes it much easier for you to move on and meet other people. This exercise could be called 'parking'. Like your car, do it carefully, watch all angles and do not knock anything!

6.9 Groups

What happens next? Look for a group of three people and move over to the edge of the circle. As you are moving towards it, examine the faces and decide who seems to be the most welcoming. Stand opposite that person at the edge of the group, catch their eye and smile. The following will happen. The person you have smiled at will smile back and one or both of the other people will turn towards you and both will take one step to the side making a space for you. When you first do this, it is not easy, but it always works. Ask in a gentle voice, 'Good evening, please may I join you?' In most cases someone will put their hand out and introduce themselves. Once in the group care should be taken not to change the subject matter. Wait for them to start asking questions. Bear in mind again, the chances are these people are from the same company or have known each other for a long time but have not got the self-confidence to break away and meet new people. As a result you are a big relief for them! When you are in a group, instinct will tell you when to move on.

6.10 Your time is valuable – use it wisely

So much time is wasted networking because nothing ever happens afterwards. Most accountants charge somewhere between £100 and £200 per hour for their services so if many hours are spent attending various functions and no useful results are achieved, the cost of lost opportunity will be high. There is a simple follow-up process – once a positive first impression has been created, and interesting comments made about various matters, try to identify areas of common ground through careful listening and discover if there might be an opportunity to do business to the parties' mutual benefit. A moment will often arise which allows the parties to bridge the gap between small talk and the possibility of big business. Networking is about building relationships, and gathering information, not about selling.

The bridging process is as follows.

1 At an appropriate time ask for their card and read it carefully. Without this is will be very difficult to move forward.

2 Always find something to comment on, e.g., the spelling of their name, or location of their business – anything to show an interest in that person and their circumstances.

3 A key moment follows. Arrangements should be made to telephone them to discuss the problem they have, e.g., 'Now is not the time or place to discuss the issue but perhaps we can have a chat and I can give you some ideas.' If the right impression has been made, the answer will be 'yes'.

4 Remember, if the question is not asked, the answer will always be 'no'.

5 This is the point when it is essential to create the right impression and avoid wasting a potential business opportunity. Not every event and not every person that is met is going to turn into business, but staying awake, alive and alert, and listening attentively and with empathy may just lead to a business opportunity.

6 Write down on their business card the day you have agreed to telephone and let them see you do this. This shows serious intention and that you are likely to telephone.

7 On returning to home or office, or even before leaving the event, it is useful to write down where and when you met the person, provide a quick description of them and mention any salient facts which may be used at a future date to show them that you were truly listening to what they had to say.

8 When phoning the following week, remind them where you met and that they were happy for you to follow up. It is useful to use small talk here (perhaps using information gathered during your first meeting) to bridge the conversation to the main matter of concern, e.g., 'So, Jo, you were telling about the cash flow issue you were having, how about a cup of coffee ...', etc.

Most people assume that the most important aspect of business cards is to ensure that you are carrying plenty with you. However, this assumption is not correct. The most important point to remember about business cards is not how many you carry but to ask for the other person's business card. Offering a business card too quickly can seem pushy and arrogant and should be avoided.

6.11 Giving and receiving

Networking is about giving first and receiving second. If a party enters into a situation considering only what they might gain for themselves alone, then the chances of success are limited. However, questions such as: 'How can I help you?', 'Who would you like me to introduce you to?', 'How will I know if someone I am talking to will be a good introduction for you?', show the abilities of a proficient and skilled networker.

On meeting fellow professionals, the usual pattern of conversation is often as follows: 'If you send me business, I'll send you ...'. Try instead, 'To build our relationship I'll do my best to recommend clients to you.' Once you are one, or even better two *up* you then have every right to ask if this firm to whom you have given these referrals whether they really do want to build the relationship with you

6.12 Systems and procedures

In a practice, there are systems and procedures for:

- taking on new clients;
- controlling and managing chargeable hours;
- assessing and studying recovery rates;
- carrying out the technical work;
- checking and review;
- sending invoices for the work in process;
- chasing up fees.

However, there is one key system missing. Where is the system for networking and, more importantly, the follow up? Most marketing partners, directors and managers would greet this question with silence. If there is no system for networking, the work will not come, and the practice will have no need for the systems and procedures outlined in the above list.

6.13 Critical role of the marketing personnel

Experience would show that marketing departments ordinarily spend most of their resources:

- organising events;
- creating written material;
- liasing with printers and PR agencies;
- creating and placing advertising.

Minimal or zero resources are put into the follow-up process. The reasons for this are as follows. By the very nature of the activity, networking is carried out by partners and senior colleagues, so it requires regular interaction with these people if networking is to be turned into real business opportunities. Now, we all know about these senior players – busy, stressed out, pulled from pillar to post by clients and their issues. As a result, being approached regularly about the follow-ups from someone in marketing is bad for the blood pressure – theirs and yours!

So, what is the solution? First, a champion is needed, preferably the senior or managing partner, who understands the importance of the follow up. Second, with the support of this champion, that person must obtain the agreement of the partnership to ensure the marketing department is an integral part of the networking process. On a regular basis, all senior people should be asked the following:

- Where have you been?
- Who have you met?
- What potential is there for a business opportunity?
- What do you think we should do about it?

An efficient filing system should be created in which to keep business cards and other details which may be of future use. CRM (Client Relationship Management) databases are vital in today's business. (Act!, Goldmine and Microsoft Access are three of the more popular packages.)

When the marketing department is given the authority and responsibility, it should ensure:

- the follow-up phone call is made;
- any literature requested is sent;
- that the call following the sending out of the brochure is made;
- that a meeting is set up where possible.

The larger professional firm is generally split into specialist departments who often do not communicate. This can be an issue when the partner has made a good contact for the firm, but it is not his or her specialist area. The hackneyed phrase 'people buy people' could not be more apt here. Each person out networking must think *firm* not *me*, and keep eyes open for firm-wide opportunities.

For example, if Janet the tax partner makes a good contact for the corporate finance partner John, it is imperative that the follow up remains the responsibility of Janet. She must go and see the contact and take John with her. She is the conduit through which she can introduce the firm to the new contact and, until the relationship is built between John and the new contact, she must remain on the scene. The marketing department should control of all these activities.

6.14 Conclusion

Networking brings great rewards, but only:

- when its many positive benefits are understood;
- when comfort zones are stretched;

- when giving is seen as the key to networking;
- when the partners are awake, alive and alert;
- when patience and persistence is in evidence;
- when the first move is made;
- when the right impression is created from the start;
- when an interesting introduction is used;
- when the ratio of listening to talking is at least 2:1;
- when the firm creates a follow-up procedure.

7 Mergers and acquisitions

7.1 Why merge?

Continued growth is vital to the success of every independent firm – to stagnate is to die. That growth, both in terms of quantity and quality of income, should result from two sources: outstanding and innovative service to clients (niche business creating added value); and mergers or acquisitions. The latter should only be considered if they make good business sense, have a real strategic objective for the firms involved, and allow both sides to achieve what they want.

Many firms believe that the route to improved profitability, and the creation of a retirement and succession strategy that will provide exit routes for the partners, is through a strategic merger or fee acquisition. Indeed, in an ageing partnership where little thought has been given to the funding of exit routes, it may well be the best of an extremely limited range of options.

If the only reason for a merger is to help build a practice of value then the partners must ensure that what they end up with has added value – or has the potential to do so – rather than simply size. Although there is a perception that mergers always confer benefits, the record of mergers in recent years does little to support this view. Few have proved disastrous, but, equally, few have resulted in clearly defined beneficial outcomes. Why is this? The principle often forgotten is that clients must benefit; the provision of service value will produce additional benefits for them, and thereby additional profitability for the practice. Other factors have a bearing, but added value is the key driver.

Accountancy practices are in the fortunate position of gaining recurring work and income from auditing, accounting and taxation services for clients. With increasing pressure on compliance fees, however, the major potential for growth must come from developing and delivering added-value services. Unfortunately, the investment in staff and resources required to grow these services organically is considerable and requires a carefully planned long-term development strategy. For this reason a merger or sale is often the preferred option.

> **Table 7.1 Reasons for a merger or acquisition**
>
> Offensive:
> - Expand to achieve economies of scale
> - Desire to improve the service to clients
> - Moving into a market where the firm is weak
> - Broaden the technical capabilities
>
> Defensive:
> - The practice looks vulnerable
> - Protection of the client base
> - Creation of partner exit routes

It is important to remember that increasing the size of the practice through a merger or acquisition will not necessarily lead to greater profitability. Few of the things that determine a firm's success – client service, developing new services, productivity enhancements – are critically dependent on size. Firms can, and should, be working on these topics anyway, long before they look to size to solve their problems.

The key consideration is whether the partners can achieve improvements without recourse to merger or acquisition.

7.2 Defining the firm's objectives

No firm can realistically attack its growth requirements unless there is a clearly defined strategy on which all the partners are agreed and in which all the partners and staff can share. The firm's strategic purpose must be examined from these four viewpoints:

1 What are the partners aiming to achieve?

2 Is a merger or acquisition required to fit an identified gap in the firm's infrastructure or service coverage?

3 Will acquired/merged growth improve the quality of service to clients and improve profits per partner?

4 Where succession planning is a major issue, will the final merged firm provide reasonable partner exit routes without damaging future profitability?

The key aim of the firm's planning must be improved profit per partner and improved service for the clients. Improved profitability can be derived from one or more of the following:

- acquisition of quality clients;
- greater geographic coverage;
- potential cross-selling of professional services;
- acquisition of specialist services;
- acquisition of specialist people;
- marketing the firm's existing and new services and adding value.

Where merger or acquisition is an identified part of the development plan, it is fundamental that any changes should contribute to improved minimum and average partner earnings within the short term. On no account should merger/acquisition augment the ranks of low-earning partners nor reduce average partner earnings. Wherever possible, fees per merged/acquired partner should be equivalent to a level which will produce the required profit share and economies of scale for cost-saving benefits.

> **Table 7.2 'Our firm'**
> - Where do we want to be in the market?
> - How easy or difficult is the aim by evolution?
> - Could merger be relevant for defensive or for aggressive reasons?
> - How easy or difficult is the aim by evolution?

7.3 The market place for merger, acquisition and fee disposal

Well over 90 per cent of accountancy practices in the UK consist of five partners or less. In the past there has been a natural cycle for small firms where partners set up, practice and retire over a 30-year period. The explosion in membership during the last 20 years, the increasing number of small practices and economic pressures mean that there are now too many firms for the market. Merger and sale activity has increased dramatically in the last few years and will continue to do so, creating opportunities for stronger firms to consolidate their market position through acquisition.

Fee acquisitions fall broadly into two categories. At one end there is a heavy demand for firms with up to £200,000 fees, a portable portfolio, no encumbrances or property issues and a retiring partner. At the other end are firms of

£750,000–£1 million in fees where a similar sized or larger practice is seeking to consolidate. Both present problems. The smaller acquisition may not provide the quality of client base that the acquirer seeks nor an actual or potential added value income stream.

With larger firms the key issues are continuity and the opportunity for providing new services to the existing client base, and developing referrals out of that client base. However, even though the merger will impact referrals, the quantity may not be what was anticipated because neither firm in the merger may be regarded by the client as more valuable than they were before.

Merger candidates tend to take a stance; most seek to be the major influence and this inhibits their vision as to what is and is not possible. In fact, there are three choices:

- merge with a smaller firm;
- merge with a similar sized firm;
- merge with a larger firm.

All have advantages and disadvantages, but unless all the options are explored, the best deal for partners and clients may not be reached.

7.4 Fee acquisition and disposal

7.4.1 Buying and selling considerations

Size

The most active market is where fees total less than £200,000. These transactions attract a higher premium multiple based on gross recurring fees (GRF). Above £200,000 the considerations extend to the feasibility of amalgamating two firms. Acquisitions in the range £500,000 to £1 million are rare, the terms and conditions are more specific and focused and the valuation attracts a lower multiple.

Information

Information available from the vendor must be sufficient to allow conclusive judgement of the benefits. In particular:

- Is there a cost impact from upgrading quality control standards?
- Are the clients price sensitive?
- Will the client base improve staff utilisation and employment costs?

Staff continuity

Clients are less likely to change to another accountant if there is a degree of continuity following a purchase. If the vendor's staff are unhappy and leave, clients may follow them reducing profitability and increasing recruitment costs.

Location

Practices in urban areas are in greater demand and the obtainable price multiple is correspondingly higher.

Fee levels

The buyer must decide whether the level of fees charged by the seller is sufficient to absorb his own costs of doing the work.

7.4.2 Valuation

General principles

The gross fee and net profit figures in themselves are unhelpful without knowledge of the staffing arrangements, type of client services and the growth trend over recent years. It is essential to note the charge rate structure, the recovery levels, quality-control standards and what passes through the profit and loss account.

Traditionally there are two methods of calculating the purchase price: either a valuation based on a percentage GRF, or a multiple of superprofits available in the practice over and above the partner's salary appropriate for the size and type of firm. The market emphasis is on the GRF multiple basis, whereas the superprofits method is of particular value for a specialist practice or as a check on the GRF basis.

Table 7.3 Small firm valuation

Sole practitioner aged 60 with four staff in the North of England

	£'000
GRF	200
Overheads	100
Available profit	100
Less: notional partner's salary for size and location of firm	(40)
Superprofit excess	60
Valuation 5 × superprofit	300
Price is a maximum of 1.5 × GRF	

7.4.3 Payout arrangements

It is extremely rare to find a 100 per cent payout of the purchase price on completion. The recommended method is to allow a phased payout with the ability to apply clawback on the unpaid balance. Payments are usually over a minimum of 12 months and a maximum of 24 months. On completion, up to 60 per cent is paid out with the remainder in an agreed number of instalments. Interest should accrue on the outstanding balance.

The most frequently adopted bases for payout of the purchase price are either a capital sum, a consultancy or a combination of both. Tax effectiveness must be considered if the arrangements include a consultancy. Any capital payment should take account of retirement relief rules and capital gains tax legislation.

There should also be a clawback arrangement where the purchase price can be reduced if any client on the agreed list fails to transfer to the buyer or does not remain as a client for an agreed period (e.g., 24 months from the completion date).

7.4.4 The sale agreement

Too often there is a relaxed approach at this stage of the negotiations, but for the avoidance of any doubt it must be absolutely clear what is and is not part of the deal. This means that competent legal drafting is required for the protection of both parties, and there should be a broad assumption that if it can go wrong it will.

The agreement should contain sufficient clauses to safeguard the positions of the buyer and seller. The following points must be included:

- parties to the agreement;
- interpretation and definition (of expressions in the agreement);
- sale price – what is included, what is excluded, clawback provisions;
- price and value of work in progress;
- debtors and agreed process for debt recovery;
- VAT;
- notification to clients;
- delivery of files;
- non-compete clause;

- completion arrangements;
- payment arrangements;
- employees/pensions (if applicable);
- staffing policy;
- creditors and liabilities;
- vendor's warranties;
- purchaser's warranties;
- professional indemnity insurance and claims;
- publicity;
- tax election;
- costs of the agreement (who bears them);
- arbitration/disputes;
- use of name;
- general;
- schedules.

7.5 Mergers

A combination of factors are present when considering a merger, but two conflicting attitudes influence the decision, affect the choice of merger partner and impact implementation:

- merger as an opportunity;
- merger as a defence against problems.

For a merger to confer a real advantage it must create additional benefit (value) for clients as well as for the partners and firms involved. In addition, the objectives of a merger candidate will include one or more of the following:

1 to improve partner income;

2 to secure specialists in a service area or for an industry type;

3 to obtain the benefits of training, recruitment and quality-control procedures;

4 to avoid the loss of key clients and enhance the range of services to those clients;

5 to obtain geographical representation;

6 to provide additional opportunities for staff and ensure staff retention;

7 to fund partner exit routes.

The concerns of a merger candidate are likely to centre around one or more of the following:

- the method of future profit sharing;
- possible lower income for mergee partners in the years immediately after the merger;
- the relative status of partners from both practices post merger;
- possible loss of name and identity in the local community;
- inability to retain key members of staff;
- the impact on clients of an increase in charge rates and fee levels;
- whether there will be less direct partner contact with clients;
- the need to shuffle clients between partners in order to establish specialisation.

7.5.1 Different types of merger

Market advantage

The aim is to add to the firm's current services, providing clients with a broader range through effective cross-selling. If there is a good track record of cross-selling then the merger idea is supported. If not, then why should the new firm be able to achieve what the old one could not?

Geographical spread

This involves the attempt to derive advantage by adding office locations to obtain local or regional (or national) spread. The question is, would clients consider such coverage to be a principal issue when choosing their accountant? Having more locations could simply mean that local partners act as independent units servicing local work. There may be some referrals, but it is more likely that costs will be shared rather than long-term client benefits developed.

Synergy

The belief that the firm will be able to create a new, more profitable entity by merging different abilities. Unless there is strong control of work spanning both areas it may not be possible to create and manage a fully integrated firm.

Solving a problem

Merger as an attempt to solve succession problems is becoming increasingly common as the age profile of partners increases. Where a firm has found it hard to attract younger partners to fund the exit routes of the older ones, a merger that creates a better age balance can help to solve the problem. However, problems of this nature can put the firm in a very weak bargaining position.

Volume

The theory in merging similar sized firms in the same location is that, through size, the firm will be better able to compete. Whilst size does help in marketing, simply creating a large unit is not a good enough reason for a merger. Most determinants of success such as client services, new services introduced, improved utilisation and productivity, are not size-dependent.

7.5.2 Initial steps

Once merger is the chosen route the following steps should be taken before selecting a suitable merger candidate:

1 obtain the full agreement of all equity partners (including an understanding of their future);
2 assemble key information (financial, clients, property, staff etc.);
3 brief a law firm with experience in the field of professional firm mergers;
4 consult a bank.

7.6 Potential problems

Every transaction to buy, sell or merge must be subject to detailed investigation by the respective parties. Potential deal-breakers must be identified and resolved. Provided there is a willingness to accept that there will be a change in the basis of the business, then careful attention to due diligence will provide a sound platform for the deal. The following potential problem areas must all be considered.

7.6.1 Goodwill

Merger with a practice which recognises partnership goodwill in its balance sheet can produce difficulties. The merged firm must make clear its policy going forward and have a clearly defined accession and retirement arrangement policy.

7.6.2 Management structure

The management structure will need to be well defined and appropriate partnership appointments made if it is to succeed. Some of the more important considerations are as follows:

- fee and charge rate structures;
- billing structures;
- alignment of staff salaries and benefits;
- appointment of a managing partner;
- management and administrative responsibilities;
- premises arrangements;
- partnership finance;
- professional standards/quality control;
- marketing and business development plans.

7.6.3 Premises

All partners and staff should operate from the same premises as quickly as possible if integration is to be successful. Problems may arise where either party is committed under the terms of a lease. However, property is not an insurmountable issue. The key is whether problems can be offset by improved profitability, thus buying time to resolve the issue.

7.6.4 Profit-sharing arrangements

This can only be considered after adjustments have been made to apply common accounting policies to both firms, including work-in-progress valuation, bad debt provisions and the application of specific overhead costs. The depreciation basis may differ, rent may vary, remuneration packages may differ and until the accounting bases are put on the same footing it will not be possible to build a profit-sharing basis appropriate for the new firm and for individual partners.

7.6.5 Capital contributions

The minimum requirements for each partner should be established.

7.6.6 Drawings and pension arrangements

A common drawing policy must be established and adhered to.

7.6.7 Working structures

The working structures of both practices may need to be revised to form a basis that is appropriate for the combined firm. Departmental structures are highly desirable as they allow streamlined work processing and present opportunities for the development and promotion of staff and overhead savings.

7.6.8 Information technology

Compatibility of computer systems is crucial. With so much of a modern firm's operations now computerised, the cost of moving to a common system should not be underestimated.

7.6.9 Professional indemnity insurance

Both firms should declare their claims history and a new policy must be put in place. Where one firm is admitted to the other firm's arrangements there must be effective run-off cover in relation to the former partnership.

7.6.10 Professional standards

Merger is an opportunity to redefine the quality-control approach and upgrade systems. Detailed inspection of one another's files will form part of due diligence and the reviews will assist in the decision on common working methods to be adopted. The implementation period usually provides a stimulus that hastens the integration of partners and staff.

7.6.11 Partner personal solvency

All partners should prepare personal balance sheets and be prepared to disclose their full situation. Overdrawn current accounts or other exposure must be resolved and a suitable personal plan put in place.

7.7 Procedures and meetings

Both firms should exchange information at meetings set up for that purpose. These meetings can be divided into five categories: initial, exploratory, investigative, technical and concluding. The following checklist should be applied to each:

- meeting objectives;
- key questions;
- participants;
- location;
- information to be exchanged;
- next step.

A record should be kept of every meeting; there must be no cause for misunderstanding as the negotiations proceed.

7.7.1 Initial meeting

The aim is for each side to acquaint one another with their respective philosophies, goals and interests. There is no commitment by either party at this stage, but there must be a willingness to share information. Key areas that both sides will wish to be aware of include:

- the nature of the other firm and the services rendered;
- whether the transaction is driven by weakness and vulnerability or from a position of strength;
- the strengths and weaknesses of the partners and personnel;
- whether there is prima facie a rationale for a deal with that firm.

Procedures will be established for further contact and agreement in writing exchanged between the parties regarding exclusivity and confidentiality.

7.7.2 Exploratory stage

The aim is to consider whether the firms are compatible and how the combination of practices will achieve one another's goals. Both parties must be prepared to divulge financial, client, staff, IT and other relevant information. The following should be considered:

- history of the firm;
- organisation structure;
- outline accounting systems;
- key features of partnership agreement;
- summary financial history and balance sheet position;
- current period results and prospects;
- outline fee analysis by principal client/client fee and service category;
- methods of accounting;
- numbers and analysis of staff;
- charge-out rates – in summary;
- chargeable hours – in summary;
- fee recoveries by partner, by service area;
- outline professional indemnity insurance arrangements;
- properties – leasehold/freehold, terms/values;
- pending litigation or contingent liabilities;
- existing and prospective pension commitments;
- exposure to historic or deferred tax liabilities (and accounting treatment);
- bad debt history/exposure;
- controls over, and level of, work in progress;
- borrowing facilities;
- background information regarding each partner (partner CV);
- insurance, retirement, death benefits and exposure of partners;
- partners' capital and capital borrowings;
- partners' outside business interests (as trustees, directors, shareholders, executors, etc.).

It must be remembered that this is the only opportunity to properly evaluate the other business. If due diligence is skimped, problems may well crop up later which will be difficult or expensive to resolve.

7.7.3 Investigative stage

The purpose of this stage is to allow the partners to broaden their understanding of the financial and operational aspects of the practice through discussion, analysis and analytical review. Particular care is required to establish the apparent reliability of accounts, budgets, forecasts, debtors, work in progress, and a full identification of contingent liabilities. At this time the following points should also be considered:

- What will be the tax consequences/implications of a merger for the partners in the merged practice?
- To what extent are performance warranties necessary for the post-merger situation?
- What are the warranties and indemnities required involving assets to be acquired?
- Is protection necessary in respect of possible premature billing of work in progress prior to merger by the prospective mergee firm?
- What procedures are envisaged to equalise partner capital arrangements?
- What is the treatment and/or valuation of assets contributed by the incoming mergee partners (for example, cash debtors, work in progress, fixed assets)?
- What are the respective values of partners' shares in the respective firms?

Meetings will be necessary to deal with concerns that arise and provide information to the partners. Just as importantly, they will provide an opportunity for the partners to meet potential future colleagues and ensure that they can work together. Indeed, consideration should be given to using psychometric testing for all partners in the new firm. This will not only establish the level of personal synergy, but will identify the aspirations of and responsibilities necessary for each partner. At this stage it is a good idea to arrange medical checks for everyone to ensure that health issues are unlikely to be a problem in the immediate future.

7.7.4 Technical procedures

A technical review will broaden understanding of the standards control procedures adopted by the prospective mergee firm. Key questions are:

- How accustomed are the partners to operating within an environment of professional standards controls?
- What is the professional indemnity claims history of the practice?

- How great is the gap between the firm's standards and those of the prospective mergee firm?
- How much training in procedures will be required for partners and staff of the mergee firm?

The technical review should be separate from the investigations covering financial and operational areas. The approach should be the same as for a hot or cold file review. The systems adopted for each service area should be examined – including standard documentation and paperwork and internal review procedures. The reviewer should note any client dissatisfaction, lost clients or potential claim, and a full report should be prepared as a permanent record.

7.7.5 Concluding stage

The objectives of the concluding stage are:

1 to establish the proposed financial terms of the merger, identify partner candidates and outline the responsibilities of key personnel;

2 to ensure that all financial and technical due diligence procedures have been followed;

3 to produce draft Heads of Agreement which can be used as a base for the formal documentation;

4 to obtain all necessary legal confirmations from the firm's solicitors and to execute appropriate merger documents.

By now all the information required for a balanced assessment of the merger candidate should be available and any potential deal-breaking issues identified and resolved. All relevant disclosure will have been made between both parties and a Deed of Accession prepared for signing by the incoming partners.

The timetable up to completion and beyond should now be prepared and agreed. This should provide adequate leeway to complete the investigative legal due diligence, and allow for approval of the deal by the partners on both sides. Although there is frequently pressure by one or other of the parties to the agreement for a speedy conclusion to negotiations, experience shows that undue haste frequently leads to complications.

7.8 The agreement

There is often a desire to minimise the legal input and proceed as swiftly as possible to the practical implementation of the deal. Unfortunately the best-laid plans can go wrong, and unless the agreed arrangements are clearly set out and comprehensively protected (for both parties) there is every likelihood of problems in the future.

Up to 90 per cent of each agreement is protective for the parties. Heads of Agreement although necessary in themselves, will not be sufficiently comprehensive to provide that protection. The agreement contents must leave nothing to chance and a typical framework for a merger should include the following:

- parties to the agreement;
- agreement to the merger;
- interpretation and definition;
- deed of Accession for incoming parties;
- specific terms for individual parties (if any);
- assets and liabilities of firm merging in;
- premises arrangements;
- partner retirement arrangements;
- integration and succession;
- employees;
- professional indemnity insurance requirements;
- pensions to former partners (if any);
- disclosure;
- tax election;
- announcements;
- notices;
- arbitration/disputes;
- miscellaneous;
- schedules;

7.9 Post-agreement follow-up

It is important that the overall business objectives for the merger are kept in view at all times and that provision is made for the successful integration of the businesses. Partners must ensure that there is a post-agreement follow-up in place and that is understood by all members of the new firm. Responsibilities must be allocated, along with a timetable for implementation; clear terms of reference must be set out and a report-back and monitoring procedure established. A typical post-agreement checklist should include the following:

- actions and responsibilities;
- objectives;
- announcements;
- known weaknesses;
- clients;
- partners and staff;
- use of time;
- management;
- premises;
- communications;
- service and quality control;
- plans and budgets;
- finance;
- administration;
- insurance;
- ethics, registration and legalities;
- associates and advisers;
- practice development;
- taxation.

7.9.1 Client review

Due diligence should have identified clients whose retention may be at risk through the change of practice circumstances and a suitable plan must be established for them with partners and staff agreeing a programme for tackling any potential problems.

7.9.2 Partners and staff

All change is a risk and most staff will have some concern over change in their organisation. All staff should be involved in conferences/meetings and other (perhaps social) gatherings in order to speed integration. Everyone should be fully aware of the aims and objectives of the combined firm and the part they are to play in achieving them.

Any uncertainty or disquiet on the part of the partners will filter down to the staff; hence the partners must provide sensible leadership through the introductory stage of the new firm. It is equally important for all of the partners in the new firm to get to know one another and co-operate to ensure the success of the merger.

8 Consolidation

8.1 Creating the right climate

As we have seen in previous chapters, the market for accountancy services has changed and grown significantly in recent years. These changes are set to continue as firms seek to expand their services in higher margin areas such as consultancy, corporate finance, tax planning, IT, etc. These higher margin areas are ones in which, traditionally, the small and medium-sized independent practices have had difficulty in gaining a substantial market share. This is partly due to the high level of initial investment required to establish specialisation in these disciplines, but the reluctance of many older partners to expand into unfamiliar areas is also a significant factor.

It is generally recognised that SMEs represent the fastest-growing sector of the UK's economy in terms of employment growth. In addition, research shows that, as well as relying on them for compliance work, SMEs seek business advice from their accountants first. As SMEs constitute the majority of the client base of most independent practices, it would be logical to assume that they are taking full advantage of the opportunities available to them. Unfortunately, due to the issues facing the vast majority of medium-sized accountancy practices – principally relating to their current partnership structure – they are prevented from fully exploiting these opportunities.

8.2 Issues facing medium-sized practices

8.2.1 Lack of investment

The traditional structure of the medium-sized, independent practice has prevented sufficient investment being made in these firms. As a result, whilst they may be able to supply some of the accounting and business services that SMEs, incorporated professional firms and high net worth individuals require, they cannot often provide all of them, which can result in clients seeking such services elsewhere.

There are three main reasons why the partnership structure hinders investment. First, the individual partners have to provide personal capital and support to any debt finance sought by the partnership. This is a limiting factor in determining how much capital is available to develop new services. Second, partnerships have no access to the equity markets and as such have no opportunity to benefit from this means of raising finance. Finally, retained profits in a partnership are generally taxed at 40 per cent, compared to retained profits in a company which are taxed at corporation tax rates of up to a maximum of 30 per cent.

A corporate structure with the ability to raise money in the public markets, to borrow money supported by a properly capitalised balance sheet without personal guarantees and to invest retained profits more tax efficiently, should therefore be a better model to capitalise on the opportunities that exist for independent firms.

8.2.2 Management structure

For sizeable organisations, the partnership concept is outdated in the modern business environment. Once firms grow beyond a certain size achieving a consensus from the partners on the approach to management is extremely difficult and compromise decisions usually have to be made in order to accommodate all their views.

Ideally, there should be clearly defined teams with responsibility for management and strategy, leaving the partners to concentrate on fee earning and the generation of new business.

8.2.3 Unlimited liability

Partners within a general partnership are exposed to unlimited personal liability. In today's business climate, where clients are increasingly litigious, this exposure to risk can be of great concern to individual partners and is a barrier to recruiting younger equity partners. In a traditional accountancy partnership, unlimited liability applies to all partners regardless of the amount of capital they have contributed to the firm and regardless of whether an individual partner was personally involved in the matter that is the subject of the litigation. Although the risks of unlimited liability in such a partnership can be mitigated by the use of professional indemnity insurance, they can never be removed.

8.2.4 Recruitment and retention

The recruitment and retention of high-quality staff is vital to the success of any business. Independent practices must compete with the big firms that offer better salaries and, with the lure of a partnership not as attractive as it once was, many are finding it extremely hard to recruit and retain people with partnership potential.

8.2.5 Capital growth

In recent years the opportunity for partners to achieve capital growth through goodwill payments has largely disappeared. They contribute to the firm's capital on becoming an equity partner and continue contributing throughout their careers. On retirement, however, partners rarely receive payment of goodwill from the firm they helped to grow.

8.2.6 Succession

Many independent firms have a strong client base but are faced with an ageing partnership considering retirement and requiring an exit route. At the same time, the reluctance of many younger people coming into the profession to commit the substantial sums that have been paid in the past has created severe succession problems.

Thus the scene is set for the arrival of a completely new concept in the history of the accountancy profession: the consolidator.

8.3 The concept

Consolidators first appeared in the US in the 1990s with varying degrees of success, and by the year 2000 the first model was being created in the UK. The aim of the consolidator is to build a fully integrated business services group that offers significant opportunities for the providers of high-quality business services to SMEs, high net worth individuals and other professional firms. This can be achieved by integrating profitable, entrepreneurial accountancy practices and bolting on other specialised services providers to enable the newly created group to deliver a wide range of business services, not all of which would traditionally be supplied by accountants.

The consolidator's first task is to raise sufficient start-up capital to establish the shell company, purchase the initial practices and continue to fund the business until it is self-supporting. Although deals with individual practices may vary slightly, partners in purchased firms will receive 50 per cent of the purchase price in cash and 50 per cent in shares which they cannot sell for a period of three years.

The compliance divisions of each purchased firm are then hived off into a separate entity and the remaining service areas are incorporated into the consolidator. Partners become directors (or paid employees) on a fixed salary and will probably have little further influence on the organisation of the business, but they will be able to concentrate on servicing the needs of their clients and generating new business.

By incorporating and integrating a number of practices, the consolidator can get rid of the unwieldy partnership structure, achieve critical mass, introduce economies of scale, build up specialist services and, through cross-selling, create a far more profitable operation than could be achieved by the consolidated firms individually, or even as merged practices in a traditional partnership structure.

8.4 Perceived advantages

For firms facing succession problems there are obvious advantages to consolidation, but successful independent firms will be looking for far more from consolidation than the provision of partners' exit routes. Bearing in mind that consolidation is still a new and largely unproven option, what is going to lure them down this route? The following are some of the advantages that consolidators believe will attract both practices and, equally importantly, investors.

8.4.1 The integrated approach

Consolidated firms will be able to capitalise on the opportunities available to accountants in being the first choice for companies, professional firms and high net worth individuals seeking business services. Using the skill available within the network they will be able to offer a full service range enabling clients to receive all their requirements from one organisation.

Integrating accountancy practices and other complementary business services providers will build a national organisation that offers a full range of business services and satisfies the needs of target markets.

Integration will bring economies of scale with regard to IT in particular. All newly acquired firms should adopt a single system that will reduce costs and facilitate the integration process.

8.4.2 National coverage

Although, should the consolidation model prove successful, there will undoubtedly be some smaller-scale companies operating on a regional basis, the current trend is for consolidators to target firms that will provide national coverage to compete with the largest national practices.

8.4.3 Local knowledge with national support

Certain functions such as IT, marketing, sales and knowledge management organised on a national basis will allow regional offices the freedom to respond quickly to their local market places. The model will enable quick access to the capital and resources necessary for investment and expansion, enabling an office to exploit local knowledge and opportunities.

8.4.4 Cross-selling opportunities

The individual regional firms acquired will generally not have the full range of services offered by the largest practices. There will therefore be a significant opportunity to cross-sell and refer services into both existing and target client bases. Business recovery, forensic accounting and corporate finance are examples of the type of services that smaller independent practices do not generally offer but which can be supplied by the network.

8.4.5 Other growth opportunities

In addition to making acquisitions and achieving organic growth through the exploitation of cross-selling opportunities, consolidators also aim to achieve growth through lateral hiring, with some incentives being offered that will benefit employment with a public company. They should explore the potential addition of other business services including recruitment, outsourcing (accounts, HR and IT) and legal services where it can be demonstrated that such services can be cross-sold into the existing and future client bases.

8.4.6 Single brand and culture

After an initial integration period, purchased firms should drop their names in favour of one joint name. The development of the brand name, as well as the critical mass gained through the acquisition strategy, should assist in the attraction of quality clients to whom additional services can be sold.

8.4.7 Incentivised staff

Share option plans are designed to maintain a highly motivated and incentivised workforce as well as to attract high-calibre staff. In addition, consolidators can use both share option plans and the ability to issue shares to attract new fee earners to the network.

8.4.8 Central support functions

As well as the common IT platform already outlined, operational efficiencies will be achieved across the group through the adoption of centralised practice management and accounting systems. These, together with a formal management structure, are expected to free up time spent on administration, enabling former partners to focus on client work and business development. This should lead to increased sales, with the acquired firms benefiting from the dedicated resources of a central sales and marketing team.

8.5 The disadvantages

Although many firms may well find that consolidation offers them the optimum route to growth, there are a number of potential pitfalls that need to be considered and a considerable number of practices, particularly the smaller independent firms, may well find that organic growth or merger are a better option. Some of the problems that could arise are discussed in the following paragraphs.

8.5.1 Undercapitalisation

Unless the consolidator has accurately predicted the amount of capital required to build the business to a stage where it becomes self-supporting there is a very real possibility that, as can happen to any commercial enterprise, it will fail due to lack of money. Practices need to be very sure that the company they are joining has a solid financial platform and can survive the odd hiccup in the development plans.

8.5.2 Market fluctuations

As a public limited company, the consolidator is subject to the vagaries of the market place. Share prices can go down as well as up, and with partners unable to sell their shares for three years they are effectively gambling that the shares will be performing well when the time comes to dispose of them. If such is not the case, then despite the initial cash payment up front, partners could find themselves worse off financially.

8.5.3 Failure to achieve targets

Consolidators expect to grow the business through cross-selling to existing clients and attracting new clients to the network. However, unless the branding is strong and full integration can be achieved between the purchased firms in a relatively short space of time, problems could arise. First, existing clients may have selected a particular firm because they wanted the service that an independent practice can provide. They may not view consolidation in a positive light, and unless the time and trouble is taken to reassure them, they could decide to seek another independent firm. Second, unless the consolidator manages to achieve a strong brand image and invests a significant amount of resources into marketing and promotion, the new clients that will be the major source of business growth may not be as easy to find as anticipated.

8.5.4 Initial income reductions and other considerations

Partners in the very successful independent practices that are the prime targets for consolidators will almost certainly have to take an initial drop in salary with a view to achieving higher earning levels as the business develops. For many older partners this is not a problem as any shortfall during the few years before retirement will be more than compensated for by the cash-up-front payment and, hopefully, the eventual sale of shares. However, for younger partners it is much more of a gamble: one that they may be reluctant to take.

Partners in independent practices will need to consider their personal objectives. If these people are in their 30s or early 40s, making reasonable money, have existing job satisfaction and enjoy what they are doing, they will be sacrificing future earnings and may be frustrated with their inability to actually make a real difference.

8.6 Conclusion

For a great many practices consolidation is undoubtedly a very attractive proposition. However, it is not suitable for everyone. Independent firms facing severe succession problems that think they can fund partner exit routes by selling to a consolidator coulddisappoint. The consolidators are looking for successful firms with a good track record and a strong client base and are unlikely to be attracted to weak or ailing practices.

There is also a substantial tranche of medium-sized firms that, although attractive to the consolidators, value their independence and prefer organic growth or judicious merger as a means of business development. They are also well placed to snap up the inevitable fall-out of clients who do not wish to be serviced by a consolidated firm but who prefer to develop a relationship with an independent practice.

9 Property issues

9.1 Introduction

For as long as there have been partnerships, there has been an argument between those who believe that a business should own its own premises and those who believe they should lease. At different times in the economic cycle, the arguments may appear to favour one or the other approach. This is not always for the reason that might be expected.

For instance, when property values are running high, the partnership could experience intense succession pains as retiring partners need to be paid out at the peak of the property market. This chapter will look at a variety of solutions both old and new, including mortgage; sale and leaseback; and the partnership pension planning route.

On the other hand, in times of recession when a business may be locked into a lease where the rent payable is higher than the market rent, disposal of surplus premises may be impossible. Property issues of this nature have wrecked many a merger (or rescue). This chapter will also look at issues of flexibility, and a range of solutions such as buying in the freehold; joint sale with the landlord; and surrender negotiations.

There are a number of new trends and financial planning products available to partnerships above and beyond the traditional options of straightforward freehold or leasehold ownership, which is part of what this chapter aims to address. It must be emphasised at the outset that no single solution will inevitably be the right answer for all partnerships. Also, changes to tax planning or partnership planning scenarios may cause decisions taken in today's climate to appear in the future to have been unsoundly based.

Above all, property decisions must be taken in the context of the strategic aims of the partnership's business plan, in which short, medium and long-term goals should be set out. There is, for instance, no point in signing a 25-year lease on 5,000 sq. ft. of office accommodation if the business plan envisages the firm doubling in size after five years.

9.2 Forms of property tenure

9.2.1 Freehold

Partnerships that own their trading property on a freehold basis traditionally regard and utilise the capital value of the property as the capital base of the firm. Thus, ownership of the property, although nominally in the name of the practice, is, in reality, in the names of the individual partners, in proportion to their share of the firm.

Owning a property freehold is the simplest form of tenure available in English law, with the owners responsible for all issues arising from the ownership and occupation of the property. There are a number of pros and cons, many of which will suggest themselves readily to the reader.

Advantages

- *Borrowing capacity* – subject to agreement with the partnership's bankers, it is open to a partnership to borrow against a tangible asset whether for investment in practice development or merely to smooth cash flow. Secured borrowing, particularly in difficult times, is likely to prove easier to arrange and cheaper than unsecured loan arrangements.
- *Subletting* – a partnership owning its own premises may have the flexibility to create additional income by subletting a portion of the accommodation to create additional income and reduce overheads. Occupiers of leasehold property may well be able to undertake the same exercise but will be subject to requirements for obtaining the landlord's consent as well as other potential restrictions on the terms they can offer.
- *Control* – ownership of the business premises provides closer control of outgoings and, in particular, limits exposure to escalating market rents.

Disadvantages

- *Responsibility* – ownership of premises brings responsibility for compliance with statutory requirements such as Disability Discrimination Act 1995 provisions, health and safety at work issues, and puts repairs and maintenance issues firmly in the partnership's court. Although many of these responsibilities may follow a leasehold occupier, many, such as disabled access, remain a landlord's liability.
- *Succession planning* – a rigid shared-ownership structure and rigid provisions for dealing with retirement may leave the partnership in financial difficulty when paying out retiring partners.

- *Partnership funding* – the ability of retiring partners to withdraw a profit on their capital injection is balanced by the need for incoming partners to make good the capital shortfall. In the event that market values and thus the capital base subsequently reduce, this can put a considerable strain on new partners who have not yet built up a capital stake. This can be a significant deterrent to taking up a partnership, a trend which is currently being seen in a variety of professions.

9.2.2 Leasehold

Leasehold tenure confers ownership rights on to an occupier for a limited period of time, typically five, 10, 15 or even 25 years. Usually, the lease document transfers virtually all of the obligations of ownership onto the tenant, including repair (which can include renewal and rebuilding), insurance and all other liabilities. However many of the rights of ownership, such as flexibility of use, or the ability to alter the building or to sublet, are retained or controlled by the landlord.

The landlord and tenant relationship is governed by the Landlord and Tenant Act 1954 (LTA 1954), which has been amended little since its introduction. Most importantly, it governs behaviour at the end of a lease, and contains the all-important security of tenure provisions (ss24–28 LTA 1954) setting out a strict timetable for the service of notices which must be complied with to preserve those rights (in which respect a competent property lawyer should be consulted).

One change there has been is the Landlord and Tenant (Covenants) Act 1995, the effect of which was to reduce privity of contract liability, sometimes called original tenant liability. This doctrine, which still holds for leases entered into before 1995, makes the original tenant (and any subsequent assignees) liable for rents and other outgoings throughout the term of a lease in the event of default by the tenant in occupation, including the cost of terminal dilapidations.

Political pressure has resulted in the introduction of a *Code of Practice for Commercial Leases* (2nd edn, April 2002) (available from DTLR or the Royal Institution of Chartered Surveyors), which is intended to promote a number of changes in the operation of the LTA 1954. These include more flexibility in the strict provisions governing lease renewal procedures so that tenants cannot lose their rights by default. Upwards/downwards rent reviews are another area where change is being enforced, although the corollary of this may be a trend towards shorter leases. Other areas include more flexibility over repairing obligations, and less strict control over alterations, change of use and assignment.

Again, a number of pros and cons suggest themselves.

Advantages

- *Transparency* – the capital base of the firm is limited to the capital contribution to the partners whilst the premises remain a tool, a business cost that can be managed effectively.

- *Succession planning* – the only issues in succession planning are to remember to apply to the landlords for a licence to assign in order to remove retiring partners from the lease. An assignment between partners does not count as a qualifying assignment for the purposes of the Leasehold (Covenants) Act 1995, and the normal indemnities will, of course, need to be written into retirement deeds to deal with this issue.

- *Flexibility* – as mentioned at the outset, it is essential that property decisions are taken based on clear business planning goals and aims. The ideal form of leasehold tenure would be a lease with a rolling six-month break, operable at the tenant's discretion. Does such a thing exist?

Well, yes, it does, thanks in part to the Code of Practice for Commercial Leases. Already, a limited number of providers, with an eye to the way Government is pushing the property industry in areas such as the upward-only rent review, believe they are in the vanguard of development of a flexible landlord and tenant relationship. After all, it is only in the UK that there is any tradition of long leases that transfer all liability for maintenance of the investment to the tenant. Elsewhere, in the US in particular, leases are traditionally shorter (three to five years) and liabilities are shared. However, there is limited security of tenure, which is mirrored here where the usual quid pro quo for a landlord agreeing to grant a short lease is for the tenant to give up his LTA 1954 security of tenure rights.

The cost may not be inconsiderable, with the rental premium in some early examples being up to 20 per cent above a traditional lease structure. A number of mathematical models are currently being developed to calculate the rental premium required for any given set of terms, where variables can include the length of lease; upward/downward or RPI-related rent review provisions; limitations on the repair liability; and tenant breaks. Such terms are not yet generally available, although it is likely they will be in the future. For the time being, the extent to which the business as tenant can enjoy flexibility dealing with its leasehold accommodation depends on the general state of the property market at the time.

In normal market conditions, the ability to assign a lease and move either to smaller or larger premises may be easier, quicker and cheaper than buying and selling a freehold. However, not having to wait for a freehold purchaser to arrange mortgage funding is balanced by the need to obtain the landlord's consent to the assignment, which will be mainly based on the assignee's accounts and financial standing.

Choice of premises is likely to be greater. Unless having one's own front door is paramount, there are office suites of all sizes, specifications and quality available in normal market conditions.

In present market conditions, a tenant might still expect to negotiate reasonably flexible terms, possibly including break clauses, a preferred length of lease term, or even an upward or downward rent review as set out above.

Disadvantages

- *Lack of control* – the business as tenant is exposed to the property market cycle. Typical upward-only rent reviews may cause a sudden doubling of occupation costs, or leave a business high and dry and unable to assign its lease if rents suddenly fall.

- *Upward-only rent review* – little needs to be said about the more or less ubiquitous upward only rent review pattern except: *Do* employ an expert surveyor in order to minimise the impact on the rent payable from review. It never ceases to surprise the experts how many businesses believe that they can do a better job. Upwards and downwards rent reviews will have some mitigating effect in recessionary market conditions, when they become more widespread.

- *Other liabilities* – a leasehold occupier is responsible, particularly if the sole occupier in a building under a full repairing lease, for all repairs and renewals (even extending to rebuilding of areas). Dilapidations at the end of a lease may also prove an unexpected cost.

- *Landlord's control* – invariably, the landlord will have to be asked for his consent to allow the tenant to take a wide range of actions. Whilst the exercise of his powers is well defined by legal precedent, and in particular the test of 'reasonableness', the right to withhold consent to a range of items including alterations, change of use, and (most important) to restrict the ability to assign the lease, can interfere with the ability of a business to occupy its business premises effectively.

Restrictions on subletting, in particular, can be insuperable. Many leases include a requirement that any subletting must be at market levels and reserve, as a minimum, the rent passing under the tenant's own lease. This is to protect the landlord's position in the event that the main tenant suffers a business failure, as the landlord's main remedy is to 'inherit' the sub-tenant (in the absence of guarantors) with the sub-tenant continuing to pay his contractual rent to the landlord. A number of ways around this, including in particular the use of a side agreement allowing the sub-tenant to pay less than the contractual rent, may work to circumvent the problem.

9.2.3 Intermission

This concludes the first part of this chapter. The arguments for and against a partnership holding its business premises on a leasehold basis have never changed significantly, but, as we have seen, there is the prospect of a new order on the horizon in the shape of the flexible lease. Before modern ownership strategies are examined, however, one particular development should be mentioned which could make much easier the role of the partner charged with looking after property issues.

Occupier management

There are opportunities these days to manage both the freehold and, possibly more importantly, the leasehold property commitment by outsourcing the business of management to property professionals. The role of the managing agent will be familiar to most occupying leasehold property, or to those who number property investors amongst their client base. Most modern property-management systems are equally capable of providing the same back-up service to corporate occupiers of property, including dealing with all bills (as well as rent and rates), and diarising action dates for break clauses, health and safety at work inspections, and all manner of similar issues. Some will also be able to offer bulk-buy discounts on insurance or energy costs After all, effective management of occupied property is not normally one of the core skills of the practice.

9.3 Property strategies – making your property work for you

The trend over the last five to 10 years for businesses to release the capital tied up 'unproductively' on the balance sheet by the ownership of property cannot have escaped anyone's notice. For many observers, watching the major corporate occupiers of property undertaking a capital-raising exercise by conducting a sale and leaseback to the ever hungry property investment market may indicate that leasehold tenure is the route of choice. However, other tax and pension-planning products available in today's market offer alternative ownership structures.

9.3.1 Ownership structures

Freehold subject to mortgage

The basic method of raising capital for property-owning partnerships is a commercial mortgage, most probably with the firm's principal bankers. Subject to valuation and the firm's ability to pay, up to 70 per cent of the value of the property can be released without the firm losing any significant degree of control. The firm will continue to benefit from increases in the value of the property, and both the capital asset and the mortgage debt will be carried on the balance sheet. There may be a requirement for periodic revaluations for compliance with FRS 15, *Measurement of tangible fixed assets* dependent on the status of the business.

Sale and leaseback

The next most common exit route for partnerships, as in the case of businesses that wish to raise capital, is by conducting a sale of the property to a commercial property investor who will simultaneously grant back to the business a lease for a term of years and at a rent to be agreed. In the case of the corporate business, this type of transaction is frequently undertaken as a capital-raising exercise, possibly to repair a damaged balance sheet. In the case of a partnership facing succession planning problems, undertaking a sale and leaseback, sometimes described these days as separating the brains from the bricks, draws a line under the firm's capital base and may allow retiring partners to be paid out without destroying the remaining business.

The apparent panacea must come with a health warning. It goes without saying (but it should be said nevertheless) that the business makes itself subject to the pros and cons of leasehold tenure already outlined. Any attempt to restrict the prospective landlord's freedom to manage the investment, such as reduced control over assignment or reduced repairing liabilities, will tend to reduce the amount of money that can be raised – or increase the cost of the capital-raising exercise through a higher rent.

Professional partnerships generally represent an attractive source of investment to professional property investors, institutions and financiers. The businesses are generally regarded as stable; less exposed to the economic cycle than retailers and manufacturers; and the joint and several liability of the partners provides built-in guarantors.

There are a number of different routes by which a sale and leaseback may be achieved, and the right one for any particular business will depend on the size of the practice and, possibly, on the nature of the business. It is also important to define what the business is seeking to achieve and, as already stated, to make the decision in the context of the general business plan.

Plan ahead

Having established that the premises are suitable for the foreseeable requirements of the practice, including the particular issue of flexibility for future growth or contraction, it remains to establish the amount of money that can be raised and the terms on which the sale and leaseback may be undertaken. In the event that the premises are deemed not suitable for future use, there is of course nothing to stop the business from selling its existing building and acquiring new premises working in conjunction with a sale and leaseback funder.

Take advice

Unless partners are fully experienced in these matters, they will benefit from the advice of professionals active in the market. Different investors or financiers will be prepared to offer different and more or less flexible terms, and there will be a variety of advisers including surveyors, some brokers, and some property investment strategists who will be best placed to advise.

It will be important to establish how much money can be raised, and to make the terms of occupation acceptable both to the practice and to the investor. The first prerequisite is to obtain a professional valuation of the building and establish the appropriate rental level. A competent investment valuation adviser will be able to advise on the capital that may be raised under a variety of leasing scenarios. The sensitivity analysis should include an estimate of the level of rent that will need to be paid to achieve a given capital sum depending on the flexibility built into the terms of the lease.

What the practice is likely to find is that the capital sum to be raised will remain much the same, whilst the variables will include the level of rent and the degree of flexibility in the lease. The greater the degree of flexibility, the less attractive the proposition is to the average investor and the more expensive the capital-raising exercise becomes.

In sale and leaseback transactions, the running is made initially by the business offering its premises for sale and leaseback. In planning the realistic outcome of the sale and leaseback capital-raising exercise, it is essential that the business is honest to itself about its attraction as a secure source of income for the prospective landlord. This is what is known in the property world as the 'strength of covenant'. It is not enough simply to offer the building at a rent and yield. Any prospective investor will wish to have close regard to the accounts, certainly for the previous three years. This will also have an impact on the yield that is derived from the rent and lease terms variables that we have already examined. If the state of the business allows for flexibility in the timing of the sale and leaseback exercise, there may be the opportunity to strengthen the accounts and therefore improve the yield.

Advantages

The advantage of the sale and leaseback structure over the traditional mortgage is that it releases 100 per cent of the capital tied up in the building. The price is the loss of control and flexibility, although a certain element of that can be bought back (at a price!).

Furthermore, it facilitates the disposal of a building which may otherwise be difficult to sell on the open market with vacant possession. At other times or in certain areas, there is however, a premium price obtainable for a sale with vacant possession and that margin is amongst the issues that need to be addressed at the planning stage.

Drawbacks

The principal drawback to the sale and leaseback route compared to the traditional mortgage route is the loss of control inherent in leasehold tenure over freehold tenure. Depending on the standing of the business, the cost of mortgage finance will be one to three per cent above base rate, and the business is likely to be restricted to borrowing say 70 per cent of the value of the premises. By contrast, a sale and leaseback releases 100 per cent of the capital, but rent, which may be equated to interest, is likely in most phases of the property market to cost between $7\frac{1}{2}$ per cent and 10 per cent per annum. When interest rates are low, ownership may appear more attractive. When interest rates are high, the leaseback may similarly appear more attractive.

In the future, following a rent review, the cost of servicing the initial capital-raising exercise increases and there is no further ability to raise capital against the building. Interest payable under a mortgage remains the same, and the business retains the flexibility to take advantage of the increased value of the building for a further capital-raising exercise if required.

Pension planning option

An option open to partnerships that may not need to raise as much cash from the disposal of their business premises as through a sale and leaseback, is to 'sell' the property into a structure that can create a self-invested pension plan (SIPP) or small self-administered scheme (SSAS) for the existing and future partners. In this scenario, a lease is created between the business and the pension fund, very much as in the context of a sale and leaseback. Obviously, in this case, it will be essential for the business to retain liability for all outgoings.

It is no part of this chapter to offer tax planning advice or advice on the structure of the pension planning vehicle, and specialist advice must be taken. There are extensive regulations governing the relationship between the individual partners, the Inland Revenue, and the SIPP or SSAS Fund if it is to be operated in the most flexible manner to allow easy ingress and exit for new and retiring members. For the purposes of this chapter, the holding body will be referred to as the 'SIPP Fund', for the reason that although there are probably more SSAS funds, SIPP funds offer more flexibility and higher gearing limits.

Creating a SIPP Fund in this way does, however, allow for a great deal of creative pension planning as well as assisting the tenant business in its operation. For a start the building can be acquired using the accumulated pension contributions of the partners (and other participants). The growth and income are received tax free by the fund.

Although the lease between the partnership and the SIPP Fund is not entirely at arm's length, and the investors retain the power of decision, the SIPP Fund will be administered by a professional pensions trustee, and the lease will need to be on normal commercial terms. Nevertheless it would be amongst the SIPP Fund manager's duties to ensure that nothing is done that diminishes the value of the property.

The rent payable by the business must approximate to open market rent, and in particular should not significantly exceed that level. Nevertheless, the rent payable can be treated as pension contributions to the SIPP by partners and grossed up accordingly.

Depending on the attitude of the partnership participants to risk, a SIPP Fund may gear up with borrowings of up to 75 per cent (an SSAS is limited to 50 per cent). This would enable the SIPP Fund to use partners' further contributions to acquire further investments, increasing the size, value and flexibility of the SIPP Fund. The use of borrowing, of course, increases the risk element in the fund, as well as leveraging returns. However, whilst it is open to the SIPP Fund to accept a lesser rent from the partnership when times are tough – in a way that a commercial landlord may not be prepared to do – if the fund is heavily geared the investors will still be liable for interest payments, whether or not these are being covered by rent from the business.

Use of a SIPP Fund does not produce as much free cash as the operation of a sale and leaseback, but it does take the property asset off the balance sheet which may be a benefit in itself. The principal benefit, however, is the creation of a useful vehicle for both existing and future partners which may have the added benefit of making the partnership attractive to potential new partners.

9.4 Leasehold strategies

We have already discussed the options open to a partnership happy to remain in occupation of leasehold property, although there are a number of issues for which it is as well to plan ahead.

9.4.1 Repair/dilapidation

Most leases of property contain a stringent clause placing liability for all repairs to the building on the tenant. At the expiry of the lease, or even in advance of that date, if the landlord believes the property is in disrepair he can serve a Schedule of Dilapidations. Failure to comply with the schedule can result in forfeiture of the lease.

In contemplating a terminal Schedule of Dilapidations, the likely intentions of the landlord should be examined in the event that the business is not renewing the lease. It may be that the landlord has quietly drawn up plans for redevelopment or a change of use of the building that would render the list of repairs completely or partially wasted. To that extent, a Schedule of Dilapidations may have no validity and can be challenged.

A useful tool for ensuring regular maintenance and avoiding the build-up of substantial liabilities is a planned preventative maintenance schedule. This should help to spread the cost of major liabilities by planning and even saving for them in advance.

9.4.2 Planning for growth/contraction

It is frequently the case that a practice will take larger premises than required for immediate occupation on the assumption that it will be possible to sublet parts of the building. Clearly, it will be important to establish that the building is capable of simple subdivision, including provision for separate meters for utilities. Other issues such as fire escapes and common reception areas need to be borne in mind also.

Most important, clearly, is the need to negotiate maximum flexibility in the subletting provisions when agreeing the terms of the lease.

When granting the subtenancies, it is important to have the strategic business plan in mind when choosing the length of term you wish to grant and ensure that there are suitable provisions for early termination in the form of a landlord's break option. Also, it would be normal to create such sub-lettings outside the security of tenure provisions of the LTA 1954 – this may even be a superior landlord's requirement.

It is also worth investigating an appeal against the rateable value of the building in the event that sublettings are entered into, as the change to a multi-occupied building is likely to create conditions for a reduction in rateable value.

9.4.3 Leasehold disposals

There are a number of strategies for disposing of unwanted leasehold premises. In the most straightforward scenario, an agent is appointed who markets the property for assignment, finds a suitable tenant, and obtains landlord's consent to the assignment. A deed is exchanged and a landlord's licence is obtained before the tenant moves out. As mentioned earlier, liabilities do not necessarily stop there, as with the pre-1996 lease the tenant remains theoretically liable for sums due under the lease until its expiry, in the event of default by the tenant in occupation. In the case of a lease granted after 1 January 1996, as part of the Licence to Assign, an Authorised Guarantee Agreement is entered into in which the tenant guarantees the performance of their immediate assignee. Only when he assigns the lease again does that liability end.

Where, for whatever reason, the accommodation turns out to be difficult to assign, a number of alternative strategies can be pursued.

9.4.4 Over-rented premises

There are two principal means of disposing of over-rented premises. First, the tenant's agents can calculate the size of a reverse premium needed to persuade an incoming tenant to take an assignment of the rental liability, or for a surrender to the landlord.

Second, dependent on the terms of the lease in this regard, you can sublet the accommodation at a loss or make a contribution to the payment of the contractual rent hidden by way of a side letter.

9.4.5 Short lease term

It is sometimes difficult to assign a short unexpired lease term as an incoming tenant may want greater security of tenure. Under those circumstances, it is sometimes possible to work together with the landlord and offer a new, longer lease direct from the landlord, who may also be happy to secure his income for a longer period without running the risk of a tenancy void.

9.4.6 Old fashioned building

Nearing the end of, say, a 25-year lease on a building which is outmoded, it might be possible to reach terms with the landlord for an early surrender of the lease to enable him to bring forward a redevelopment or refurbishment of the accommodation and its subsequent reletting. As an example, there have been instances of landlords approaching tenants to prompt a surrender of outmoded office buildings which it is their intention to convert, perhaps to residential apartments, and sell at a significant premium to commercial values. This is an example of the opportunity to create premium value from a position of liability. Whilst this is less likely to be an available option in a declining market, the option should be examined.

9.4.7 A declining market

In a declining market where neither a subletting nor an assignment may be possible, many landlords will see the economic sense in modifying a contractual rent passing in preference to insolvency of the tenant and the subsequent void period. Such negotiations should never be ruled out, but the approach should not be made lightly, or other than as a last resort, if the remedy is not to fall away for over use.

9.5 Conclusion

The property market is constantly evolving to provide solutions to the many and varied requirements of occupiers and users of property. It should not be forgotten that the property industry exists to provide a service to those occupiers, and it is more and more the occupiers of property who are the masters. However, without adequate planning, or in the event of misfortune, the masters can become prisoners of their properties.

Solutions that seem right today may be crafted quite differently in 10 years' time. It should not be forgotten that the biggest problem facing businesses 10 years ago was being locked into an over-rented leasehold scenario to which the most popular solution was to try to negotiate the purchase of the freehold, thereby swapping rental liability at a cost of, maybe, 10 per cent for an interest liability at, maybe, seven per cent. Today the trend is for a business to divorce itself from property ownership by way of sale and leaseback. In 10 years' time, business may be struggling to redeem itself from those leasehold commitments once again.

The readiness of investors to accept upward and downward rent reviews, and the trend towards shorter and possibly more flexible leases will make leasehold tenure a more acceptable form of occupation for many businesses. It will not happen overnight, but in 10 years' time a flourishing flexible leasing market would be expected.

It may be that the SIPP Fund option provides something approximating to the balance between freehold and leasehold ownership that many businesses would like. One thing that is sure is that no one solution will suit all businesses.

10   IT (internal/external)

10.1   Information technology (IT)

The world of IT encompasses a massive industry in itself as well as playing a part in all aspects of life from social to scientific. In its own world business has seen exponential growth which has resulted in the largest companies in the global economy coming from out of nothing in a matter of two decades. The 'dotcom' bubble which burst in the year 2000 was not based on real business. However, the main computing industry is reality and based on firm business foundations. The impacts of IT throughout the business cycle both within itself and within the accounting profession, has been, and continues to be, remarkable in its speed.

It is worthwhile identifying the elements of what we mean by the term 'Information technology' in its combined form (see **Appendix 1**). It is defined as business jargon – often the name of the part of an enterprise that deals with all things electronic. Another interesting aspect of the definitions is that applied to the term information, which includes:

- a message received and understood that reduces uncertainty;
- a collection of facts from which conclusions can be drawn;
- knowledge acquired.

This chapter concentrates on the use of technology and its application of information rather than any technical aspects of the systems involved in hardware, communications and software development. In many ways the technical aspects move and change so rapidly that any detailed discussion would be out of date before published and also is not relevant to a discussion on a practice of value.

The fundamental question that could be raised is: has the dream of what IT could do for the profession come true? Some of the dreams of the early 1980s, when the microcomputer brought IT to the smaller practice, were that:

- the presentation of information to clients would be such that clients would understand the underlying figures instantly and be better informed;
- the sources of information to back up the work of the professional would not only be readily available but would also be in a form to enhance performance and knowledge;

- there would be seamless integration of the application areas, such as tax and accounts, to allow both central access to data as well as automatic transfer of common data;
- there would be great efficiencies in the work flow and reductions in the time to deliver;
- the automation of routine tasks would be commonplace;
- the amount of time created by the efficiencies and automation of routine tasks would allow more proactive client-facing activities for the professionals.

This chapter will try to address this question, offer possibilities and also ask the question as to whether the dreams of the early 1980s are still dreams that will come true.

10.2 IT practice survey

A survey on accounting practices is conducted annually by the IT Faculty of the Institute of Chartered Accountants in England and Wales (ICAEW) the results of which can give some insight into the current use of IT. This survey is available from the IT Faculty, in full at www.itfac.co.uk; the elements extracted for the purposes of this chapter are as follows.

- Sixty per cent of practices have networked systems, this is a little misleading as a number of practices surveyed are sole practitioners. However, it is true to say that there is not universal networking of PCs in practice.

Figure 10.1 Results of IT practice survey

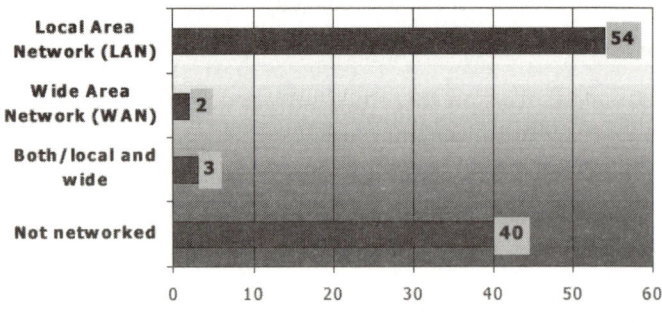

Eighty-eight per cent use the Microsoft Office suite, illustrating the dominance of this product in the professional business market. Use of word processing and spreadsheets is universal throughout practices.

Figure 10.2 Results of IT practice survey

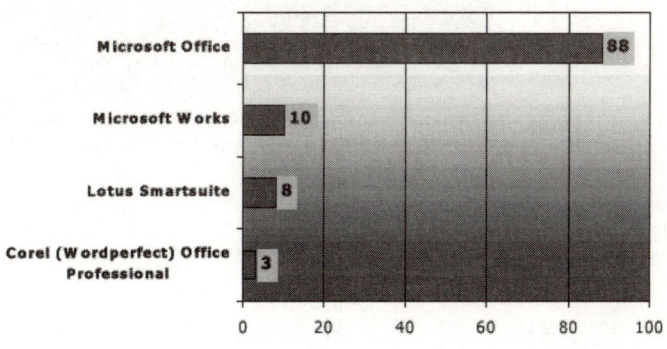

- IT support for systems is varied, with 38 per cent provided internally within the practice and 31 per cent with no support at all. This excludes application support from software houses but does indicate that backup systems are likely to be inadequate in general terms – a weakness identified by the survey.

- Sixty-six per cent of firms are providing IT related services to their clients. This statistic surprised many at first glance but should not be taken in isolation as much of this was on the back of other accounting related services provided, not specific IT services.

- The expectation was that client databases would be electronic almost universally. However, this has been dispelled as only 58 per cent of practices had electronic client databases. Of those with electronic databases some 22 per cent had two or more with common fields of information greater than 80 per cent of these were not linked electronically.

- In terms of the Internet and its usage, the expectation is that 92 per cent will have web access during 2002, the figure being 87 per cent in 2001 at the time of the survey. Interestingly only 25 per cent felt that web access was critical to the running of the practice.

Figure 10.3 Results of IT practice survey

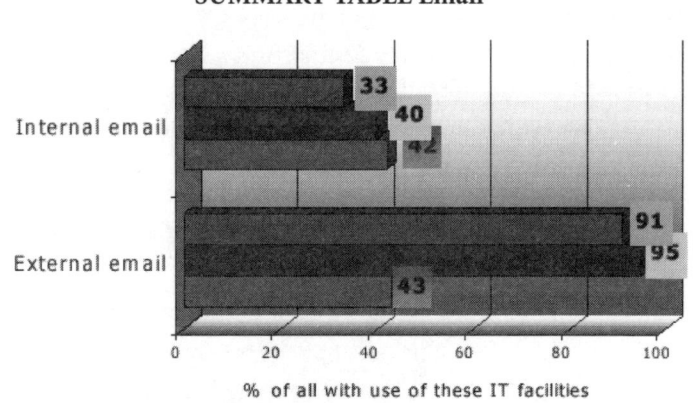

Figure 10.4 Results of IT practice survey

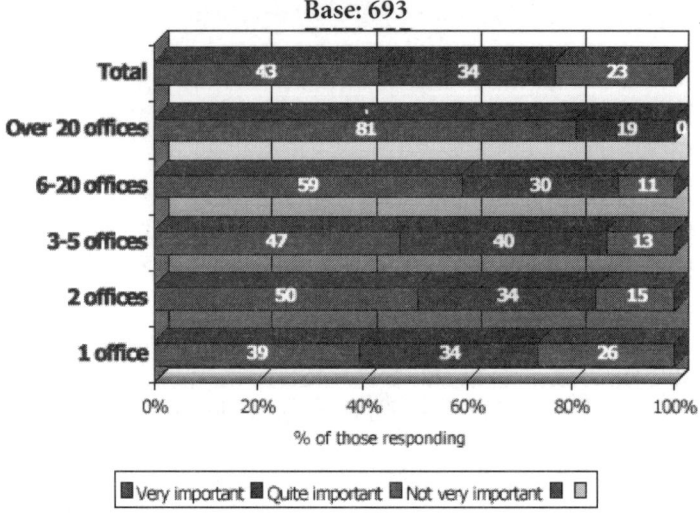

- Thirty-eight per cent had their own website with that figure expected to rise to 46 per cent during 2002. In addition the survey indicates that only four per cent offered Internet bookkeeping services to clients, expected to rise to 18 per cent during 2002.

- Usage of professional practice software statistics showed that the universal acceptance of packages to assist with the work was not a reality. Accounts production came out on top with 71 per cent, with the other main application of personal tax, payroll and accounting showing 57–64 per cent utilisation. The next tranches of packages were in the 30 per cent range and included time and fees, corporation tax and audit. Nine per cent of those surveyed used no professional practice application packages at all. The most surprising statistic is the usage attributed to time and fees recording which shows at only 37 per cent.

Figure 10.5 Results of IT practice survey

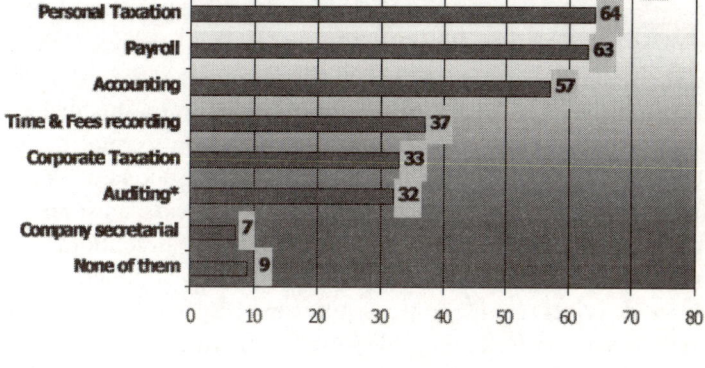

The usage of IT and packages and thus answers to the question of whether the dreams of the early 1980s are coming true, can be illustrated by a Due Diligence report for a prospective acquisition produced by a major firm recently. The report was in Microsoft PowerPoint, which was innovative, yet the use of graphics and the intrinsic presentation capabilities of the application were completely ignored. The use of PowerPoint as a word processor can be likened to the saying that '... accountants are the best group at taking a computer and making it into a 2Gigabyte typewriter'.

What the survey does not say, but indicates, is that the aspect of building value for the client is almost totally ignored in terms of the existing services, much of the added-value thinking being additional services. The use of graphics in accounts production, wealth pie charts in personal tax, benchmarking and meaningful industry comparisons are very rare. Firms are coping with technology by replicating manual processes and not making innovative use of technology to add value.

The survey does not indicate that accountants are any worse than other professionals. However, there are indications that the use of IT is not yet an integral part of the work flow of a practice. Dan Simms, CPA, is the partner responsible for IT at the Atlanta-based US practice of Habif, Arogeti & Wynne (HA&W). This is a paperless practice, the principle of utilising technology as an integral part of the work flow is fundamental. The question to ask is whether the goal of a paperless practice is the route to achieving the dreams.

It is a potential conclusion from the outcome of the survey that the use of technology within practice has primarily been simply to turn manual systems into computerised systems. . This in itself is not necessarily a bad thing, however, any gains may well be hard to achieve. The principle as illustrated by HA&W at one extreme is that of ensuring that many manual processes are not just made more efficient by technology but are in fact largely eliminated. Dan Simms states that they cut out $125,000 of paper costs in the last financial year alone, costs driven out of the system by eliminating the manual process of printing and filing. Effective use of voice recognition technology is another aspect of the HA&W revolution which has proved so successful. Voice systems have been available for practices in the UK for some years; however, there have been reliability issues along with the unwillingness of practitioners to change their way of working to eliminate manual processes. Suppliers such as Pyxis Computer Services (www.pyxiscomputerservices.co.uk) have utilised the more reliable current technology platforms to provide innovative systems that are likely to be more prevalent in the future.

10.3 Technology and practice

IT has meant change and change in itself is part of today's business environment. Other chapters deal with aspects of change in some detail, but the fundamental point of overhead cost changes is relevant here. IT now occupies second place in most practice overheads whereas only a few years ago it was regarded as mainly a capital investment with some maintenance overheads. A further aspect of overhead to be added to the calculation is that of communication costs as Internet usage gathers pace. It is now considered good practice to include all communication costs, including telephone, as part of the IT spend – following on from the definition earlier of IT as '... the part of an enterprise that deals with all things electronic'.

The internal management of firms' systems based on the ability to monitor and control the fees billed against the time records. This underlying role of practice management systems has hardly moved over the last 25 years, the development of systems generally being in the analysis, ease of billing process and demonstrable recovery. This also raises the question of traditional billing, but the whole topic is addressed elsewhere in the book. The more innovative systems have developed by being more client-centric than most practices have been either aware of or utilised. Access to client information is two-fold: first in relation to hard facts and figures (hard data); and second the 'softer' data to do with relationships, such as notes and correspondence. The soft data is the key to developing systems that add value to the practice in terms of succession, retirement and building value.

The IT jargon for such systems ranges from CRM (customer/client relationship management) to PSA (professional services applications). As such, many of the current packages available in the UK address this area of the practice with varying degrees of success. The integration solutions, such as Iris (www.iris.co.uk) are strong on the transfer of data between applications. Whereas there are more PSA-based solutions, such as PROcost Control Desk from PROacc Systems Limited (www.proacc.co.uk) and Practice Engine (www.praceng.co.uk) are looking at client profiling to provide better service and effective marketing. These systems are leading the paperless practice initiatives, although it may be that the market is such at the present time that the term can switch off the more traditional partnership.

10.4 Knowledge management systems

Knowledge management became the new jargon some years ago and the uptake of systems and processes based on this environment must not be underestimated in the corporate and large-practice arena. Current marketing of such systems in the UK to the smaller firm is centred on the term 'document management'.

At the document management level the case for investing in such systems is strong in terms of simply the storage space saved versus the usable/chargeable space freed. Robin Klein, Managing Director of Singleview (www.singleview.co.uk), adds to the case through a cost benefit analysis of retrieval of documents only: if 25 individuals retrieve five documents per day that leads to 25,000 documents per year. If it takes three minutes to manually retrieve the document, at a charge out-rate of £100 per hour, the saving is £125,000 annually. If it takes 15 seconds on a system to retrieve the document, that equates to around £10,000 per annum; a saving of £115,000 per annum. Robin Klein does, however, recognise the difference between knowledge and the application of knowledge by stating that, '... knowledge is deemed to be power which thus enables progress'.

However, the current position from the perspective of Simon Hurst is that often firms have structured filing systems for documents, but he has not come across smaller firms with knowledge management and rarely with document management systems.

Referring to the issue of technical staff, discussed again under IT Staff in a Practice at **10.7** below, this is an area that needs consideration for knowledge management. Mark Ryan (www.ryaninternational.co.uk) has strong views on those qualified to create knowledge. A new type of staff support is required in this area, namely a knowledge manager or librarian, whose role is to convert information from the specialists/partners into knowledge for the practice. He sees two distinct databases of information. The traditional hard data of the mainstream applications such as tax and accounts production, and the soft data. He does not believe that these can be one database although they should be linked.

10.5 Learning

In the world of estate agents the saying is 'location, location, location' and this can be applied to the IT aspects of professional practice over training. The term 'training' in itself should be used with caution. Two expressions are applicable here to reinforce the distinction between training and learning:

- parents being asked whether they would be happier for their child to have 'sex training or sex education';
- 'you train dogs, people learn'.

The Gartner Group research has shown that five hours are gained in productive time for every hour of technology training. This is true of the individual and also of the group where there is common training, to quote from the author Ken Blanchard; 'none of us is as smart as all of us'. If this is taken to conclusion, then for every 40 hours there are an additional 200 hours of capacity, the effect on the staff model is evident.

The way forward to enable universal confidence and capability in IT for a firm is to start with the training budget and then lead on to the hardware and software budgets. Simon Hurst of the research consultancy 'The Knowledge Base' (www.tkb.co.uk) illustrates this with a simple table of results:

Table 10.1 The effect of training

System choice	Implementation and training	Success expectation
Good	Adequate	Excellent
Bad	Adequate	Reasonable
Good	Inadequate	Minimal
Bad	Inadequate	Minimal

The use and abuse of e-mail is currently a hot topic in larger business. In the smaller practice this has not come onto the radar but is causing untold harm to both productive and relationships. E-mail is a new method of communication that does not have the interaction of face-to-face or telephone communication, nor the formality and caution associated with correspondence by mail or fax. It must be treated with respect as a new medium of communication and need to be the participants trained in its use and administration.

10.6 Technology assessment

One of the gurus in this field is Gary Boomer of Boomer Consulting (www.boomer.com) and he has written extensively on this area. 'Boomer's Technology Physical' (below) illustrates the type of hard questions a practice should ask itself.

Table 10.2 Boomer's Technology Physical

1 Does your firm have a current three-year technology plan and budget?
2 Are your partners and staff adequately trained?
3 Is your firm in compliance with software licensing agreements and are you using current versions of the software?
4 Does your firm have a quality PC for every person attached to the network?
5 Does your firm have an outside facilitator for technology planning?
6 Do you have adequately trained network supervisor and support personnel?
7 Has your firm implemented Windows 2000 as your desktop operating system?
8 Do you have a qualified partner providing technology leadership?
9 Do you have a written disaster recovery plan?
10 Have you upgraded at least one-third of your network nodes during the past year and are you planning to do the same in the current year?

Boomer Consulting have updated and modified the original technology physical to produce a formal leadership scorecard to assess where a practice is in

IT (internal/external)

terms of technology. The scorecard can also be used for strategy planning by scoring the ambitions of the practice. Interesting comparative data for benchmarking can be achieved through the associations that many practices have developed in the UK and internationally, or through training consortia (**Appendix 2** *The Technology Leadership Scorecard*™).

One key benchmarking criteria lies in the amount of investment required for IT in a practice. As a benchmark, the high-tech practices who are investing heavily in IT are approaching an investment of 5–7 per cent of gross turnover. This includes the training budget and also assumes the wide definition of IT to include such overheads as communication costs. The ability of the firm to invest in this level is best achieved through a 'technology surcharge' within the billing to clients. In the example of HA&W this is exactly what they did, and continue to do, in order to be a profitable, paperless practice.

10.7 IT staff in a practice

A key to the success of the US firm HA&W mentioned earlier is that they had a technology champion and technology team responsible for the management. It has been estimated that the ratio of 1:25 IT person to chargeable person is the right mix. However, care must be taken to hire the right people, not accountant-clones.

Figure 10.6 Microsoft Corporation, 1978

There are various methods for looking at the cost benefit of employing adequate IT staff, – adequate in terms of both expertise and productivity. One such example is based on the following underlying data – daily charge-out rates for the various levels of chargeable staff are: partners £2,000; manager £1,400; senior £800; junior £400. If five minutes per day is wasted due to technology inefficiencies or lack of adequate training, over three years this amounts to £13,800 or 23*Pentium 1.7Gb desktop PCs!

10.8 Broadband and its impact in the UK

Broadband is essentially high-speed transmission. The term is commonly used to refer to communications lines or services at T1 rates (1.544 Mbps) and above. It is a method of transmitting data, voice and video using frequency division multiplexing (FDM), such as used with cable TV.

George Cox, Director General of the Institute of Directors, sees the increasing use of the Internet being materially affected by the take-up of broadband and its associated increase in speed. The productivity gains and the ability to have fixed identified costs will mean that business can communicate more effectively with high-quality sound and images. The key applications we can already see being affected include:

- web surfing – removing the frustration of slow speeds;
- e-mail – always-on and instant delivery even away from the office;
- file downloads – large files, especially graphics files, can now take a fraction of the time and therefore are more usable;
- real-time data – always-on means real-time information such as news or share prices;
- audio/video streaming – allows audio and video content to be broadcast over the web by a continuous stream enabling live broadcasts for example, and video films utilizing technology from entities such as Forbidden Technology (www.forbidden.co.uk);
- video conferencing – this area is seriously underused in business at the present time but could be one of the main winners with the increasing use of video conferencing as a standard business tool;
- B2B – the impact on the world of business to business (B2B) e-commerce is likely to be high. The ability to exchange invoices and basic business forms at such high speeds, along with the already prevalent large Acrobat Reader files will be affected favourably.

The other side of this broadband revolution is that of collaborative working practices. There are some trends in the new working regime that will all benefit from Internet speed and they include teleworking, mobile office environments, and work flow management within teams from remote locations. It was predicted in 1997 that by 2001 five million people in the UK would be collaborating remotely whereas the actual figure in 2000 totalled 1.5 million. Of this 1.5 million, 312,000 were home working, 805,000 were teleworking with home as the base, and 477,000 occasionally telework. Why such a limited uptake? There are many reasons, but one of the primary issues has been Internet speed.

It will be interesting to watch the experimental town of Modalen, situated at the end of a fjord in Norway. The town has had broadband connection linked to the Internet in all aspects of social and business life – to read meters of household energy usage on the net, send invoices and payments electronically through the net, use cheap local telephone rates with telephony systems linked to the net. Another specific opportunity is to be able to send class assignments when the children cannot get to school because of adverse weather conditions.

Finally, the area of outsourcing should not be ignored. There are increasing worries over capital depreciation, skill and staff shortages and maintenance/upgrades, which lead to the possibilities of outsourcing. Broadband is an enabler in this sector.

This all ties up with the strategy of the main player in the IT world, Microsoft Corporation. The Gartner Group made a statement about the future of IT:

> 'we believe that by 2005, the three features common to leading businesses will be that they approach zero latency with information flow, they will have moved to real-time monitoring of business activities, and device independence will be a standard feature of information access.'

Microsoft uses the easy-to-remember phrase to summarise this in its Microsoft.net philosophy, namely: 'Anywhere, Anytime, Any device'. This .net platform from Microsoft is for XML web services allowing applications to communicate and share data over the Internet, regardless of operating system or programming language.

The IT Faculty survey did indicate that the great majority of practices had access to the Internet, some 87 per cent with the expectation of 92 per cent during 2002.

Figure 10.7 Summary table: web browser/Internet access

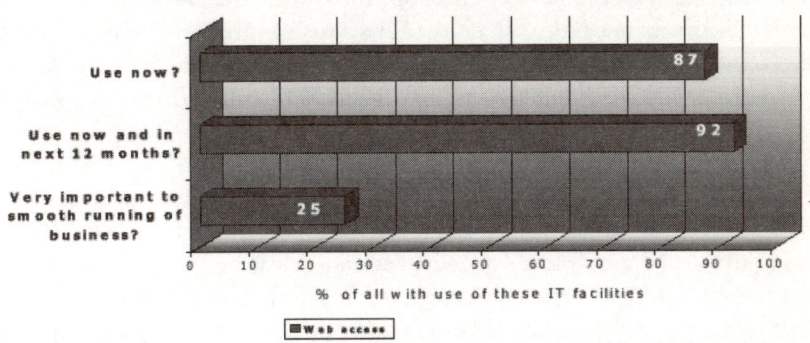

The access routes to the Internet, illustrated below indicated that 65 per cent have modem access, which is likely to indicate slow speed and therefore different expectations and working practices. Only 25 per cent felt that access was very important to the running of the business this is likely to change dramatically with broadband speed.

Figure 10.8 Results of IT practice survey

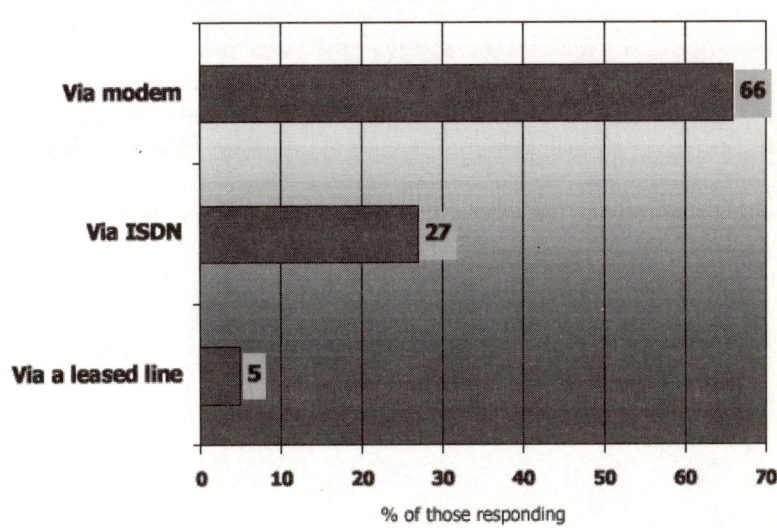

10.9 Security is the best policy

Simon Hurst uses the phrase 'Look out the world wide web's behind you' to highlight the issue of security on the Internet and through e-mail. This is the first aspect affecting most smaller practices and individuals in recent times. It has been a bad time for viruses with some very nasty examples spreading extremely quickly.

Perhaps one of the most worrying trends has been the level of automation that many of the latest macros have achieved. Until recently, even the more notorious viruses such as 'I love you' and 'Melissa' did at least require someone to double click on an e-mail attachment to activate and disseminate them. Recently, several viruses have emerged that can either travel directly across the Internet by exploiting security shortcomings in server software, or use other security vulnerabilities to run automatically as soon as an e-mail is opened. So at least you have to open the e-mail – well no actually. If the preview pane in Microsoft Outlook is used, just selecting the e-mail to delete it could be enough to trigger the virus.

However, 'a virus checker and a few passwords written on notes stuck on a computer does not amount to a security policy' (Institute of Director's Guide). The biggest single obstacle to e-commerce trading is acknowledged as security, both from virus infection and hacking. A database of information in a practice is not only the single most precious asset, the practice also has a duty to protect the information under the legal framework of the Data Protection Act 1998 as well as corporate governance issues under the Turnbull Guidelines. There is no doubt that whatever systems are put in place it still requires awareness and commitment from staff to ensure security and monitoring of this is essential.

Options include off-the-shelf packages from suppliers such as Symantec (www.symantec.com) with the Norton suite, and outsourced specialist providers such as Star Internet Group (www.star.net.uk). These do give the required security but are not the total answer and the practice must implement a security policy and guidelines. Guidance in choosing the right supplier includes some due diligence work on the supplier itself in term of their procedures and processes for contingencies.

The major security elements for practice protection are:

- anti-virus software;
- hacking detection software – Intrusion Detection Systems (IDC);
- data encryption;

- firewalls;
- user authentication.

> 'Making security a priority … could mean the difference between a successful practice and no practice.' (Simon Hurst, TKB)

10.10 Extensible business reporting language (XBRL)

The Profitable and Sustainable Practice task force of the Institute of Chartered Accountants in England and Wales, created to discuss this heading, held a consultation session on IT issues specifically. The group looked at IT trends, they believed would affect the general practice over the next decade. Two main trends were identified:

1 the Internet;

2 knowledge management systems.

These areas have already been discussed at some length in this chapter but the synergy with the task force is interesting. The area specifically mentioned and debated within the task force relating to the Internet is that of the development of xbrl. This is being promoted as the new 'digital language of business'. It will allow financial information to be published, exchanged and analysed in a standard way. It may underpin many other developments regarding finance and IT. It could, for example, make it easier to extract tax-return information automatically from accounting packages and submit it to the appropriate authorities (www.xbrl.org).

The potential XBRL applications are as follows:

- XBRL for Financial Statements – financial statements of all sorts used to exchange financial information;
- XBRL for Taxes –specification for tax returns which are filed and information exchanged for items which end up on tax returns;
- XBRL for Regulatory Filings – specifications for the large number of filings required by government and regulatory bodies;
- XBRL for Accounting and Business Reports – management and accounting reporting such as all the reports that are created by the accounting system rendered in XML to make re-using them possible;
- XBRL for Authoritative Literature – a standard way for describing accounting-related authoritative literature published to make using these resources easier, with 'drill downs' into literature from financials possible.

For different classes of user the potential benefits are as follows:

- companies who prepare financial statements – more efficient preparation of financial statements because they will be created one time and rendered as printed reports on Web sites as regulatory filings;
- analysts, investors, and regulators – enhanced distribution and usability of existing financial statement information. Automated analysis, significantly less rekeying of financial information from one form into another form, receiving information in the preferred format for a specific style of analysis;
- financial publishers and data aggregators – more efficient data collection lowers operating costs associated with custom, idiosyncratic data feeds and reducing errors while concentrating on adding value to the data and increasing transaction capacity;
- independent software vendors – virtually any software product that manages financial information could use XBRL for its data export and import formats, thereby increasing its potential for full-interoperability with other financial and analytical applications. General benefits also arise, in particular:
- facilitation of data transfer and processing – data derived from different systems can be transferred, presented, sorted, analysed and compared in a standard form;
- elimination of re-entry of data;
- international convergence on the standard.

Benefits will also accrue from international convergence towards the XBRL standard, which is well under way. Reuters has become the first publicly listed company in Europe to release its financial results on the Internet, using a prototype of XBRL to publish its third quarter 2001 trading statement. This interim statement is a simple one, primarily involving a breakdown of revenue figures by the business sector, but demonstrates that XBRL is a practical as well as a theoretically sound reporting tool. A sample balance sheet is available on the www.xbrl.org site based on Great Plains Software and an illustration is shown below.

Figure 10.9 Sample balance sheet

	CONSOLIDATED BALANCE SHEET		
	Great Plains Software, Inc.		
		MAY 31,	
(Dollars in thousands)		1999	1998
ASSETS			
Current assets:			
Cash and cash equivalents		$ 26,983	$ 18,197
Investments		96,700	48,721
Accounts receivable, net		12,593	8,790
Inventories		746	542
Prepaid expenses and other assets		6,340	2,914
Deferred income tax assets		5,542	4,630
Total current assets		148,904	83,794
Property and equipment, net		19,126	8,501
Goodwill and other intangibles, net		3,838	4,946
Deferred income tax assets		3,091	3,318
Other assets		5,293	2,286
		$	$
Total assets		180,252	102,845
LIABILITIES AND STOCKHOLDERS' EQUITY			
Current liabilities:			
Accounts payable		$ 8,392	$ 4,135
Accrued expenses		11,590	6,941
Income tax payable		--	3,257

XBRL Financial Statement Viewer
- Document Information
- Entity Information
- Accountant Report
- Balance Sheet
- Income Statement
- Stockholder's Equity
- Cash Flows
- Notes
- Taxonomy Used
- GPSI Custom Taxonomy Added
- Instance document (Raw XML)
- How this sample was created

Copyright 2000, XBRL.ORG

It is likely that XBRL will increase the need for companies to have more information as it becomes more readily available through the technology. It may be that the role of the accountant changes because of the speedier analysis and they become an intermediary for this analysed information, much in the role of an information broker. David Rankin, Managing Director of Tenon Technology (www.tenongroup.com/services/technology/), is often quoted commenting about the failure of most firms to capture the 'reseller' market for computerised bookkeeping in the 1980s. It is hoped this opportunity in the area of XBRL information broker is not also lost. The accountancy professional might be seen as an information adviser rather than being about numbers, utilising the skills of forming opinions, analysing data and making figures understandable.

An initiative by the IT Faculty of the ICAEW, in terms of the skills of practising members, may be relevant in this context and well as others to do with IT more generally. The IT Faculty promotes the concept that IT expertise for the ACA should be examined and then be part of the continuing professional education programme with the recommended CPE element being 20 per cent IT related and the IT content of examinations being 20 per cent directly IT related.

Appendix 1   Definitions

Information

'1 The act of informing, or communicating knowledge or intelligence.

2 News, advice, or knowledge, communicated by others or obtained by personal study and investigation; intelligence; knowledge derived from reading, observation, or instruction.

3 (Law) A proceeding in the nature of a prosecution for some offen against the government, instituted and prosecuted, really or nominally, by some authorized public officer on behalf of the government. It differs from an indictment in criminal cases chiefly in not being based on the finding of a grand juri. See "Indictment"'.

Source: *Webster's Revised Unabridged Dictionary* (© 1996, 1998 MICRA, Inc.)

Technology

'1 The application of science, especially to industrial or commercial objectives. The scientific method and material used to achieve a commercial or industrial objective.

2 Electronic or digital products and systems considered as a group: *a store specializing in office technology.*

3 *Anthropology.* The body of knowledge available to a society that is of use in fashioning implements, practicing manual arts and skills, and extracting or collecting materials.'

Source: *The American Heritage® Dictionary of the English Language* (4th edn, 2000, Houghton Mifflin Company).

Information technology

'<business, jargon> (IT) Applied computer systems – both hardware and software, and often including networking and telecommunications, usually in the context of a business or other enterprise. Often the name of the part of an enterprise that deals with all things electronic.

The term "computer science" is usually reserved for the more theoretical, academic aspects of computing, while the vaguer terms "information systems" (IS) or "information services" may include more of the human activities and non-computerised business processes like knowledge management. Others say that IT includes computer science.'

Source: *The Free On-line Dictionary of Computing* (© 1993–2001 Denis Howe)

Appendix 2 The Technology Leadership Scorecard™

To help you clearly understand your current situation, complete The Technology Leadership Scorecard™. Rate your reactions to each pair of phrases. Decide where you lie on the scale from 1 to 10. Add up your total from each column.

	1	2	3	4	5	6	7	8	9	10	
We don't have a clear vision.											We have a clear well-defined vision.
We don't have clear goals with regard to technology.											We have clear goals with regard to technology.
We don't have confidence in our IT department.											We have confidence in our IT department.
We don't have a written game plan and the budget to achieve our goals.											We have a written game plan and the budget to achieve our goals.
Employees don't understand the game plan and their responsibilities.											Employees understand the game plan and their responsibilities.
We don't utilize a Technology Team and Task Forces to accomplish our goals. (No leverage)											We utilize a Technology Team and Task Forces to accomplish our goals. (Leverage)
We don't have a Coach to insure we follow the game plan.											We have a Coach to insure we follow the game plan.
We don't have a Training Coordinator and well-defined training curriculum.											We have a Training Coordinator and well-defined training curriculum.

Appendix 2

	1	2	3	4	5	6	7	8	9	10	
We don't have a Training facility.											We do have a Training Facility.
We do not have as much confidence in the future as we would like to have.											We have a strong sense of confidence about our future.
ADD COLUMN TOTALS											YOUR SCORE

References and acknowledgements

IT Faculty of the Institute of Chartered Accountants in England & Wales (ICAEW)	www.itfac.co.uk/
Dan Simms, CPA, of Habif, Arogeti & Wynne	www.hawcpa.com
Pyxis Computer Services	www.pyxiscomputerservices.co.uk
PROacc Systems Limited	www.proacc.co.uk
Practice Engine	www.praceng.co.uk
Iris Group	www.iris.co.uk
Robin Klein of Singleview	www.singleview.co.uk
Mark Ryan	www.ryaninternational.co.uk
Simon Hurst of The Knowledge Base	www.tkb.co.uk
Gary Boomer of Boomer Consulting	www.boomer.com
George Cox of the Institute of Directors	www.iod.co.uk
Forbidden Technology	www.forbidden.co.uk
xbrl	www.xbrl.org
David Rankin of Tenon Technology	www.tenongroup.com/services/technology/
Symantec with the Norton suite	www.symantec.com
Star Internet Group	www.star.net.uk

11 Professional indemnity insurance

11.1 Housekeeping to build your business

The Institute of Chartered Accountants in England and Wales has made it compulsory for accountants to provide professional indemnity insurance to levels that are thought to be adequate to cater for the normal yet unexpected errors that do occur in practice.

Accountants have, to a great extent, put in place a very high level of 'housekeeping' and work very much more closely with their Institutes in achieving those high levels which has resulted in the number of Professional Indemnity claims reducing or being eradicated, especially in the last five to 10 years.

Many practices will have seen the introduction of the Joint Monitoring Unit as a detriment to their business and, at the very least, a nuisance in terms of trying to maintain standards. There is no question in the writer's view that the introduction of the Joint Monitoring Unit played a key role in reducing the number of circumstances, and ultimately professional indemnity claims, within the accountancy profession.

As a specialist broker handling professional indemnity for all professions, the writer believes that many other professions could learn a lot from what he believes is the success of the control over potential claims against accountants that is currently in place.

Another important feature that has helped reduce potential claims against the accountant is the education area within the profession. There are a number of highly professional training bodies that have enabled accountants to achieve and sustain their practice development to a high level. Organisations such as Mercia and other specialist accountancy training groups continue to maintain the high level of standards required within the profession on behalf of the Institute.

In general, providing that accountancy practices maintain their levels of education and housekeeping, there is no reason why a practice should not continue to build without any likely pitfalls arising in the future. There is no question that the value of a practice can be reduced considerably if 'skeletons are found in the cupboard' for a practice that has not maintained the high levels required by the profession as a whole.

As a specialist in professional indemnity for the last 20 years, and manager of an insurance brokerage that looks after somewhere in the region of 2,500 firms of accountants, the author is in a strong position to recount some incidences that have occurred to practices he has dealt with over that period of time. Later in the chapter, specific case studies on professional indemnity issues will be examined, but the overall message that should be passed on to accountants when trying to continue to add value to their business is, 'Stick to what you know – not what you would like to know'.

It is likely that every practice has had the opportunity to earn significant fees in areas linked to accountancy that, on the face of it, would appear to be extremely attractive, but if honesty prevailed, the practices in question would probably refuse to become involved in the work if they were asked to produce a CV of their past knowledge of particular areas.

Mergers and acquisitions is one potential minefield where although the fees involved can be considerable, if the due diligence is not carried out correctly the potential losses can be extremely significant. When these losses occur, although adequate insurance may be in place, this will reflect in the premium increases to the practice. More significant will be the increased difficulty in being able to sell or merge the practice at a later date, as the adverse history of the practice would have to be disclosed.

Another area of concern is the careful selection of partners in a practice, especially if the practice is acquiring fees or purchasing a smaller practice without the full knowledge of the individuals that have handled the business in the past. On the face of it this may seem a very quick way of increasing the fee turnover of a business, but unless it is known that this is going to be a perfect match, experience shows that it is very much safer to grow business from within rather than purchase from an outside source. The poor acquisition of a partner and their fees can result in a number of claims arising, rather than one-off claims. This can result in not only significant increases in the cost of the insurance, but insurance companies could impose a large policy excess, thus resulting in a very high level of self insurance. If the situation becomes difficult in this regard, the Institute have put in place what is known as an assigned risk pool where the Institute have guaranteed that you can have insurance in place but for those few practices that end up in this particular pool. However, the cost is usually so high that it is almost not worth continuing in practice.

In the event of purchasing a block of fees or a smaller practice, great care should be taken to establish the history of that business. This can be easily done by obtaining full details of the history of the professional indemnity (e.g., copies of proposal forms, copies of policies, etc.). This, again, is an exercise that could be carried out by one of the experienced training groups that also operate in such areas as peer review systems.

11.2 What level of cover should be taken?

The Institute of Chartered Accountants has strict requirements on the minimum level of cover required, which is dependent on the practice's fee income. This should be treated as it is intended, i.e., minimum. As to the level of cover, this is a decision that can only be taken by each individual practice. No other person/company (e.g., broker or insurance company) will know or understand the practice's clients and, therefore, exposures as well as the partners themselves do.

If a practice becomes involved in the more unusual areas of practice, e.g., mergers and acquisitions, directorships, financial services, then any potential loss that could arise in these areas should be considered carefully. If practitioners are acting for publicly quoted companies, they could consider that the quantum of losses would be well above the average of a non-quoted company client.

Until recently (pre-11September), the cost of what is known as top-up insurance was relatively low and even after that date, as a comparison against the cost of primary insurance, the top-up levels have still been cheap compared with the potential losses that can occur at, for example, a claim above £1 million. Normally a top-up insurance would come into place above at least a primary policy of £1 million for any one claim.

11.3 Financial services – a way to increase the turnover of your practice and add value

Most practices have looked at ways of increasing fees by networking existing clients. Advising on financial services products is a potential minefield and most practices choose to refer their clients to specialists within the financial services world. There is no reason why an accountancy practice should not set up a financial services operation and, indeed, those that have done and have ensured that they have individuals properly qualified within the practice, have generally made a success and have increased the fee income of the practice, on average, between 10 and 15 per cent.

Importantly, it should be understood that where such areas as financial services run alongside accountancy, there are rules and regulations that are in place for the financial services side that must be adhered to and if they are not, the potential for a professional indemnity claim is increased many fold. This stability helps to prevent professional negligence claims, caused by staff, arising in the long term. Financial services operations working away from accountancy practices have probably had more claims on their own professional indemnity due to their lack of knowledge of individual clients. This could have been avoided if they were working either within an accountancy practice or very closely alongside one.

The statement of 'sticking to what you know' still prevails, but a practice should not avoid giving expertise to clients where they have a considerable knowledge of their business or financial position. There is obviously an opportunity for other accountants who have financial services operations in place to take on those clients if that advice is not offered – but care should be taken.

11.4 Run-off

What is run-off? It is a bit like the term 'comprehensive' in motor insurance. Many people believe they understand what it means but do not understand how it should be put in place correctly.

Under the Institute's requirements of an insurance policy, when a partner retires it is compulsory that the existing policy provides cover for that past partner's liability.

Likewise, in the event of a practice being sold, it is important to ensure that the past partner's liability is correctly protected. There are two ways of protecting the insurance requirements. First, if a practice is being sold, it is possible for the partners selling the practice to continue to arrange the insurance for past run-off liability, thus giving peace of mind that cover is in place. Also, if the selling partners arrange the insurance, this can be more economically beneficial. If the past partner's liability is lost into the practice that has been acquired, the purchaser may end up paying a disproportionate premium and also may be required to pay a much higher excess than experienced in the past.

The second method is for the acquiring practice to take on the past liability of the business. This is the normal way that cover would be put in place, but it may well be worth getting a comparison of cost as well as cover (including the excess to be applied). The best advice is to speak to a professional indemnity insurance broker when considering a change in structure.

11.5 Succession planning from within

The possible problems that can be caused in acquiring practices and thus increasing the fee income of a business have been touched on. The more natural way of planning succession would be from within the business and, therefore, the importance of recruiting high-calibre employees that are going to be loyal and therefore supportive of a practice over many years should be emphasised.

Experience shows that it has proved extremely difficult to obtain what is now needed in a modern-day accountancy practice, i.e., the ability to maintain high standards of technical knowledge coupled with the opportunity and equal need to encourage new clients and to, therefore, grow the practice. Very often it is difficult to satisfy the needs of the enthusiastic 'youngster' who may not stay the course with the practice where he has served his apprenticeship.

Providing incentives to staff (financially or otherwise) encourages them to stay within a business, thus creating a high level of loyalty and diligence. This helps to prevent claims arising in the long term. It will also improve the value of a practice by allowing it to boast long-serving staff who enjoy close working relationships with both partners' clients and other members of staff. This would appear to be fairly obvious but is perhaps more complex in terms of being able to satisfy individual staff both by way of financial rewards and job satisfaction.

There is no question that if this standard can be obtained, then succession planning is very much in place and if this is done on a very regular basis to ensure a complete diversity of ages of potential future partners then, again, a much more professional practice will have been formed and problems are far less likely to occur from a professional indemnity point of view.

Problems usually arise where three to six individuals of the same age group form a practice and a long period of time passes before they see the necessity to involve other individuals as partners. This is a natural self-protection mechanism but, in the long run, if the partners are prepared to involve other junior partners, perhaps on a salaried basis, sooner rather than later, it will leave a more stable practice.

Examples of claims that have actually occurred, follow. They paint the picture of avoiding growth in a practice unless it is well within the control of the partners. The examples also illustrate that a practice should not get involved in areas about which the partners have no knowledge, even though the fee may be extremely attractive.

11.6 Examples of claims within the profession

11.6.1 Complacency and bad habits

An accountant's brief was to prepare and submit a client's tax returns to the Inland Revenue. Despite several requests for additional information to complete the returns, the information was either late or not forthcoming at all. The returns were submitted late for several years running and penalties were imposed. The client alleged negligence against the accountant and sought compensation.

11.6.2 Turning a blind eye

An accountant acted as the company auditor to a client for 15 years. During this period, the bookkeeper/secretary misappropriated funds and submitted false receipts into the company books. The accountant was aware that the books were not kept up to date and that there were some minor discrepancies, but never brought this to the attention of his client. However, he did not detect fraud and in fact went on to certify that the accounts represented the true financial position of his client when clearly they did not. When the client finally discovered the problem, he pursued the accountant for negligence on the basis that the poor books should have aroused suspicion and prompted further investigation.

11.6.3 Offering advice on a subject you do not specialise in

An accountant was employed by a client to advise on the purchase of another company. The client wanted to offset the profits of their own company against the losses of the purchased company with a view to limiting any tax liability. The accountant's instructions were specific. They gave advice on how to achieve the least tax liability and recommended that the best way was for the two companies to abridge their accounting periods to the same length. This advice was not entirely correct and the client company did become liable for stock relief claw-back. The accountant was pursued for negligent advice.

11.6.4 Failure to understand a potentialy complex subject

An accountant acted as an auditor for a client who was the proprietor of a firm of solicitors. The client did not operate incoming/outgoing funds correctly and, instead of having two accounts (clients and office) in accordance with the statutory regulations, he used only the one account. The client was also in fact responsible for misappropriating funds. This led to an official investigation and the client was struck off. The client then pursued the accountant for failing to advise that he was dealing with the accounts incorrectly and for the loss of livelihood.

11.6.5 Loss of document cover

A client found themselves in hot water when they lost 10 years' worth of electronic filing which they had for a major customer. It took four weeks' work to research and reinstate the records. Their policy paid for the extra staff needed to do this.

12 Financial management

12.1 Introduction

There has been much discussion on building shareholder value in quoted companies, but what is true for large businesses is equally applicable to accounting practices. Whilst the fortunes of large companies are in the hands of professional managers working to build value for their shareholders, professional practices are more usually typified by the same individuals combining the interests of shareholder, worker and manager. The aim is to concentrate on the first of these.

The emphasis is not on window dressing for short-term gains, but on developing strong and stable businesses that will provide the owners with a useful basis for negotiating a disposal. At the same time, a prospective acquirer will see sound prospects for developing the business in the future.

Other chapters cover several strategic areas where the business can build value. This section shows how financial management helps to set up a framework to manage and monitor progress in a positive and complementary way. An effective system must reflect the business goals with sufficient feedback to alter course and condition behaviours to adapt to them.

The aim is to build a business delivering an acceptable return on capital over the medium/long term and a positive cash flow. Few want to pay good money for transient profit, but many would acquire a business, which has a secure and growing fee base, and a lean cost structure reflecting efficiency and effectiveness. At the same time it will not have neglected to invest in the future. In other words, a business which:

- makes steady long-term profits;
- generates surplus cash;
- uses its assets efficiently;
- has sound information and control systems.

12.2 Strategy and planning

It can be very exciting running a business on a wing and a prayer, but there is no substitute for devoting time to look at the firm's long-term potential and the financial imperatives that flow from it. Indeed, it can be that finance, in itself, becomes a key to its success. Some cynics might argue that 'if you want to make God laugh, tell him your plans'. An organised approach still provides a view of the future and goals to work towards, albeit that we live in an uncertain and dynamic environment with no guarantees. Firms who have thought through options are usually better equipped to respond to change than those who rely on intuition. Partners owe it to all other stakeholders in the business as well as themselves. It is impossible to do full justice to the subject within the confines of this chapter, but merely to note its overall importance and a few guiding principles.

The process itself is becoming much simpler. There is good forecasting and spreadsheet software available to evaluate options, and generally a great deal of data is available within the business or externally through the Internet and other public sources. Less plentiful, is the time to allocate to the task. An open mind, a conceptual approach and capacity for 'blue skies' thinking are also crucial.

Much depends on the partners' own objectives. What is the collective will and over what time scale? The remainder is the interaction of the environment, market place and available resources to achieve these goals. All these aspects are both dynamic and interactive. To make some sense of a complex structure calls for careful analysis of each segment by moving down through the layers of each major item and making a strategic choice (see **Table 12.1**).

Table 12.1 Strategy and planning considerations

Layer 1	Layer 2	Layer 3
Owner expectations	Shape of firm	• Size • Geographic coverage
	Profitability time scale 1/3/5 yrs	
	Culture/lifestyle	• Attitudes to risk • Relaxed/intense
	Succession disposal	Merger/sale
Environment	Economic	Buoyant/depressed Market size Threats and opportunities Legislation Competition Communications

Profitability and scope for improvement

Markets/clients	Market share Pricing policy Service standards	
	Product areas	● Diversification ● Specialisation
	Clients	● Size ● Type ● Business sector
Resources	Qualified/skilled/support	● Availability

Some of the elements may be speculative, others can be gauged more precisely, but the exercise should identify the key drivers that will determine the way forward and the forces of change that will shape the destiny of the firm.

Having chosen the strategic path, the firm needs to be clear about the way it wishes to implement the plan and what options it has when conditions change, as they certainly will. There are many dimensions to a successful business but one of the key outputs from the exercise should be a financial statement for the medium term.

Strategic planning is not an exact science, given the many unknowns, and cannot be tied up in a neat package to be dusted down occasionally. It is more like a river, where the flow is the contribution from many sources, not always of equal importance. Even great rivers have to change course and firms should be constantly on their guard against pursuing strategies that become out of touch with the environment. There are many sad cases of those who have. A sense of direction combined with vigilance and flexibility are the watchwords, and everyone must buy into it.

Has the practice attempted a formal planning exercise? Is it regularly revised? Is the annual budgeting process tied into it?

12.3 Profitability and scope for improvement

Surprisingly the balance between cost and price is not always understood. One senior partner recently bemoaned an acquisition where only five clients out of 40 were really profitable, the rest losing money; not so much a business as a charity. To another, getting work was hard but getting profitable work was even harder.

Whilst these are real issues, professionals are prone to explain away or sublimate poor profit performance rather than concentrate on:

Financial management

- pricing and fee growth;
- planning and project management;
- outputs, efficiency and the control of cost;
- IT support and organised, accessible data;
- reusable know-how;
- positive behaviours.

Every firm should be setting performance standards, but to quote Alan Bennett:

> 'Franklin:
>
> "Have you thought, headmaster, that your standards may be a little out of date?"
>
> Headmaster:
>
> "Of course they're out of date. Standards are always out of date. That's what makes them standards".'

At the very least, budgets should be based on reasonable expectations. Whilst *budgets* usually predict a safe financial outcome, there is scope for improving results by setting *targets* to motivate and stretch performance, particularly in key areas. How aggressive they will be depends on the firm's culture and competitive spirit. Well judged, they can raise the game significantly. Badly pitched, they can be demotivating.

Budgets and targets should be well understood and introduced at all levels of the firm. The budget then becomes a reference point for the financial period against which all major variations are explained. Whilst budgets provide the necessary financial disciplines, they should not become a straitjacket which often produces negative behaviour. Running alongside should be a parallel forecast of the expected out turn for the year that is modified as the year progresses and as conditions change beyond control.

In searching for improvements the firm should re-examine the operating processes involved from start to finish. A broad outline gives some idea of the leakage that needs close attention (see **Table 12.2**).

Table 12.2 Operating processes and leakage of profit

£ Shrinking value	Where it went	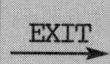
Available Working Hours		
Time worked	• Holidays, sickness, other absence	
Time booked	• Unbooked time	
Available for billing	• Non-chargeable time	
Charged to client	• Inefficient time written off	
Received from client	• Discounts and bad debts	

12.4 Fees

The central planks of a solid client base are investment in market development and a reputation for quality, know-how, value for money, customer care and efficiency. This can be strongly supported by effective financial management to generate fees and profitability.

Competition and a healthy awareness by clients now mean that fee rates have to reflect market dynamics. Margins of the past are just a distant memory.

> 'To my professional charges for crossing the street to greet you, and on discovering it was not you, crossing the street again – 25 guineas.' Anon.

To pitch realistically requires a sound knowledge of the market place and an appreciation of clients' bargaining positions. The firm equally needs to value fully its skills and accumulated know-how, and set its cost base at an economic level relative to fee income.

At the risk of over-simplification, two major forces affect fee earning, as shown in **Table 12.3**:

Table 12.3 Forces that affect fee earning

Market led	Supply led
• Economic climate	• Trained specialists
• Demand for services offered	• Innovators
• Competition	• Problem solvers
• Market share	• Balanced mix of staff/leverage
	• Back office and technical support

How it can improve on any of the factors within its control or respond adequately where they are outside it? Before quoting for fees, whatever the task, the system should define it, plan it, and cost it, particularly fixed-fee work. This is not always straightforward where tasks are 'one off' or have uncertain outcomes and usually require special provisions to cover additional work or an allowance for contingencies.

Even armed with this information, fee negotiation can still be uncertain but benefits from positive behaviours such as:

- confidence and high esteem;
- resilience to client's pressure;
- appreciating and demonstrating the added-value content of the work;
- willingness to 'premium price';
- resisting the desire to please the client or fear of losing client/missing fee targets.

Not everybody is a natural negotiator and there are major gains from structured training programmes. To provide confidence and support the firm might also set up a peer review arrangement to agree the fees charged by individual partners who balk at the idea of charging for fair effort.

More commercial considerations include:

- market rates;
- fixed/statutory fees;
- discount for large or long-run repeat contracts;
- introductory rates for new clients;
- competitive tenders;
- the added-value content of the task.

Managers should routinely monitor and investigate major variations in pricing from standard charging rates.

12.5 Managing time

People are the most expensive resource in any professional business and their use and effectiveness hugely impacts on profit. This is not the place to discuss the ways in which skilled teams should be motivated, trained or organised to work efficiently, but rather to emphasise the importance of comprehensive reporting and controls.

Business managers should be comfortable with performance standards, benchmarked against best-practice levels in each area of operations. This applies to all members of the firm, but particularly to the most highly skilled and remunerated. Managers will then be better placed to tender for work more accurately, assess performance and plan future staff requirements.

For the fee earner population, the crucial numbers are:

- total available hours;
- proportion chargeable;
- proportion non-chargeable.

How many hours is each individual expected to work in the year at each level of seniority? This gives a theoretical standard capacity for the business and when combined with the chargeable/non-chargeable ratio provides the clue to additional profit and efficiency.

The subdivision is simpler to start by analysing the non-chargeable areas, e.g., allowance for:

- sickness/compassionate/maternity/paternity leave;
- holidays;
- training and know-how;
- management;
- administration;
- marketing/client development.

The list can be surprisingly extensive. All major activities should be given time codes and a genuine estimate should be made of the likely cost at standard charge-out rates. This will produce some very interesting statistics to create a formal budget. Overall this gives a far better idea of resource allocation, particularly over the discretionary areas, and can determine the size of the investment in the 'softer' issues such as training, know-how development, quality and practice development.

There will obviously be a higher proportion of non-chargeable effort at partner level, given the usual managerial/administrative responsibilities and the need to 'rain-make'. As this is often as much as 40 per cent of their workload, it needs to be linked logically with their individual business objectives.

The remainder is available for client work and this balance needs to be firmly controlled. The boundaries are frequently breached and non-chargeable areas become the wastelands, somewhere to charge irrecoverable time, particularly when there is a fall-off in commercial activity. Surges in non-chargeable time are often the bell-weather for overcapacity.

This prompts several questions. Is non-chargeable time in balance? Is it involving the right people? Are there are different ways to manage it? Does it provide value for money and are the partners and fee earners accountable for performance?

Chargeable time is normally understood better by fee earners. In seeking profit improvement there are, nonetheless, some important factors to watch for, particularly administrative and behavioural.

It should be simple to allocate time to client files, but there are complex processes in many firms and, a real chore that conditions fee earner attitudes. Better investment in IT for online data input, clear instructions and precise coding systems can create the right environment. Responsible management and a code of conduct should reduce the number of missing/late/illegible/wrongly coded time lines that result in undercharging the client.

Fee earners need convincing that they should not be the judges on whether time should be charged to the client. Many hours are lost because they are afraid to book time in case it reflects inefficiency or overindulgence, or they are worried that the client will not perceive it as worthwhile effort. The client manager is the appropriate person to make these decisions when the bill is raised. Only then should any excess be written off and carefully recorded. Major losses or profits should be categorised and trends analysed against:

- individual fee earners;
- teams;
- work types;
- clients.

Booked time is, of course, only the consequence. Firms are increasingly aware of the need for better job/project planning and use of case management software. This has certainly helped in scheduling and costing work and finding the appropriate mix of staff to optimise profits. It also helps in tracking progress, highlighting inefficiency or defining changes in the scope of work.

Are there robust systems for managing fee earner time and highlighting variations on a job-by-job or client basis in place? Do post completion reviews take place after each major job?

12.6 Other expenditure

This will differ from firm to firm depending on size, range of activities and location. Property costs, IT and professional indemnity insurance usually loom high. All expenditure including support staff should be benchmarked and assessed for its value to the business.

Space can be as much as 10 per cent of turnover depending on location, but by nature is relatively immovable in the short term. Strategic questions surround the future use of space/working practices, market demand and rents and the extent of the commitment to the property through lease or purchase. Normal capital investment decision-making rules apply.

Professional indemnity costs are closely linked to the firm's risk management policy, including quality, systems of monitoring and control, and the level of risk inherent in the service. A good track record is important in any exit strategy.

IT is a major issue despite falling costs of hardware. Rapid technical obsolescence implies constant spend to keep up with market expectations and support business efficiency. Expenditure needs a good business case and formal approval, but with wildly different options in software, hardware and communications across the market, a coherent exit strategy is very hard to get right.

Is all other operating cost and are support function processes subject to review? Are there operating standards? Does the outlay match the business plan and provide value for money? Are there alternative ways in which the service can be provided at less cost or made more flexible?

12.7 Working capital

Efficient businesses control the working-capital cycle and generate strong cash flow. Indeed, in the words of a senior partner, 'To me, profit is the cash that I have in the bank at the end of the day'. So many firms fail to grasp the issues. Severe cash crises, short-termism and an inability to seize long-term

Financial management

opportunities as they arise, are common. A CEO of a large building society once commented, 'Having cash puts the business into a privileged position. It's like going into a restaurant and looking at the à la carte not the table d'hôte'.

Any financial management system worth its salt provides plenty of information to communicate throughout the organisation to obtain maximum commitment. Whilst the central objective is to generate cash, poor management directly reduces profit through write-offs of irrecoverable work in progress or bad debt. Cash shortages and increased borrowings are warning signals. A firm wanting to protect the value of its short-term assets must therefore ensure that its routine housekeeping is smart and that the process of turning fee earner effort into cash is swift. At its best, a firm should be striving to work on negative working capital by controlling its investment in clients, i.e., debt and work in progress (WIP), seeking payments on account and using the credit shield provided by suppliers and VAT. It has been done.

Best practice firms are constantly tightening the standard for lock-up of working capital/investment in clients. Have processes and benchmarks been reviewed thoroughly to release the benefits of early cash? How saleable is the WIP and book debt?

Figure 12.1 Practice cash flow

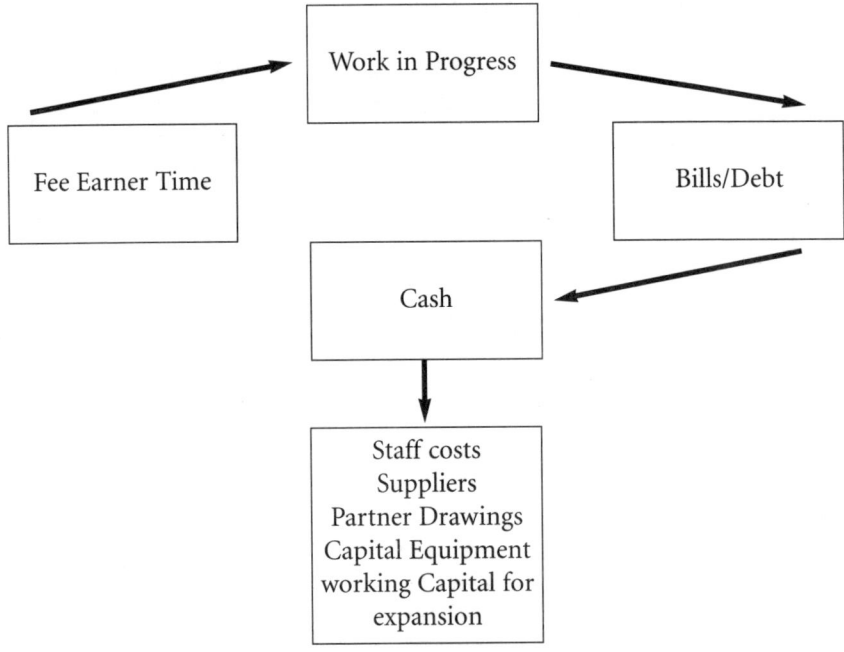

12.8 Cash management

In some businesses, this is almost an art form. Without recourse to external shareholders, the only option is to fund a practice personally, or through a bank loan. Neither is in infinite supply and the need to work within limits is vital. Prospective purchasers do not normally like large overdrafts, or an obligation to pay out significant undrawn partner current accounts. Both of these are unmistakable signs that cash management can be improved.

The sections on work in progress and debt pick up several pointers to speeding up cash delivery, but some relate to cash management itself.

- Developing a cash forecast integrated with movements in debtors and creditors. Relatively cheap IT software eases this process. An 18-month rolling forecast will alert managers and allow time for corrective action or to seek extra funding.
- Smoothing fluctuations in income or expenditure and reducing unnecessary pressure on bank lending limits. Classical targets would be the elimination of the annual billing rush by fee earners to meet their budgets, anticipating seasonal effects or fixed dates for major outflows, e.g., tax payments, quarterly rents and VAT, professional indemnity premiums and capital expenditure.
- Surprisingly, not everybody takes full credit from suppliers, a useful and free source of finance.

Partner financial issues are particularly tricky. The regular monthly drawings schedule is usually pretty conservative, leaving a number of distribution problems. If cash is particularly tight, balances remaining are usually paid out 'as available'. Better forecasting provides a more informed view and reduces uncertainty for partners in planning their own financial affairs. Clear rules need to be drawn up in prioritising different elements of the 'draw down', to cover issues such as performance bonuses, pension contributions and other payments affecting individual tax positions, as well as the general distribution of profit. These rules should be clearly understood and applied pretty strictly. Certainly, the sooner profit is paid out, the more contented the partnership will be and the business aim should be to close the gap between profit generation and its distribution. Linking partners' distributions to their cash-collecting efficiency can be a worthwhile incentive to manage debt and WIP levels better.

By linking cash forecasts with balance sheet items, it will be possible to see the impact of reducing/extending WIP and debt on cash balances. Ideally they would be updated monthly and segregated into:

- *Cash from operations:*
  - receipts from clients;
  - suppliers;
  - staff;
  - other;
  - VAT;
- *Financing:*
  - receipts/(payments).
- *Capital expenditure.*
- *Partners.*
  - capital accounts;
  - current accounts;
  - taxation.
- *Net change in bank balance.*

12.9 Managing work in progress

As a store of human effort, work in progress (WIP) is frequently ignored, treated as a dumping ground and only relevant when compiling the annual results of the practice. Taking a positive approach and applying close management, the firm will see real improvement in both profits and cash flow.

Detailed WIP information provides practice managers/supervisors with a fuller understanding of the status of each task in hand. Modern IT systems provide alternative valuation options and if data is valued at cost, it is easy to compare the accumulated sum with the agreed fee for the job to check on profitability as the job progresses. Detailed monitoring identifies inefficient areas, concentrated on:

- booking time;
- monitoring costs, task by task;
- recognising and providing against unbillable time cost;
- delays in converting WIP into fees.

12.9.1 Booking time

Some problems arising from poor time recording have been discussed, and, in particular, the effect on profits of under-recording where fees are time based.

Equally, in fixed-fee tasks there is a tendency to treat time records as irrelevant as they do not affect the size of the client's bill. Both actions are harmful. First, there is an obvious loss of potential profit when a bill is based on booked hours. Second, you end up with a wholly distorted view of the profitability of the task. There is no pointer to the efficiency of the fee earner or the accuracy of the original client's fee quote and there may be an opportunity for renegotiation.

12.9.2 Monitoring and analysing work in progress

If the business wants to improve its performance, it has to understand the reasons for its overall holding of WIP and how many days' turnover it represents. More detailed data can explode out the holdings of the various departments/teams or fee earners. If this is recorded and analysed at each month end, the trends will certainly focus management attention.

The detail is equally important, providing partners/supervisors with control information on the progress and profitability of each task/project. As has been emphasised, the analysis is only as good as the quality of the booking. If this is high, then the job review will produce a confident view of progress. Emerging problems can be tackled early, opening up opportunities to change the staff mix, address inefficiencies or renegotiate terms with the client if the scope of work has altered.

12.9.3 Recognising unbillable time

Work-in-progress records become notoriously out of date and need regular review. Time cost sometimes remains on file for months or even years and fee earners are reluctant to treat it as irrecoverable; a convenient way of avoiding uncomfortable post mortems. Typically, this is time spent on abortive tasks, introductory/exploratory interviews that fee earners hope will lead to future income, or post-completion work, which has to be done after the fee has been rendered. Regular weeding out maintains the integrity and reliability of management reporting and avoids self-delusion. That said, the management team needs to pay attention to the size of provisions and investigate the reasons for larger items.

12.9.4 Converting work in progress into fees

The quicker chargeable hours are billed out, the earlier the recovery of cash. Two factors apply here:
- the length of time taken to do the job;
- fee earner inertia in starting the billing process.

And the solutions can be found by:

- analysing and re-engineering the task and better scheduling;
- making billing a priority issue and finding ways to make the billing process administratively easier.

12.10 Managing debt

In building a business which is attractive to prospective purchasers, the quality of the book debt and the adequacy of provisions, the management controls and the speed of collection are vital.

Long gone are the days when partnerships could afford to issue fee notes and just wait for the bill to be paid. Serious recessions have been brutal reminders of the need to collect cash efficiently and with as much emphasis on speed of settlement as the client's ability to pay. At the same time, we have experienced far greater competition and there is a growing danger of relaxing strict management controls as part of the 'marketing mix'. Successful firms believe that they have a lot more to offer their clients than a lax credit policy. Partners need clear policies on managing client debts in order to avoid risk or raising funds to support the extra capital employed. Indeed, if the firm's capital is invested in unnecessary debt, there is little scope for allocating money to more productive areas such as capital investment, training, know-how or working capital for business expansion.

The best practices have developed a comprehensive approach to debt management including:

- overall policy and control;
- terms of business;
- risk assessment;
- invoicing and collection;
- monitoring and recovery;
- qualified support staff and infrastructure to implement it.

12.10.1 Responsibility for overall policy and control

As debt is usually one of the firm's largest assets; the resources to manage it should reflect its importance. Far too often these are insufficient, lacking in professional expertise, and attitudes are frankly indifferent. Well-managed firms make sure that policy is determined at the highest level and that there is a disciplined approach throughout the business, particularly amongst the partners. As the commercial scene is constantly changing it calls for continuous review and close scrutiny of economic trends and internal debt-management performance.

A useful way to agree the business-wide policy, monitor performance and deal with major problems is to set up a formal credit-management group. This needs to be given appropriate powers to operate effectively, apply sanctions and make commercial judgements that will stick. Ideally, it would agree through regular meetings:

- credit terms for the business;
- client credit limits;
- doubtful debt policy and conduct regular reviews of old debts;
- write-offs and recovery procedures;
- targets for accountable managers and fee earners.

Good two-way communication between the group and all levels of the business is essential to create a positive approach to debt management. Whilst individual partners may regret the loss of autonomy, they will gain from the independence and the consistent approach that the group provides, and it often relieves the more faint hearted of difficult decisions and avoids impaired client relationships.

Have you set up formal credit policies and the means to implement and monitor them?

12.10.2 Risk management

It is now widely accepted that successful firms understand the balance between risk and reward. In a competitive market or in the dash for growth or personal/team billing targets, there is a natural instinct to accept instructions without regard to the creditworthiness of the client or the risk element in the job itself. A standard reference to a reputable credit agency will certainly provide the former, whilst a short enquiry with the client partner should determine the latter. The client credit limit should cover not only the debt exposure but also all unbilled WIP. Client managers should be encouraged to work inside these levels and be asked to produce a business case before exceeding them. This not only contains risk but will encourage client managers to collect cash faster to remain within limits. The task of the credit-management team will be to ensure that the firm's debt portfolio reflects a sensible spread of risk.

Have you set up a formal process to evaluate and manage risk? Do individual clients or market sectors form a disproportionate percentage of outstanding debt?

12.10.3 Terms of business

The trigger point for raising a fee note needs to be clearly understood and link with effective WIP management. In routine cases, the main criterion is the completion of the job in line with the client's instruction, e.g., audits and taxes returns. There are often more complicated tasks where fees are contingent on successful outcomes such as corporate finance deals.

The important task here is to agree on standard terms for each type of transaction, in line with normal commercial practice. This should help reduce the scope for individual discretion, to create a credible, fair and consistent policy.

Where a standard policy is clearly inappropriate there should be a well-understood mechanism to co-ordinate the approach by referring to a credit management group or responsible partner or professional credit manager. The problem areas are often special transactions including:

- third-party bills;
- large clients exerting pressure for longer credit terms;
- large client disbursements;
- unusual settlements, e.g., accepting equity stake in the client's business;
- long-term agreements;
- completion at some uncertain future date, e.g., realisation of property.

12.10.4 Invoicing and collection

If the business is to speed up the movement of WIP into bills and cash, it has to create a slick and well-understood operation. Systems have to be geared to make the process user-friendly in compiling and issuing bills. Clients should receive bills that are clear and they should be given supporting information. This avoids the uncertainty that provides them with an excuse to delay payment. The sobering fact is that a significant percentage of clients do not pay because their queries are unanswered. Wherever possible, invoice on a regular quarterly or monthly basis and issue interim bills on account. There is always scope for offering prompt settlement discounts. Remittance advices and reply paid envelopes are an added incentive.

Have you examined your invoicing/collection procedures to see whether they can be smarter? Does your firm see the credit function as an essential part of 'customer service'?

12.10.5 Monitoring and recovery

The process should include a series of staged reminder letters and regular statements of account. Effective credit managers should be employed to follow up accounts that are not paid to terms. As delays increase, so too should the attention of the credit controller. A good relationship between the credit manager and the client's bought ledger section usually pays dividends. Where more serious action needs to be taken, the credit manager should recommend it to the credit-management group, whose decision should be final.

Do you have clear guidelines on recovery action and is late payment followed up quickly?

12.10.6 Criteria

This is difficult to define precisely as it will depend on the type of work undertaken. What is good or bad for the firm depends on the credit terms set by the business and should be judged by the divergence from these standards. Other yardsticks are the levels of bad and doubtful debts written off as a percentage of fees. Additionally, credit managers' performance might be judged not only on their success in recovering bad debt but also on the profile of debt and consistency of cash collections.

Do you have a competent and independent team managing debt collection and working to set performance standards? How can they be improved?

12.11 Performance data

Ultimately, all business activity has a financial impact, although the firm needs separate measures in place to judge other critical success criteria, for example quality, client service, brand loyalty. As Professor Robert Kaplan cogently describes in his work on the 'Balanced Scorecard', these are equally important in developing a successful firm.

Purely financial data needs to be interpreted carefully. As much emphasis should be placed on trends and continuous improvement, as on absolute numbers which are often based on an arbitrary annual time scale. Several measures have been mentioned above and their precise structure and organisation will depend on the shape of the practice and the goals that it has set for itself. Depending on the sophistication of the accounting systems, regular reports and comparisons with budget and plan should include the points set out in **Table 12.4**.

Table 12.4 Information to be included in reports and comparisons with budget plans

Revenue	Fees per partner/fee earner/specialist group
Profits	Gross contribution after deducting all directly attributable costs per team/department/client Net profit per equity partner share
Productivity	Hours worked per fee earner
Lock-up	Days' debt outstanding Days' work in progress Cash collections and outflows
Overhead expenses	Percentage of fees and variation from budget

There is also the important question of communication. Practices that have an open culture appear to achieve more through good communication of corporate objectives. If everyone has a clear understanding of what is expected of them and regular feedback on how they have performed individually or in groups, it is easier to see what extra contribution they can make to firm's success.

13 Quality control

13.1 Why have quality control?

The most obvious benefit of quality control in building a practice of value is its capacity to preserve the practice's right to continue working in and earning income from regulated areas. Clearly, if a practice allows its quality control to deteriorate to the point where it loses something as valuable as its audit registration, a large stream of fee income will disappear. Even if the practice improves its procedures to the point where it regains its registration, the lost clients will long since have moved on to new accountants and will not be won back easily if at all. With this in mind, most practitioners would agree that some minimum level of quality control is necessary to preserve certain key income streams. This view, although valid, is somewhat limited. If all that the firm seeks from its quality control procedures is to maintain its ability to operate in regulated areas, it is surrendering many of the benefits that a good quality-control system can provide.

Any firm seeking to create a practice of lasting value should have a system of quality control in place whether regulations require it or not.

There is far more to quality control than mere compliance. Strict compliance with no added features means little more than staying out of trouble. This view is both negative and reactive. It guarantees that quality control will add nothing to the value of the practice. Quality control has far more to offer an accounting practice than the mere prospect of staying out of trouble with regulatory bodies. If quality control is done properly and taken seriously it can make the firm more profitable and improve its capacity to generate new business. Firms that work on the principle that quality control relates only to compliance with laws and regulations are lowering the equity value of the their practices by encouraging the delivery of services that only just scrape through. Quality control, if it is to create and maintain a valuable practice, must be about making sure that the firm does the best that it possibly can in every aspect of its operations.

13.2 What should quality control cover?

The short and simple answer to this question is 'everything that the firm does'. The more areas that quality control covers, the more value it will add. A dispassionate, well-planned and clearly focused quality-control system is often the most effective way of exposing the firm's strengths and weaknesses in areas as diverse as:

- profitability;
- gaining new clients and retaining existing ones;
- fee negotiations;
- recruiting;
- training;
- technical skills and competence;
- standard audit documents;
- staff and job planning;
- performance appraisal;
- promotion policies;
- client relations (including responses to letters);
- inefficient practices by individual partners and managers; and
- the structure of the firm.

If the quality of a firm's work in any of these areas is low or in danger of deteriorating then the firm's value as a continuing business entity will be reduced.

13.3 Why should a firm with competent partners and staff need quality control?

It is all too easy for any service based entity to become so involved in the day-to-day business of serving its existing clients and seeking out new ones that it has no time to run a health check on the quality of the services that it provides. This is particularly true of soft services.

The fact that accountancy services are amongst the softest of all marketable commodities helps to blur the distinctions between excellence, mediocrity and even inadequacy. One audit report looks very much like another. No practice can legally offer its clients a special set of tax laws not available to any other taxpayer.

If a firm has no rigorous process for evaluating its services and internal operating systems, it has no worthwhile way of knowing how well it is doing.

Professional partnerships are particularly susceptible to complacency in this area. A professional partnership is the ultimate owner-managed business but usually with rather more in the way of owner-managers and less in the way of corporate strategy than a limited company of similar size would have. In reality, some professional partnerships are little more than groups of sole practitioners sharing a name and some common facilities. In such a situation, it is all too easy for partnerships and even individual partners to judge themselves by their own criteria with no reference to any external standards – rather like an athlete comparing his own times without knowing what the world record is.

13.4 How can quality control help?

Quality control, provided that it is done properly, will allow a firm to look at itself objectively and assess how well it is doing. The follow paragraphs give some examples of how effective quality-control procedures can appraise a firm's performance and offer suggestions for improvement where weaknesses are identified.

Many partners in highly successful practices would see these matters as being well outside the normal province of quality control in spite of the fact that they are precisely the areas where a practice can lose value quickly and easily.

13.4.1 Profitability

Where a firm is not as profitable as the partners believe that it should be, every partner will have a theory to explain why this is so. In most cases, these theories deal with what their proponents would like the truth to be rather than what the truth actually is. A partner is far more likely to attribute a poor recovery on a job to staff inefficiency or client incompetence than to poor fee negotiation or the partner wasting time making trivial review points. This view is likely to find favour with other partners because it has the attraction of placing the blame outside the partnership. It is unlikely to be contradicted too vigorously by members of staff other than those whose exit strategy has reached a fairly advanced stage. Thoughts generated in this environment may be comforting but if they are inaccurate, profitability will continue to be a problem. Any problem that is diagnosed incorrectly will either remain a problem or emerge somewhere else as a completely different and usually more serious problem.

If a firm attributes poor recoveries to staff inefficiency when in reality they are due to something else (such as poor fee negotiation or excessively detailed reviews), the most likely outcome will be that staff will not record all the time that they spend on jobs. Recoveries may look as if they have improved but the results are illusory. All that has happened is that the partnership has moved from making poor recoveries to drawing conclusions from inaccurate information. Such tainting of information can be hard to detect and even harder to rectify.

An experienced but disinterested quality controller should notice any marked discrepancy between the fees charged and the amount of work needed to do the job properly and give an objective view of where the problem arose, even if the partners did not like what they were being told.

13.4.2 Retaining existing clients

It is amazing how many clients are lost in circumstances beyond the firm's control. The classic examples are fee disputes and takeovers. There always will be cases where a smaller practice will struggle to retain clients when certain things happen, but there are other cases where unforeseen events were not necessarily unforeseeable. They just were not noticed soon enough or dealt with appropriately. A sole shareholder and director approaching retirement age is always going to be a client at risk. In this case, a takeover offer should not be a surprise. If anything it should be totally obvious.

The same is often true of fee disputes. All too often they are shrugged off with an argument that runs along the lines of, 'He wants a Ford Fiesta, we deal in Rolls Royces'. If that is true, why did he come to your firm in the first place? The more probable explanation is that the departing client felt that he was paying for a Rolls Royce but only getting a Ford Fiesta for his money.

Proper quality control should be able to highlight any problems with the firm's service before the client decides to move away. In extreme cases, it can even identify the true reasons for a client's departure and prevent further losses from the same cause.

13.4.3 Gaining new clients

Quality control can also help partners to pitch for new business. Far too many partners sell the features of their firms or even themselves rather than the benefits that they can offer to a potential client. An independent review of a proposal document can make sure that it offers a genuine prospect of good service rather than eulogy on the firm and its partners and very little else.

13.4.4 Fee negotiations

This is one of the darkest recesses of all partnerships. Some partnerships are saddled forever with uneconomic fees because a partner simply underpriced the work in a desperate bid to expand his client portfolio. The technique is to pass the guilt on to the members of the engagement team by insisting that the fee is realistic and any under recoveries are down to inefficiency. This approach depletes the value of the practice. If carried to extremes it can result in the firm having so much low-margin work on its books that it has no capacity to take on anything really profitable.

The effect on staff performance and retention can be devastating and costly. Good audit staff members are generally too intelligent and possibly too motivated by self-interest to accept the blame for poor recoveries without question. Unfortunately, they do not see it as a topic for serious internal debate. They just see it as a good reason to find another job. Quality control can expose this highly damaging practice for what it is by detecting cases where the agreed fee is too low for anyone to do the work to the firm's standards.

The second area where quality control can help in fee negotiations is detecting extra work that was not agreed as part of the original service. The most common example of this is on audits where members of the audit team help the client with accounting work simply to have some chance of meeting the audit timetable. Staff members are often unwilling to admit to having done this because it suggests a failure by them to communicate the problem on time. A quality-control review should highlight any discrepancies between the time charged to a particular audit section and the amount of pure audit evidence on the file.

13.4.5 Recruiting

One of the all too common problems that cold reviewers find on files is evidence that tests are being done by people who do not understand fully what the purpose of the test is. Any deficiencies in evidence are likely to be made good by someone who is seriously overqualified doing some belated and inefficiently timed remedial work.

A combination of last-minute repairs, time pressure and internal assumptions means this problem is rarely identified with any real accuracy. Internal training, if it exists within the firm, is a favourite first target. The staff cannot do the work, therefore training must be to blame. It looks like a fair argument but it is usually well wide of the mark. More often than not, the cause of the problem is having the wrong people on the job rather than having the right people with the wrong training.

Problems with producing quality work within budget are rarely put down to an incorrect recruiting policy. It is much easier to blame the labour market for failing to deliver the kind of staff that the firm's existing recruiting policy demands.

In many cases firms change their approach to work without actually changing the type of people that they recruit to meet the demands of the new approach. For example, a number of firms have moved away from procedural auditing to a combination of analytical review and directional testing, but they have carried on recruiting as they have always done.

They have not adjusted their recruiting policy to fit the changed staffing requirements of their new audit approach. This usually means that the firm will have too many inexperienced staff and not enough people with the higher skills necessary to apply the new approach effectively. Conventional accounting wisdom is more likely to result in the audit approach being changed to fit the recruiting policy instead of the recruiting policy being changed to suit the new approach. If this happens, the value of the practice will suffer in two ways. It will have lost a more cost-effective audit approach and will continue to be saddled with an unnecessarily expensive and uncompetitive cost structure.

Accountancy is, after all, a 'people business'. Having the right people in the right places is vital to creating a practice with a value that can be passed on to the next generation of partners. If the firm is succeeding in spite of its staff and therefore because of the current partners' skills in crisis management, then the firm's heritable value is negligible. When the partners go, the value will go with them. The practice has become too dependent on its existing partners to survive as a viable unit once they have moved on.

Unfortunately, far too many partners like to believe that the practice will decline if they leave. It is an excellent boost to their egos but a definite barrier to people interested in buying their way in.

A successful partnership can only be passed on if it has the right staff in place to do the basic work effectively, regardless of who is in charge.

13.4.6 Training

The link between quality control and training should be obvious but it is often missed. In all too many cases, the only connection that a firm's partners choose to make is blaming their trainers for failures in quality control. As we have seen earlier, this is probably unfair, but it obviates the need to look in less comfortable places for a more probable and realistic cause of failure.

Quality controllers should be good trainers. They need to be able to communicate what they find effectively to all levels of the firm. Even if we ignore the problems of client confidentiality, it is rarely effective for an outside trainer to deal with problems that are specific to the firm's own clients, procedures or people. Any good quality control programme will have a significant impact on the firm's training policy.

13.4.7 Technical skills and competence

Imparting the appropriate level of technical skills and competence may well be the job of the firm's training side, but identifying the skills and competence clearly is not. Training must be responsive to the firm's needs if it is not to find itself working in a vacuum or imparting skills and knowledge that the firm does not require.

Some of the most successful courses (in terms of participants' responses) may well do little or nothing to increase the firm's value. All that many of them do is increase the value of the firm's staff to another employer. It is easy to confuse the success of a course as a training event in itself with its success at contributing genuine value to the firm.

Quality control can be a very effective mechanism for identifying gaps in skill and knowledge and developing carefully targeted training to cover the deficiencies. Close co-operation between trainers and quality controllers will help to give the firm's training programme relevance and credibility. It is not the whole solution to a firm's needs for skill and competence. Training must to be reinforced if it is to have any credibility at all. Nothing undermines training more that a partner or manager telling more junior colleagues to ignore what they hear on courses.

13.4.8 Standard audit documents

There are two approaches to selecting standard audit documents. One is buy an off-the-shelf package that satisfies the JMU and apply it warts and all. The other is for the firm to develop its own documents and try to keep them up to date with the endless stream of new technical developments.

Neither approach is very satisfactory. Off-the-shelf packages, however well designed and however frequently updated, are likely to result in inefficiency and ineffectiveness if someone does not monitor how they are used. In some cases, the firm may have chosen a package that looked attractive when they decided to use it but it is no longer suited to the way the firm approaches its work.

Internally developed documents are equally prone to these ills with the added danger of their becoming out of date if nobody takes the responsibility for updating them seriously.

Most accounting and auditing work requires a degree of original thought that cannot be embodied in a set of standard documents. It is better to use a reasonable package intelligently than to search for the non-existent perfect 'foolproof' package. Quality control can ensure that the firm gets the best possible value from its audit documentation by concentrating on areas where it is being used inefficiently or ineffectively.

13.4.9 Staff and job planning

If you were to ask the partners in a firm how much money they lost through poor job scheduling or allocating jobs to the wrong people, they would be unlikely to have an answer. Part of the problem undoubtedly lies in the difficulty of measuring wasted time, but there is also a serious fear of the truth. In extreme cases, the cost of remedial work for a misallocated job can exceed the total cost budget.

There is an argument that repairing the damage and making good the inadequacies of the fieldwork are part and parcel of quality control. It is an argument of sorts but a very weak one. Most successful entrepreneurs will tell you that there is no profit in making good something that should have been right in the first place.

Allocating the right people to the right jobs is an integral part of providing a top-quality service. It is no defence to say that the firm gave a good service considering the experience of the staff that it had to provide it. That is a bit like saying that an orchestra gave an acceptable performance once you allow for the fact that nobody really knew how to play their instruments properly. Quality control can and should be used to monitor this side of the practice.

13.4.10 Performance appraisal

Performance appraisal is the Achilles heel of many accountancy firms. It is not just that partners are often poorly equipped and trained for the job, although they often are. It is more a question of building genuine objectivity into a process in which too many of the parties have a vested interest. All too often performance appraisals degenerate into nothing more than futile exercises in blame allocation.

Some descend to the even murkier depths of becoming attempts to justify low pay increases because of financial problems elsewhere in the firm.

If the quality of the firm's appraisal process is poor, good staff will leave even if their appraisals result in promotion and better than average pay increases. This reaction is not in the least unfair. The people concerned see the appraisal process as the lottery that it is and have no wish to ride their luck too far. A poor performance appraisal system can leave the firm vulnerable to staff shortages just at the time when it can least afford them – when the economy is strong and new businesses are starting up.

Quality control on its own cannot compensate for the human failures (ego, pride, the desire to be 'right', etc.) that so often afflict the worst appraisal systems, but it can identify where and why the systems are failing in the firms that use them. It may even be able to produce constructive suggestions such as allocating appraisals to partners with the requisite skills and knowledge to carry them out effectively.

There are a number of objective criteria that can be used to assess compliance (frequency of appraisals, time spent with each staff member, how soon after the event they were completed, whether any coherent action plan emerged, etc.). These are useful indicators of the quantity of appraisal that the firm is providing but they say nothing of the quality. Unfortunately, most appraisal systems fail on quality. Quantity can be supplied easily by making time available. Making the best use of that time, far more difficult.

Appraisers may well spend the requisite amount of time in appraisal sessions but what they do in that time does not always add much in the way of value to the firm. In some cases it may even detract from it.

13.4.11 Promotion policies

Does your firm really have a promotion policy? The mere fact that people are promoted every now and then is no proof that there is a policy in place. Some promotions are no more than desperate attempts to retain staff without resorting to across-the-board pay increases. Others may arise by default: a vacancy may have arisen, the firm has no really suitable candidate to fill it so the closest fit, however inappropriate, will be given the job. If this method works at all, it is by accident rather than design. A mediocre senior may turn out to be a good manager because the managerial role brings out latent organisational skills of a kind that the senior's role did not require. If this works, it is seen as living proof of the partners' corporate judgement and shrewdness. If it does not work, it is the senior's fault for failing to adapt to the new role. 'We gave him the chance and he blew it.'

In fact, the whole thing is down to pure luck. Any practice that trusts to luck in selecting members of its management team is sitting on a valuation time bomb. Sooner or later the firm's luck will run out and an expensive remedy will be needed to put things right.

Quality control can help focus the firm on what its needs are. It can also give an objective view of what skills are required by the various grades within the firm's structure and possibly how to adjust the requirements of each grade to suit the skills of the firm's people.

13.4.12 Client relations (including responses to letters)

This is one area that often gets overlooked even in those firms with effective and well-established quality-control procedures. This is surprising given that it is one of the few areas where a firm can genuinely set its service apart from the competition. Auditing, tax and accounting are rendered uniform by law and regulation. Payroll and management accounts are often constrained by standard software. In reality, any client can obtain any of these services from any reasonable practitioner with only superficial distinctions between them. The one area where a firm can stand out from the competition is in the way in which it communicates with its clients. Could your firm easily give a measure of the quality as distinct from the quantity of its communication with its clients?

Communication or lack of it is also an area of considerable risk. A badly written letter to a client could do irreparable damage to the firm's image. A disaffected client could show it toother potential clients or use it as a conversation piece with business associates.

Failure to visit the client at appropriate times could also damage the firm's reputation for service. It would be difficult to convince a client that a firm is committed to giving the best service when the client has to go the inconvenience of visiting the accountant's offices rather than the accountant taking the trouble to visit the client. Obviously circumstances alter cases. Some clients' business premises may not be suitable for anything other than social site visits. If this is the case, site visits could be restricted as an inherent feature of the approach to serving that particular client. The risk is that partners will use it as an excuse to let all site visits fall by the wayside.

Quantity of service in this area is easy to measure, but quality will always be a bit subjective. Bombarding the client with every press release that the firm issues may be counter-productive. The client may see copious irrelevant correspondence as an indication that the firm is out of touch with the true nature and needs of his business.

There will always be those who will argue that the quality of client service is too subjective to measure at all. The true reflection of quality is the fact the client is still with the firm. This is fine until the client takes his business elsewhere.

Without wishing to deny that some aspects of quality are highly subjective and down to the client's perception rather than to anything tangible, there are some ways of avoiding sudden and allegedly unforeseeable departures from the client base.

One of the easier aspects to measure is response time to letters. This is a question of fact. If the firm has a standard maximum response time, the letter was either answered within that time or it was not. What is more difficult to measure is the quality of the response and that is often where the more serious problems are to be found.

The frequency of telephone calls should also be measurable – especially in this litigious age when prudence dictates that all telephone calls should be noted on the appropriate file.

One area where firms could improve greatly in the service that they offer their clients is in letters and other written communication. Accountants' letters are often badly written, poorly organised and difficult to understand.

Does the firm have a clear language campaign? If it has one, is it monitored? If it is monitored, does the monitor have enough linguistic skill to detect the plethora of ills that can afflict accountants' letters (faulty grammar, inscrutable language, needlessly long sentences, unnecessary and time-wasting content, etc.)? Most official accounting pronouncements fail most of the established tests of readability.

Quality-control campaigns to improve firms' written correspondence can be very effective if they are given the right degree of prominence. One enterprising firm actually used its newsletter to highlight howlers appearing in outgoing correspondence. Names were obviously changed to protect both the innocent and the guilty but the firm's letters did improve when some of the more literate partners became aware of exactly what their colleagues were committing to writing in their firm's name.

13.4.13 Inefficient practices by partners and managers

Some reviewers pride themselves in being exacting and meticulous. Views like this are rarely based on reality. A large number of review points on a file normally indicates that the job was managed inadequately somewhere along the line. More often than not, the problem will have arisen at the planning stage and the review is being used to mop up the mess caused by a poorly considered plan and inadequate briefing of the field staff.

In some cases it may be the result of an unwillingness of partners and managers to review work on site. Most quality controllers will be quick to point out any correlation between off-site reviewing and poor recoveries. Too many partners are loath to visit their client's premises because they like to give the impression that they are always at the end of a telephone. This is an astonishingly reactive approach to client service.

People who are set in their ways show remarkable inventiveness when it comes to thinking up reasons for not changing what they do or how they do it. Quality control, if done properly, can make the link between changing practices and adding value to the firm as a whole.

13.4.14 The structure of the firm

Some quality-control failures arise purely from the structure of the firm. Rigid departmentalisation can result in one department having staff to spare while another one is paying staff overtime to complete its work. Work done in excessive overtime will always be of a lower quality than work done within a normal working day. Even the most influential senior partners cannot overcome the design features of the human brain.

Where structural defects in the firm are causing problems, there are too many vested political interests for the firm to be able to deal with the matter internally. It is too easy for individuals to see themselves as winners or losers even if the firm as a whole is improved.

Proper quality control can identify where the firm's structure is a genuine problem and which the structure is being blamed for shortcomings elsewhere.

13.5 Establishing and maintaining effective quality-control procedures

13.5.1 Complying with quality-control requirements where the firm is a registered auditor

SAS 240 sets out the minimum requirements for the people who should be involved in quality control. Under SAS 240, the first requirement is to have a designated senior audit partner who is responsible for quality control. SAS 240.1 states:

> 'Firms should establish and communicate to audit engagement partners and audit staff, and others who need to be aware of them, quality control policy and processes; this will involve the establishment of an appropriate structure within the firm, including the appointment of a senior audit partner to take responsibility for these matters.'

The guidance notes in the standard make it quite clear that the partner appointed to this role must have enough seniority and experience to discharge the duties effectively.

Features that could invalidate the appointment include:

- appointing a salaried rather than an equity partner or appointing any partner with insufficient seniority to be able to enforce compliance;
- appointing a partner with little or no current auditing experience;
- appointing a partner who has consistently failed to comply with CPE requirements;
- appointing a partner who does not have the time to discharge the duties properly.

The standard (SAS 240.14) also requires firms to appoint a senior audit partner to monitor the quality of audits. This is a separate appointment from the policy-making partner required by SAS 240.1. The standard does not specifically require two separate partners, but it recommends very strongly that different 'senior audit partners' discharge each set of duties where possible.

SAS 240.14 reads:

> 'Firms should appoint a senior audit partner to take responsibility for monitoring the quality of audits carried out by the firm.'

The difference between the two roles is essentially that the first partner is responsible for making and communicating policy. The second partner is responsible for making sure that the firm complies with the policies that have been made. Obviously, the monitoring side will involve compliance with statutory and regulatory requirements as well as the firm's internal standards. For many senior partners, both these roles have potential conflicts of interest between the need to generate acceptable profits and the need to comply with standards.

One of the main duties of both the partners involved in compliance is ensuring that commercial pressures do not prevent compliance with standards. The explanatory notes in the standard go to great length to make this clear.

This aspect places considerable constraints on the conduct of the partners involved. Any attempt by them to overemphasise recoveries at the expense of strict compliance could put the firm at risk. The auditing standard makes it quite clear that potentially poor recoveries, however they may be caused, are no excuse for failing to follow standards.

13.5.2 Striking the balance between standards and profitability

There is always a risk that a firm could overspecify its audit and accounting requirements if quality control is not linked to the firm's commercial objectives. This is one of the dangers of over zealous standard setting. There is little point in setting standards of evidence that exceed the requirements of the profession. It is far better to set acceptable standards that the firm is capable of maintaining than to develop a set of standards that may well be the 'highest in the profession' but are either too difficult or too costly to maintain. There is something farcical about a firm setting standards that are too high and then failing to keep them. One of the aspects of quality control should be weeding out standards that are neither necessary nor cost-effective. It is not unknown for some partners and managers to have their own unofficial standards that do little more than add cost without adding any real value to the firm's services (e.g., testing prepayments totalling £500 in an audit where materiality is £10,000).

13.5.3 Quality control beyond compliance

As mentioned earlier in this chapter, quality control really starts adding value to a practice when it moves beyond mere compliance into something resembling an operational audit.

13.6 Using external quality controllers

13.6.1 What are the advantages of using an external quality controller?

External controllers will see things that the firm's partners either cannot or will not see. Very few organisations, especially professional partnerships, are capable of solving their own internal problems. Partners are rather prone to believing in their own omniscience and perspicacity, whether justified by the facts or not. In most cases, the barrier to solving the problem is not so much lack of skill and experience as a strong and very human tendency to be attracted to explanations that are comfortable rather than explanations that are accurate. It is very easy for an organisation to conduct a rigorous internal examination of criticisms made against it by outside (or inside) parties and to conclude that the criticisms are unjustified (always with the rider that 'we do not wish to be complacent'). The trouble with this approach is that the criticisms and perceptions of the organisation remain the same and continue to damage the organisation much as they did before. If anything, their effect is exacerbated by the added perception of complacency.

If criticism is costing your practice money or clients, it is safest to assume that the criticism is fair. The greatest difficulty is seeing why it is fair. An external consultant can often be the key. It may mean allowing the consultant to interview your clients and it will almost certainly mean allowing them to interview your staff in strict confidence and total anonymity. It is only by doing this that they can detect discrepancies between the way the partners see their firm and the way in which their clients and employees see it.

It is not always easy for internal quality controllers to be dispassionate – particularly about their own work or work in which they have been heavily involved. Sometimes the relative seniority of the reviewer and the reviewed may also influence the degree of criticism and objectivity. In extreme cases this could lead to shortcomings being given less emphasis than their seriousness warrants, or even being overlooked completely because of the possible internal repercussions of a junior partner criticising a more senior colleague. ('Professional licence if carried too far, your chance of promotion will certainly mar.')

Where this is likely to be a problem, it is worth considering an external reviewer. The advantages of using an external reviewer are:

- a reduced risk of the reviewer being influenced by the internal status of the responsible individual (RI) whose work is being reviewed;
- experience gained in reviewing other practices;
- a greater degree of objectivity than an internal reviewer would have;
- fewer problems with continuity;
- the reviewer is not conditioned to the firm's culture, which means that he will see things differently and will, more likely to find the blind spots in the firm's own review procedures. (There will always be aspects of a practice that will be left alone by mutual and often unspoken consent.)

The main disadvantages of using an external reviewer are:

- it costs more – external reviewers have to be paid at a rate that includes their profit margin. Their time will never be the recovery of a fixed cost or the notional (and often highly artificial) opportunity cost of lost chargeable hours. It involves paying out real money;
- the review will be limited in scope – external reviewers will usually have a limited amount of time, which means that the extent of their review will be constrained by the time available, the timing of their visits and any limitations in scope that the firm may impose to make the review more focused;
- external reviewers are unlikely to understand the firm's true 'corporate culture'. This makes it more difficult for them to detect certain internal problems. Members of the firm are not always willing to confide in outsiders in quite the way that they would with their colleagues.

13.7 Keeping the quality-control system running

It is all too easy to set up a quality control system with great enthusiasm only to see that enthusiasm wane very quickly as the daily grind of running the practice asserts itself. In essence, the problem is one of commitment. If everyone in the firm understands the firm's quality-control objectives and is committed to them, the system will continue to add value to the practice. If either the understanding or the commitment lapses, so too will the benefits.

13.7.1 Essential steps to maintaining effective quality control

Treat quality control as an integral part of the firm's operations. Everyone in the firm is responsible for quality control – not just those nominated specifically for the purpose.

- Make sure that everyone knows what the standards are. Standards, like business objectives, should be clear to everyone who has anything at all to do with attaining them. It is not easy for people to achieve a target unless they know what the target is.

- Appoint a competent and effective auditor as the head of quality control. If the appointment carries any suggestion at all of being a useful place for a poor performer, the entire quality-control process will have no credibility and will fail.

- Make the brief as wide as is reasonably possible. Quality control is relevant to everyone in the firm, not just the fee earners. It should not just be about complying with standards and regulations. A rude or offhand switchboard operator can do far more damage to your practice than a visit from the JMU.

- Give the quality controller time to do the work properly. This means doing the bulk of the work in normal office hours. If the work is allocated to overtime, it will be seen as unimportant, as will any recommendations that arise from it. Commitment to quality control means committing serious time to it.

- Set up a formal system for file reviews. Many of the problems with work files relate to what is missing from them rather than what is actually on them. Use a checklist as the basis for the review, but do not let the checklist become a constraint.

- Keep a written record of the results of the reviews. Distribute the results as widely within the firm as is necessary.

- Make sure that there is an effective means of dealing with the results of any review. A formal report to the partners meeting will rarely be enough. It is too easy to read reports and ignore what they recommend or even to avoid reading them at all.

- Draw up a proper and measurable action plan. Any action plan should not just list the actions that the firm intends to take. It should also set dates by which the actions are to be accomplished and by whom.

- Use the action plan to identify success and failure. An action plan will only be effective if it sets measurable results (e.g., 'Improving the general standard of signing off on our working papers' is too subjective to be measurable. 'All subsequent events reviews must be signed by the partner and carry the same date as the audit report' is totally objective and easy to measure. Either the document will have a partner's signature or it will not. Similarly, the date will either coincide with the one on the audit report or it will not. Nothing is open to speculation.).

- Concentrate on a few important items. The action plan should deal with matters that are serious, prevalent and practical. A firm-wide action plan is not the most appropriate way of dealing with individual aberrations. It is also a relatively ineffective way of dealing with 'soft skill' problems such as attitudes to clients, telephone techniques, etc.

- Make sure that the results of the review reach the appropriate levels in the firm. For some firms, this may be difficult as it may involve partners sharing information with staff in a way that they have not done before.

- At all costs, avoid using the action plan as a device for allocating blame. The action plan should be the means of putting things right. Any attempt to work out why something went wrong should be focused clearly on avoiding a recurrence. It should not be seen as a witch-hunt.

- Monitor the progress of the action plan. Make sure that it does not lose momentum. The price of quality, like the price of freedom, is eternal vigilance.

13.8 Succession planning and quality control

What happens when the quality controller is promoted, leaves or retires? In all cases apart from sudden death and a few other rare occurrences, the departure of the quality controller is a foreseeable event. The problem is that it is not always foreseen in enough time to ensure a seamless transition from the old incumbent to the new.

It is easy to be lulled into a false sense of security by a successful and effective quality controller who is working entirely by experience and instinct but with little in the way of written procedures. The assumption may be that any successor will be able to do the same, but this is leaving far too much to chance. If the firm's quality control procedures are to remain intact in a period of transition, it is important for the outgoing controller to brief his successor as soon as possible. This means identifying the successor as early as possible and creating enough time for an effective transfer of duties. Typically, anyone responsible for quality control should be at a level where three months' notice would be the minimum. By taking this approach, the firm should have enough time to select a properly briefed successor, provided that the process of identifying the right person for the role is not left too late. Replacing the compliance officer is a serious matter and needs to be given proper consideration.

Appendix 1   Questions that an effective quality-control system should be able to answer

Note that this list is not exhaustive. All that it seeks to do is give an idea of areas in an accounting practice where quality control can either solve problems or maintain existing successful practices.

Technical and compliance matters

1. Is the firm complying with legal requirements and professional standards?
2. Are the accounts that the firm signs being checked properly before being released?
3. Are the firm's work files complete, accurate and easy to follow?
4. Is the work being done as efficiently as possible?
5. Are work plans being tailored properly to the clients' circumstances?
6. Are we doing work that proves nothing of value because we are regurgitating old work programmes instead of thinking about the client as it is now?
7. Is the firm's structure resulting in the wrong people being put on the wrong jobs at the wrong time?
8. Is work being planned properly before being carried out?
9. Is work being scheduled far enough ahead to ensure that no key dates (e.g., stocktaking and circularisations) are missed?
10. Is all work being reviewed at the appropriate level?
11. Are ethical matters (such as independence and competence) being considered at the appropriate level and are they being documented adequately?
12. Are the engagement letters complete and up to date? (e.g., does the scope of the audit include special reports to regulators as well as the normal statutory report?)
13. Are permanent client files complete and up to date?
14. Is the firm complying with money laundering procedures when taking on new clients?

15 Is the firm obtaining proper professional clearance before taking on new work?

Client service matters

16 Are we giving clients all the services that they require? (e.g., is the client likely to retire from business in the near future? Is the business paying too much in interest?)

17 Are the field staff identifying opportunities to provide additional services that may be of real value to the client?

18 Is the frequency of client contact appropriate?

19 Is the quality of the correspondence (written and oral) appropriate? (e.g., is there any suggestion that clients are being ignored or being deluged with publications that have little or no bearing on their businesses?)

20 Is there anything to suggest that some clients are unhappy with the firm's service?

21 Do clients ever complain about the way their telephone calls are handled? (Have you ever asked them?)

Staffing matters

22 Are assignments being staffed with people at the appropriate level?

23 Are there any areas where special training is required?

24 Is work being delegated properly and to the right people?

25 Are work appraisals being done regularly?

26 Is there anything to suggest that appraisals may not tell the whole story? (e.g., is the true appraisal being done orally with something much blander being written down?)

27 Is there an imbalance in the staff structure?

28 Does the firm need to change the type of people it recruits?

Profitability and recoveries

29 Are the fees reasonable in relation to the time needed to do the job properly?

30 Are significant budget variances being investigated properly?

31 Is the allocation between planning and finalisation the most cost effective?

32 Is work being finalised within a reasonable time of the completion of the fieldwork?

33 Are partners and managers making too many trivial review points?

34 Are accounts being adjusted unnecessarily for immaterial items?

35 Are files complete when they are handed in for review (or are managers and partners completing an unacceptable amount of routing fieldwork)?

Matters affecting the firm as a whole

36 Does the firm have the right number of Responsible Individuals for its client portfolio? (Are there some Responsible Individuals with only a handful of audits?)

37 Is staff morale at an acceptable level?

38 Is the firm overloaded to the point where standards could be compromised by pressure to complete the work?

39 Is the firm responding to its clients' needs promptly and effectively?

40 Does the firm have adequate procedures for making sure that tax returns, Companies House filings, tax payments and similar matters are dealt with on time?

41 Have all partners and qualified staff complied with CPE requirements? (Does the firm have a system in place that allows it to answer this question accurately?)

42 Is the firm complying with requirements regarding such matters as confidentiality, 'fit and proper persons' and prohibited investments? (Do the office cleaners and computer maintenance contractors, whether employees or not, have to sign a confidentiality agreement?)

43 Is the firm adequately insured?

44 Is the firm promoting the right people?

45 Is the firm carrying too many unprofitable clients?

Appendix 2 Qualities of an effective quality controller

The purpose of this checklist is to help identify the person most suited to the role of quality controller in a practice with a sizeable audit portfolio. It is unlikely, although not impossible, that the person chosen will have all the qualities on the list, but some of them at least should be in evidence.

The ideal quality controller should be:

1 a competent practical auditor;

2 knowledgeable about the regulatory regime, although knowledge alone is not enough. It is the practical application of the knowledge that matters;

3 innovative and receptive to new ideas;

4 a good listener. Often, the solution to a problem lies somewhere in the firm. The quality controller needs to be able to listen to people and coax solutions out of them;

5 a good communicator;

6 above and beyond the firm's internal politics. The job may involve criticising some of the firm's most senior people. Anyone who balks at this is likely to devalue the practice by leaving certain serious problems unidentified and unresolved;

7 committed to the task. Commitment is determined as much by the firm's attitude to quality control as by the quality controller's own attitude. If the firm supports the quality controller, there is unlikely to be any a problem with commitment. If the quality controller is succeeding in spite of the firm's commitment rather than because of it, then the controller's own commitment is likely to be eroded over time;

8 a skilled trainer. If quality control is to become embedded in a firm's culture, everyone in the firm must be trained in its standards and empowered with the skill and authority to maintain them;

9 good at delegating and empowering. All effective quality controllers know that quality control is not their job and nobody else's. Every partner, line manager, supervisor and assistant must take responsibility for the quality of their work. If a quality controller does not share responsibility in this way, the role, apart from becoming impossible to fulfil, will be seen as remote and possibly irrelevant;

10 a strong motivator. It is all too easy for a quality controller to be seen as a nitpicker and mistake hunter. Effective quality controllers need to inspire people to work well rather than make them feel inadequate by concentrating unduly on compliance failures. People with the kind of ego problems that like to catch other people getting something wrong are unsuited to the role. The ideal quality controller likes to catch people getting it right. Paradoxically, people with this positive attitude are usually better at eliminating errors than people who are unduly negative.

14 Marketing and promotion

14.1 Introduction

Over the years there has been an abundance of definitions of the marketing function from different sources. One of the most simplistic and yet meaningful descriptions is: 'Marketing is the creation of an environment in which business is generated and sustained profitably'.

This is effectively saying that marketing encompasses the entire business as seen from the client's viewpoint. It is a mechanism of involving the whole business in identifying and understanding client needs and offering solutions. Creating this environment involves the key tasks of:

- formulating a strategic business plan including setting goals, planning and use of strategic tools;
- marketing planning – both internal and external;
- building an effective communications strategy.

14.2 Strategic business plan

Strategic planning is the process of developing and maintaining an organisation's resources and capabilities to take optimum advantage of changing market opportunities.

Before firms start setting goals and deciding on how to achieve them, some fundamental soul searching is required through asking the questions: 'What is our business? Who is our customer? What is *value* to the customer? How are we perceived? What will our business be? What should our business be?'

To find the answers a whole mix of issues needs to be addressed including;

- a market survey of existing clients;
- an internal (strengths and weaknesses) and external (opportunities and threats) analysis of the practice;
- assessing the risks as well having an open mind and the will to reposition the firm to successfully exploit developing market opportunities and determine its future direction.

This then allows realistic and manageable goals to be set in the areas of turnover, profit, positioning, awareness, market share, and the adoption of growth and marketing strategies to attain them.

A case which typifies the above is that of the fictitiously named accountancy firm Smart&Smart but which represents a real case scenario of a practice redefining its role in the dynamic business market. Smart&Smart was a small practice with the traditional mainstay of tax and audit work but which, like many other firms, was becoming aware of other opportunities either through some limited informal experience, indirect involvement, observation or a combination of all three. These ancillary areas included consultancy in improving financial performance, a payroll service, IT expertise in financial software systems and financial services.

Based on their existing resources and capabilities, client relationships, and assessment through research of the potential growth of these services in the business market, they made the major strategic decision to redefine the firm as a business solutions provider by formally adopting them as sub-brands that make up the overall Smart&Smart offer. The corporate identity now reflects the dominant brand accompanied by the individually branded styles of each service as Smart&Smart – consulting, Smart&Smart – payroll, etc. The firm made the further relatively radical decision to drop 'Chartered Accountants' from their name and give it equal status with the other disciplines.

This repositioning of the firm creates a clear differentiation from competitors who, although theyhave gone down a similar route in meeting market needs, have on the whole presented the services as ancillary to the core of Chartered Accountancy. It is a business model that projects clearly defined areas of specialism and expertise. In achieving this greater breadth of offer, the firm employed growth strategies including: product development; market development; acquisition and strategic alliances.

The opportunities in cross-selling within the existing client base are obvious and are dealt with in the marketing planning section under marketing strategy in **14.3.3**.

14.3 Strategic tools

14.3.1 Brand development

Where marketing was defined earlier as generating business, branding could be similarly defined as 'creating an environment in which clear communications happen'. The aim of a brand is to create a dialogue of trust and reassurance in the mind of the client that will lead to preference and loyalty. Brands must be consistent in value but not static in nature.

The business brand

Business brands reflect a combination of the product and corporate characteristics, and the firm's differentiation. They are built on six key areas:

- the firm's vision of the business;
- the wants and needs of the market;
- its business culture;
- the products or services;
- the competitive environment; and
- the clients.

It is having a clear understanding of all of these that will help to create the desired competitive positioning.

Positioning

Positioning is a reflection of the firm's performance and image in the task of meeting market expectations.

For example, the desired positioning of Smart&Smart is as a provider of practical business solutions delivered in a personable but professional environment.

Tim Hazelhurst Chairman of ABBA, the National Association of Business to Business Advertisers states, 'The strength and relevance of your brand is directly proportional to your ability to locate and convert business opportunities'. This could apply equally to the situation of a firm gaining a client through referral by a third party who has experienced the brand, or indeed directly, through the reputation of the firm.

Values

An important element of the brand make up is the less tangible and more emotionally based 'atmosphere'. Although the product range and added-value features are crucially important elements of the brand promise, they are increasingly being matched by competitor firms. In the final instance, therefore, the brand choice and loyalty will be heavily influenced not by 'what a firm does' but 'how it does it'. That is to say, how the firm behaves and interacts with clients and prospective clients.

This has particular relevance in the professional service market place where people and procedures within the business culture are major contributors to the embodiment of the brand promise. It effectively defines the personality of the brand where clients' own values are reflected in those of the brand, creating in turn an emotional security and preference.

14.3.2 Website

From its popular beginnings in the mid-1990s when having a presence on-line was deemed to have entered the 'cyber era,' the website was a simple communication tool offering an e-profile of businesses, their products and services. Great advances in both interactive and design software since then has resulted in the emergence of the website as a strategic business tool which can effectively complement existing non on-line activity, but which has the potential to replace much of the latter in the long term.

Unfortunately there are numerous firms stuck somewhere between the e-profile and e-information status, asking why being on-line is not working for them – having spent several thousand pounds on its development. The answer is undoubtedly that there was an absence of both a clear objective and strategy from the start.

The basic building blocks of an e-business strategy are as follows.

Relevance and value

People visit a site to answer a question or solve a problem. It is now accepted that 90 per cent of a firm's website must be of value to its clients. This means asking them what they want to see that would offer solutions.

Examples of the kind of information could be using the website as a client coded 'portal' for the following:

- directory of the firm's clients which could be used as sources for potential sales targeting or suppliers and provide a link to their websites;
- use of the new accounts-on-line software which promises to process financial information sent on-line by the client to the accountant firm who returns it on-line within 24 hours in a management accounts format;
- business sector information.

Intelligent dialogue

This can exist at several levels.

- A selling opportunity would require your website to have the ability to influence the client's decision making. In the case of Smart&Smart whose IT department is a preferred supplier of software packages, the possibility of 'e' transactions should be effected.
- An enquiry from a client making a specific request in the consulting, payroll etc., activities would require an informed response;
- An information update level for clients on items such as fees incurred, IT project status.

Managing these interactive processes efficiently is a crucial part of the overall e-business process.

Design and travel

Keeping it simple but entertaining are the key elements to maintaining functional interest. Research shows that it takes only four seconds to convince new visitors to remain in a site otherwise they move on. It is important that they find what they are looking for within three clicks. Getting the balance right between graphic style and ease of travel around the site is crucial.

Promotion

Recent research has shown that the most effective way to drive traffic to your website is to have joint arrangements where the co-partners are motivated by commission to link to your site and promote your offer. This can be local banks, insurance brokers and management consultants where no conflict of interest exists.

Test market

Before going 'live' it is important to test the overall effectiveness of a website with a selected group of clients representing a wide range of business sectors. This could be expedited through a focus group using the firm's website and evaluating whether the site delighted or disappointed them in meeting their needs. From this analysis further development or adjustment should result in finally launching the site with confidence.

The website is as important in embodying the brand promise as the people and procedures of your firm itself.

14.3.3 Marketing planning

Internal marketing planning

In the professional sector there is normally a high contact level with clients. This has major implications for a firm's brand image where all the contact people involved in the delivery have a major influence in the client's perception and interpretation of what that brand means to them. As already discussed in Brand Values (see **14.3.1** Brand development), it is how the service is delivered – as opposed to what is delivered – that is usually the memorable experience of the firm by the client.

It is therefore essential that firms show equal importance to the role of their internal customers, namely their staff, as they do to maintaining and targeting external clients.

Internal marketing describes the work needed to develop and motivate both client contact personnel and support staff to be client focussed in the areas of competence in skills and knowledge; courtesy; credibility; responsiveness; understanding of their needs. This equips employees with the abilities to successfully handle the client contact process.

These employee attributes are major contributors to the overall service quality. It also promotes the culture that a firm's employees are effectively working for its clients, which in turn should motivate them to make that extra effort to please.

A mystery shopping exercise can be very effective in identifying weaknesses in how contact staff handle enquiries and complaints.

Of course this internal marketing process applies equally to the firm's partners. With the 'business' branding approach to the market it is important that the firm's partners adopt a more collective management stance in support of the brand. It is effectively promoting a culture of clients belonging to the firm and not to individual partners. In practical terms generating business from new or existing clients must be executed for the good of the firm and the brand.

External marketing planning

Having decided on the direction the firm should take through strategic planning, the next phase in the marketing process is the marketing plan that focuses more narrowly on the products, services and markets. With the nickname of 'blueprint for success', the marketing plan is regarded in the marketing profession as the central instrument to successfully direct and coordinate the front-line marketing effort.

In the case of Smart&Smart, the offer has been extended to services that are designed to fully exploit opportunities with both existing and new clients. To achieve a clear focus on each of these targets, separate marketing plans should be considered.

The plan for existing clients will be more straightforward because of the already established relationship and the knowledge gained of their business and its needs.

The components of the client marketing plan are as follows.

Current situation

This describes the current status of the firm throughout the client base in terms of their needs and behaviour profile, the services already being provided and competitors in these services. This analysis is an ideal opportunity to review the extent of existing business with clients, its profitability and any competitive involvement.

As background information, a wider market analysis should be made of the market situation in terms of the size, growth and trends of services like business consultancy, IT software, payroll services, and financial services, and the more qualitative client needs, preferences and perceptions.

This indicates the big picture, which can then be interpreted in the context of the firm's target catchment. The data can be obtained from market information agencies (Keynotes, Mintel, etc.) and use of local research techniques (questionnaires).

SWOT analysis

A strengths/weaknesses and opportunities/threats analysis is simply a way of confirming the ability of a firm to be competent and competitive in the provision of its services to the market. The strengths/weaknesses analysis is internal and considers issues like the firm's people and skills, procedures, delivery, complaints, fee levels, etc., where the opportunities/threats analysis reflects market issues like competitors and environmental factors such as economical and technological.

Objectives

The two types of objective to be set are financial and marketing.

In the case of Smart&Smart where the individual services are regarded as profit centres, then the financial objectives will include turnover, profit and, in the case of acquisition, return on investment. This would then dictate the marketing effort required to realise the financial objectives. It would include setting objectives first in, client awareness and second in client adoption of each of the service products.

Marketing strategy

This centres around the existing relationship of the firm with clients and the trust and reliability that has been built up between them over a period of time. In the majority of cases this relationship has been developed around the core accountancy role of the firm where the client has experienced the people, procedures, competency and understanding of the firm.

From the firm's standpoint it is this intimate knowledge of the client business that makes the targeting for Smart&Smart – consulting, payroll, IT and financial services – more efficient. This could include knowledge criteria like the client's growth objectives or potential, size, productivity and financial management record. It therefore becomes easier to convince clients of the perceived value of adopting the Smart&Smart solutions.

As more existing clients experience a part or more of the wider brand offer, so the potential of business generation through referral and reputation increases. However, to maximise business opportunities, a marketing strategy needs to be considered for targeting potential new clients. As in the plan for existing clients, the driver for effective marketing in this market is the established role of Chartered Accountancy. It provides the necessary authority from which any other related service can be developed and promoted with credibility.

The fundamental difference lies in the marketing strategy. Where previously it revolved around the relationship with existing clients, it is now based on its overall attractiveness as a multi-specialism solutions provider.

Using appropriate databases and targeting criteria this positioning will be heavily dependent on effective promotions discussed under **14.3.4** below.

Action plan

This cross-marketing in the existing client market, will obviously require a team approach consisting of the marketing person and those partners involved in the different activities. The team should be actively involved in personally promoting and implementing their offer to meet the set objectives.

A 'marketing committee' meeting monthly could provide a platform for setting time limits for promotion or visits; cross-consultation for further potential business; monitoring progress and promoting a cohesive marketing culture in support of the Smart&Smart business brand.

14.3.4 Marketing communications

In services marketing, the objective is to create tangibility from something which lacks physical evidence. This can be manifested in all the marketing communications disciplines in a way that the audience can relate to the experience on offer. This is the first step along the brand experience continuum, the final step being the actual adoption of the brand.

In this sense, marketing communications could be more accurately described as contact strategy where the effort and direction is in creating a 'dialogue' with target audiences and developing relationships.

Tim Hazelhurst of ABBA takes the view that: 'your brand is the sum of all your relationships. They are strategic assets with both clients and prospects, and are created through all market contact including both personal contact and indirect methods'.

The three key elements of communications are:

- *brand strategy* – what we wish the market to think of us – positioning;
- *contact strategy* – how we deliver the message – disciplines;
- *creative strategy* – how we express it – attention/interest.

Contact disciplines

The standard mix includes: advertising; direct mail; public relations; personal; sales promotion; website; corporate literature.

These can be used individually or in any group combination to create an integrated approach, for example advertising, direct mail, personal contact and PR. Integrated marketing communication is particularly powerful in establishing the desired positioning of the brand. It depends heavily on such factors as coordination, consistency of message, timing, duration and budget.

Advertising

Of all the disciplines advertising is the one which seems to create fear, uncertainty and doubt in the minds of accountancy firms. This is due, in the main, to its perceived inability to produce direct, tangible results in increased business which in turn creates a reluctance to allocate future spend to advertising.

What may not be considered in this argument is the ability of the advertisement to gain attention and interest. In other words the days of simply listing the firm's services and contact details are past. Business markets are now demanding a more creative approach to advertising which targets the 'heart' as much as the 'mind'. This effectively means including emotional factors like empathy and understanding, as well as service benefits in the advertisement design. Knowing your audience is critical for this exercise.

A major factor in gaining attention and interest within the statistically proven time of 1.4 seconds, is the 'likeability' of the advertising. According to Erik du Plessis, head of Impact International, a leading advertising research company, successful campaigns have three general characteristics:

1. they are likeable because of their entertaining qualities;
2. they are visual rather than verbal;
3. they say something meaningful about the brand.

Other crucial issues in any campaign are targeting, choice of media, insertion frequency, the duration and budget. It is the latter that will dictate whether it is feasible to employ an agency, even a small one, who will plan, implement and manage the whole campaign with both the required creativity and cost effectiveness. Local press, regional business publications and radio would be the obvious media choices for business-to-business promotion.

If the budget level means that a firm decides to go it alone, then at the very least they should employ an outside graphic agency to achieve the desired creativity in advertisement design. Another saving is to take advantage of late slots and bargain spaces in the press. The downside to this is the ad hoc approach rather than a planned programme, and this can reduce the overall effectiveness.

It is the synergistic effect of advertising in conjunction with other disciplines that is a measure of its true effectiveness.

Direct mail

Unlike the more indirect targeting nature of advertising, the direct-mail method is about narrow and efficient targeting. With the development of database technology and management, precision targeting of potential clients can be achieved using a whole range of parameters. There are numerous companies that supply business listings for purchase or rent, at a more sophisticated level which further includes turnover, growth, profit, etc., to the standard business directory profile of name, company, contact detail. In these cases firms pay for what they get.

Mailings can include a promotion of the firm, announcing a new product or service, a questionnaire, or an invitation to a seminar or hospitality event. Any mailer should be accompanied by a letter addressed to the appropriate person by name which lends both professionalism and personalisation to the process.

As in advertising, it is important to incorporate creativity in both the design and copy in order to encourage attention and interest, and for response, a reply card mechanism should be included. In its role of promoting the firm's services, the message of the mailer is most effective when it identifies a problem with the target business and offers a solution in a creative, attention-getting style.

Although strictly a response mechanism, a mailshot can play a significant part in awareness building. Statistically, for a business-to-business direct mailing project, the expected average response is around six per cent.

Public relations (PR)

PR is about building and sustaining positive relationships between the firm and its publics to inspire their confidence and loyalty as well as to stimulate action. The publics are all those who have both an actual or potential impact on the firm's ability to achieve its objectives. They include suppliers, employees, financial institutions, other potential sources of business referrals and clients – both existing and prospective.

The key tools of PR that effectively serve to reach the publics include the press, events and sponsorships.

Achieving effective press PR is the combination of good media management in targeting the publications, feature list awareness, relations with the editorial staff, along with quality writing, story interest value and regular publishing. All of this is essentially the function of PR agencies who will try to secure a monthly retainer for their services in preference to project payment. The PR agency's real skill is in recognising or creating newsworthy stories, writing them and achieving a high publishing rate with the right media titles at the right time.

Again, if the budget prohibits the appointment of an agency, an in-house marketing person must attempt to fill the role. Events can vary from corporate hospitality, receptions, seminars and public speaking. All are designed to offer goodwill, expose the firm's people to its publics and generally to raise the firm's profile in the business community. The obvious advantage to this invitational activity is in the potential business opportunities created through meeting face to face.

Sponsorship performs a similar goodwill and profile-raising role in the general community by, for example, supporting sporting or local cultural affairs.

PR is generally accepted as the most influential and cost-effective form of marketing communications. As far as the press PR is concerned this only applies if you achieve frequent publication. The cost if you do not, can be significant if not prohibitive.

Personal contact

The personal involvement has been discussed under **14.3.3** Internal marketing planning. A further important personal contact is in telemarketing as a follow up to a mailing campaign. This role requires the attributes of courtesy, understanding and persuasion to determine the interest and secure a meeting with a partner or attendance at a seminar.

The person employed to carry it out is an intrinsic part of the selling process without blatantly showing it. If the decision is to use an external agency, it is crucial to select those who have experience in the professional sector.

Sales promotion

In the professional services market, sales promotion needs to be projected as added-value features. The objective still remains to incentivise business generation but it must be perceived to be presented in a credible and professional fashion.

In the case of Smart&Smart for instance the following could be considered as incentives:

- the consulting unit offers a free half-day consultancy that would be a snapshot of the key areas of the business such as tax, liquidity or profitability and business plan guidance for the smaller company;
- the payroll unit offers a month's trial of managing salaries and wages at a discounted rate;
- in targeting smaller businesses the financial services unit offers a free consultation to the owners/directors on their personal financial situations. This could be an incentive to employ other services or financial services for the whole business.

Website

The website as a communication and business tool has already been discussed in **14.3**.

Corporate literature

The corporate brochure concept is the visual representation of a firm's brand strategy.

In the case of Smart&Smart it reflects both the firm's skills and resource credentials as well as the personal, practical and professional way the service is delivered.

In these days of immediacy where 'less is more', the copy should be minimal but meaningful. It is the overall look, feel and message of the document that will make the right impression. There has been great expense incurred by firms in producing brochure material that bears little relation to their actual positioning. Getting the right style, finish and content is vital to communicate effectively with the target audience.

The newsletter as another corporate communication is a way of talking to clients about the issues that could affect their businesses. This proactive approach promotes a feeling of client involvement, increases the perceived value of the firm and helps to sustain client loyalty.

14.4 Conclusion

It does not seem that long ago since the accountancy profession's view of marketing was, to say the least, 'frosty'. It is somewhat ironic therefore that there is a growing acceptance of the fact that without adopting a strong marketing stance accountancy firms will find it difficult to survive in an increasingly aggressive, competitive market place which includes financial institutions and management consultants.

For the marketing effort to be successful it must be planned, implemented and managed within a business environment with a focus on key strategies, like new product and market development, branding, marketing communications and e-business.

This business environment will promote a culture in which all employees, including partners, will be responsible to the brand and what it stands for.

15 Motivational leadership

15.1 Introduction

It has often been said that the only constant in business today is change. Rapid changes in technology, growing worldwide competition and ever changing client demands are contributing towards the continuous need to produce or provide more for less.

Change affects every organisation, large or small, public or private, and success for them all depends upon their ability to produce the right goods and services of the right quality, at the right price and time, and to continually meet customer needs efficiently and effectively.

A recent study of over 100 of the best-performing companies identified that they have several characteristics in common – whether in service or manufacturing, the key elements contributing to their success are the same. They all demonstrated three key ingredients:

- customer satisfaction;
- employee satisfaction;
- champions of change.

These organisations focus on the needs of customers and clients, welcoming the challenge of demanding customers to drive continuous improvement, innovation and competitiveness. They thrive on change and have a style of leadership that supports and encourages others to challenge the status quo. Change is seen as a continuous process – a way of life – not a 'quick fix' short-term project with an end date, or a 'bolt-on extra'.

They also appreciate that change can only be embraced by realising the full potential of all employees. Effective communications, continuous development and greater involvement has led to flatter organisation structures with decision-making closer to the customer.

The challenge is to increase the number of UK organisations joining the ranks of 'Business Excellence'. The more that can be learnt about successful implementation of change, the winners and the also-rans, the sooner we can join the premier league and legitimately call ourselves 'world class'.

15.1.1 What can be changed?

The next decade will require businesses to examine every aspect of their organisations. One thing is clear, whether businesses want to improve quality or client care, or even take the drastic approach of totally re-engineering their business, people are the very heart of any change. If the support or commitment of staff is not won and they are not brought on side, any change will be slow and unlikely to achieve optimum benefit. Thus, if a business wants to restructure, change shape, change direction, improve performance, change the behaviour of partners and staff, or develop new services, people can either help or hinder the process.

15.1.2 Is there a choice?

Is it possible to stand still? Does there have to be change to achieve goals in the longer term? For answers to these questions it is helpful to look at history, i.e., what happened to the industries that did not change? For example, who now dominates the manufacture of motorcycles, pianos, watches and hi-fis? Service organisations have not been bypassed either. Many banks and building societies have been absorbed by more efficient predators and refuse is being collected by French and Spanish operators.

It is possible to stand still and not effect change, but as one Quality Guru once said in the long distant past 'survival isn't compulsory'.

There are two kinds of change – that which is threatening and that which is exciting. The difference is subtle but powerful. Change that is threatening is imposed on you – change a person has little influence or control over – change that is exciting you encourages involvement in. Many projects fail because people are merely spectators in the change process rather than participants.

Thus, successful change, to enable achievement of the practice's future goals, requires effective leadership and excellent management. Motivation of people is required at all levels if a practice is to drive change, to accept it and thrive on it, and to make sure that the business is ready to deliver the long-term objectives.

15.1.3 Are leaders born or made?

With the possible exception of major religious leaders of the world, leaders are made, not born. It is quite true that some people have more highly apparent skills and qualities of leadership than others, nevertheless, they become good and effective leaders only by working on these and, where necessary, presenting them to best advantage. For example, one of the reasons Julius Caesar was able to exert his authority for over 20 years was because, as a political leader, he never took rewards – especially illegitimate rewards – that were available to him in his position within the Roman Senate. Also, as a military leader, he never asked his men to do anything that he himself was not prepared to do (if they walked, so did he; if they went without food, so did he). He also walked with them in triumphal processions at the end of his campaigns.

William the Conqueror was able to put together a force to invade England in 1065–1066 because he was able to persuade others with influence in northern France (Normandy) of the rightness and merits of his case (the throne of England had been promised to him and then usurped by Harold the Saxon). This relied on his powers of persuasion, which he had to develop.

Richard Branson has used his own achievements to help build the reputation and brand of Virgin. He has reinforced the values of the brand through a series of high-profile activities – the fastest sea crossing of the Atlantic, attempts to circumnavigate the world in a balloon, media coverage of him serving drinks to customers on his airline, dressing up in bridal gear to launch the Virgin Bride arm of the group.

In each case, traits, styles and the relationship with the environment are apparent and exhibited. In order to be able to do this to best advantage, each has to be identified, learned, developed and improved, in the same way as any expert in any other field. Also, as with other expertise, some parts come more easily than others. However, they each have to be tackled. For example:

- determination – Caesar only managed to cross the Channel to England at the fourth attempt; Richard Branson had three attempts at the Blue Riband crossing of the Atlantic and four at the non-stop balloon flight (at which he remained unsuccessful);
- commitment – William the Conqueror burnt his boats (hence the expression) on the south coast of England before setting off to do battle at Hastings; Branson committed himself to a five-year plan at Virgin Rail and refused to be put off by difficulties that became apparent in the first two years.

There has always been a debate about the differences and overlaps of leadership and management. Current opinion is that they are different concepts but they overlap considerably.

So if this is leadership, what is management? Management is usually described as achieving results through other people – in practical terms achieving the business vision and plan by working with colleagues and staff, managing what people do and how they do it, to achieve business results. Perhaps management has the overtone of carrying out objectives laid down by someone else. It is certainly true that a well-managed business, in the sense of having perfect organisation, still needs that 'extra something'. That 'extra something' is often identified as being the contribution of 'leadership'.

Leadership has some distinctive nuances not always found in management. A leader must:

- give direction;
- provide inspiration;
- build teams;
- set an example;
- be accepted.

Leadership can be 'specific to the particular situation' and its 'authority' can derive from:

- position (as in job title, rank or appointment);
- personality (as in natural qualities of influence); and
- knowledge (as in technical professional skills).

A leader is the kind of person (with leadership qualities) who has the appropriate knowledge and skill to lead a group to achieve its ends willingly. Personality and character cannot be left out of leadership. There are certain generic leadership traits and seven of the most important ones are as follows.

- Enthusiasm – try naming a leader without it!
- Integrity – this quality makes people trust a leader.
- Toughness – demanding, with high standards, resilient, tenacious and with the aim of being respected (not necessarily popular).
- Fairness – impartial, rewarding/penalising performance without 'favourites', treating individuals differently but equally.
- Warmth – the heart as well as the mind being engaged, loving what is being done and caring for people – cold fish do not make good leaders.
- Humility – the opposite of arrogance, being a listener and without an overwhelming ego.

- Confidence – not over-confidence (which leads to arrogance), but with self-confidence which people recognise.

Leaders must also inspire others. In 1987, James Kouzes and Barry Posner identified five characteristics of what they call exemplary leaders.

1 Leaders challenge the process. Leaders search for opportunities. They experiment and take risks, constantly challenging other people to exceed their own limitations.
2 Leaders inspire a shared vision. Leaders envision an 'enabling future' for people, and enlist those people to join in that new direction.
3 Leaders enable others to act. Leaders strengthen others and foster collaboration.
4 Leaders model the way. Leaders set the example for people by their own leadership behaviour and they plan small wins to get the process moving.
5 Leaders encourage the heart. Leaders regard and recognise individual contributions and they celebrate team successes.

The leader has a responsibility in three key areas of need in the business:

1 task need – to achieve the common task;
2 team needs – to be held together or to maintain themselves as a team;
3 individual needs – the needs which individuals bring with them into the group.

These three needs (the task, team and individual) are the watchwords of leadership and people expect their leaders to:

- help them achieve the common task;
- build the synergy of teamwork, and
- respond to individuals and meet their needs.

The task needs work groups or organisations to come into being because the task needs doing and cannot be done by one person alone. The team needs are present because the creation, promotion and retention of group/organisational cohesiveness is essential on the 'united we stand, divided we fall' principle. The individual needs are the physical ones (salary) and the psychological ones of:

- recognition;
- a sense of doing something worthwhile;

- status;
- the deeper need to give and to receive from other people in a working situation.

The task, team and individual needs overlap and this overlapping is evident in that:

- achieving the task builds the team and satisfies the individuals;
- if team maintenance fails (the team lacks cohesiveness), performance of the task is impaired and individual satisfaction is reduced;
- if individual needs are not met the team will lack cohesiveness and performance of the task will be impaired.

Leadership exists at different levels:

- team leadership – of teams of about five to 20 people;
- operational leadership – essential in a business or organisation comprising a number of teams whose leaders report to you;
- strategic leadership – a whole business or organisation, with overall accountability for the levels of leadership below you.

At whatever level of leadership, task, team and individual needs must be constantly thought about. To achieve the common task, maintain teamwork and satisfy the individuals, certain functions have to be performed. A function is what leaders *do* as opposed to a quality, which is an aspect of what they *are*. These functions (the functional approach to leadership, also called action-centred leadership) are:

- defining the task;
- evaluating;
- planning;
- motivating;
- briefing;
- organising;
- controlling;
- providing an example.

Leaders need to be able to undertake these functions with a high level of skill – skill which can be learned as part of the process of developing an effective leader.

Decision making provides a good example of how these skills can be applied, and different styles are appropriate in different circumstances. The leader may:

- make the decision, and tell the team what the decision is;
- make the decision, and persuade the team to accept it;
- make the decision, but allow discussion and questions, before implementing it;
- make a preliminary decision, but then allow the team to change part of it;
- present the facts to the team, and make the decision based on their ideas;
- allow the team to make the decision after the leader has defined certain boundaries or limits;
- allow the team to make the decision by themselves, without interference, and tell the leader what it is.

It is important for an individual to be aware of their own style of decision making in different situations, and the impact that has on the different teams and individuals that person leads and manages, as this is key to developing a more effective style of leadership. Sometimes it is difficult for us to identify our own style of leadership – we need to ask others who are affected by it, and consider the impact our style has on their performance and motivation.

At a practical level it is not possible to let everyone share in all decisions. For example, a leader or manager would probably not want the whole team deciding about a disciplinary matter, or wish to spend time consulting everyone over a decision that had to be made very quickly. But if, for example, the workspace layout was under consideration, the team members might be upset if they were not asked for their views and preferences. Also, if work was being allocated that required a considerable amount of overtime, there may be no choice but to ask for volunteers.

Some people in teams prefer to be told what to do rather than have to think things out for themselves. A leader of an inexperienced or unskilled team may provide very specific instructions, knowing that this is essential if the job is to be done correctly. But a team which is used to using its own judgement will resent a leader who is overbearing.

In reality, a person's natural style is more likely to be effective than an assumed style that does not match their personality, and the way decisions are made should be appropriate to the circumstances.

15.2 Motivation

One of the biggest challenges faced by a leader or manager is creating a team of motivated people. Motivation is what makes a person want to do something, and the key word here is want. There are things that people all have to do that they may not want to. Motivation is when people give willingly. People can always be made to do things, but to have them feel motivated is quite different. A simple definition of motivation in the work context is: 'Getting people to do willingly and well those things that need to be done'.

Ned Herrmann, in *The Whole Brain Business Book*, talks about how you cannot motivate people, they can only motivate themselves. He believes:

> 'The facts of the matter are that we all motivate ourselves. This inner self motivation can be encouraged in a number of ways by supervisors, managers and executives.'

It is becoming increasingly obvious that the most a manager can do is remove the barriers to motivation and create an environment in which people are able to motivate themselves.

It is quite easy to distinguish people who are motivated from people who are not. There is a distinction between being unmotivated and demotivated. Unmotivated people have no desire to do a particular task. Demotivated people did have the desire to do it, but have lost the motivation. It is easier to remotivate those who are de-motivated than it is to inspire motivation in people who really have no interest in doing the task in the first place.

15.2.1 Possible characteristics of motivated, demotivated and unmotivated people

Table 15.1 Characteristics of motivated, demotivated and unmotivated people

Motivated	Demotivated	Unmotivated
Asks questions for clarification	Asks rhetorical questions which are unanswerable	Does not ask questions
Seeks to solve problems	Points problems out to others	Ignores problems
Wants to share knowledge with others	Wants to complain about difficulties to others	Does not talk about the task/job at all

Puts in the time to achieve a good result	Wastes time	Does the bare minimum to get the job done
Is generally quick to respond to requests	Responds to requests reluctantly	Forgets they have been asked
Seeks to help others	Cannot help others and does not ask for help himself	Does not occur to them that they might need or offer help
Generally seems positive	Generally seems negative	Neither positive nor negative because they are disengaged from the task
More likely to cope with things going wrong with good humour	More likely to overreact to things going wrong or complain about them	Doesn't care if things go wrong
Positive attitude to problems – 'I can sort this out'	Negative attitude to problems – does not think they can sort the problem	May generally be positive, just not interested in this particular job

There are many theories about what motivates people, and all of them have some value. The key thing is to make them work in practice. In order to learn how to create an environment in which people can help to motivate themselves, there first needs to be some understanding of what makes people 'tick'. People, despite having a lot in common, also have very specific individual differences. There are 'generic commonalties' of values and motivation and yet each individual finds a different stimulation.

15.2.2 Understanding people

There are many different theories about what does make people tick. Many theories of personality are linked to motivation, although the emphasis they place on it varies. All of this knowledge is useful in attempting to understand what motivates people. However, for the most part, one theory alone does not provide the whole answer and so an overall understanding of different theories can help to inform actions and thinking when trying to inspire motivation in others.

One theory by H Eysenck says that people have three personality dimensions and that people's personalities are linked to their biological make up – there is not much anyone can do to change them. Another theory is that people act as scientists in that they form a theory about how the world works and then test out the theory. That is, our personalities are formed by what happens to us. So we take each experience, process it and use it to make judgements about future experiences. This theory says that fundamentally people's motivation is based on their need to predict their environment, and thereby reduce uncertainty and increase mastery over the world. Yet another theory is that people have personality traits which help them to have predictable behaviour. Personality grows and changes, and people have the potential to become something different. Personality is formed by present circumstances and conscious experiences.

All of this is useful information when thinking about what actions we can take to help motivate people.

15.2.3 Maslow's hierarchy of needs

These kinds of thinking encouraged Maslow, who was one of the founder members of the American Association for Humanistic Psychology, to publish a theory of motivation in 1954 which is still widely accepted as relevant today, particularly in the world of work. He called it the hierarchy of needs. He identified four kinds of basic human needs which he termed 'deficiency needs'. Deficiency needs are those needs which can be satisfied. He then identified a fifth and highest kind of need, which is only identified when the other four needs have been satisfied. That is the need for what he termed 'self-actualisation'.

Figure 15.1 Maslow's hierarchy of needs

Need for self-actualisation – 'becoming what one is capable of becoming'
Needs for esteem – competence, adequacy, self respect and respect by others
Needs for love and belonging – affection, intimacy, roots in the family or group
Needs for safety – physical, economic, psychological security
Physiological needs related to survival – food, drink, sleep, basic sex

Self-actualisation relates to an individual's need to achieve their potential, but Maslow argued that they would be unable to do this until the other four deficiency needs are satisfied.

So what does this mean for a leader or manager? Well, if a member of a team feels insecure, or is worrying about how to pay the bills, then they are unlikely to be motivated to develop themselves or improve the quality of tasks. If they feel isolated from the rest of the team, they are less likely to be motivated. If they feel that they are not cared about or not respected, they will not be so well motivated. All of the four deficiency needs are something that a leader and manager can do something about. They concern environment, pay, health and safety, being part of a team and being respected.

Psychologist Carl Rogers talked about the conditions for personal growth. He said that people are dynamic and goal directed. Essentially people have two ways of identifying their own concept of who they are. First, their own experiences of what they can and cannot do, and second, evaluations of them made by other people. People have a need for unconditional regard, i.e., to be liked for themselves, regardless of what they do.

So, a leader or manager needs to think about how they see their team and how they are treating them. As leader, do they feel valued by their team? Does the team feel that their leader cares about them as individuals, as much as they care about the work they do? Are they given the opportunity to test themselves, to try out new ways of doing things? Are they given positive and helpful feedback about their behaviour and their actions?

The above theories, in particular the work of Maslow, was taken further by Douglas Macgregor. He talked about this theory of motivation at work in terms of Theory X and Theory Y. The two theories are representations of assumptions that people, in particular managers, may make of other people with whom they work.

Theory X assumes that people basically dislike work and need to be directed and controlled in order to produce results. Theory Y says people like work and, under the right conditions, will seek to take responsibility for it.

15.2.4 Macgregor's theory (the X-Y theory)

Table 15.2 Macgregor's theory

Theory X	Theory Y
1 People dislike work and will avoid it if they can.	1 Work is necessary to people's psychological growth.
2 People must be forced or bribed to make the right effort.	2 People want to be interested in their work and under the right conditions they can enjoy it.
3 People would rather be directed than accept responsibilities.	3 People will direct themselves towards an accepted target.
4 People are motivated mainly by money.	4 People will seek and accept responsibility under the right conditions.
5 People are motivated by anxiety about their security.	5 The discipline people impose on themselves is more effective, and can be more severe, than any imposed on them.
6 Most people have little creativity – except when getting around management rules.	6 Under the right conditions, people are motivated by the desire to realise their own potential.
	7 Creativity and ingenuity are widely distributed and grossly underused.

15.2.5 Hertzberg's motivational theory

After extensive research, behavioural scientist Frederick Herzberg identified two groups of factors that affect employee performance: motivation factors and maintenance factors.

Motivation factors are the things that must be present to make employees want to improve their performance. According to Herzberg, employees will be motivated to improve when:

- they experience a sense of accomplishment;
- they are recognised for their achievements;
- they are given something interesting to do;
- they have responsibility for themselves and their work;
- they have opportunities to grow.

Maintenance factors are essential to helping employees remain satisfied with their jobs:

- *management is willing to teach* them new skills and delegate;
- employees feel good about the organisation and personnel policies;
- physical working conditions are good;
- employee relations at all levels are good;
- employees feel secure in their jobs;
- employees feel that they are paid adequately;
- employees feel that their jobs do not cause problems in their personal lives.

The presence (or absence) of maintenance factors has no effect on motivation. These factors only maintain performance. On the other hand, motivation factors will cause employees to improve their performance.

15.2.6 Leaders/managers and motivation

Performance reviews provide a practical framework in which motivation can be managed on an individual basis in a practice (see **Chapter 5** Developing New Skills). To get the best out of this process, managers and leaders should take a realistic and visionary view of people who work for them and with them. Individuals can be managed better if it is recognised that they are:

- individuals, but become fully developed and achieve their potential as a result of their relationship with other people and the undertaking of meaningful work;
- creative and imaginative, but only in concert with others through working on their own or in teams;
- driven by achievement (as individuals) but know that they achieve more as part of a team;
- self-motivated and self-directed but need management/leadership (if only to co-ordinate activities);
- intelligent enough to know the difference between rewards such as money and those less tangible rewards that meet value needs;
- interested in leaving work and the world a better place.

Managers should check that individuals have:

- a sense of achievement in their job and feel that they are making a worthwhile contribution to the objective of the team;

- jobs which are challenging and demanding with responsibilities to match capabilities;
- adequate recognition for achievements;
- control over delegated duties;
- a feeling that they are developing personally as well as gaining experience and ability.

15.2.7 Getting the best out of people

The starting point is for the manager/leader to be motivated! Enthusiasm and motivation inspires others and the badges of good example, setting are that the person setting the example should be:

- public – make sure you act in the open;
- spontaneous – do not appear calculated;
- expressive – do things because they are natural, not for effect;
- self-effacing – setting a good example is not glory-seeking.

Motivation is contagious so a manager/leader should be infectious! If the motivator is not motivated, they will be unable to motivate others and should examine the reasons why they lack motivation. Symptoms include having little or no interest in the job, wanting to arrive late and leave early, wanting to leave the job, feeling active dislike for it and feeling out of place in it.

Motivation can be strengthened by remembering:

- to feel and act enthusiastically and in a committed way in work;
- to take responsibility when things go wrong rather than blaming others;
- to identify ways to lead by example;
- to motivate by word and example rather than manipulation;
- to set an example naturally rather than in a calculated way;
- not to give up easily;
- to ensure it is the right job for personal abilities, interests and temperament;
- to be able to cite experiences where what has been said or done has had an inspirational effect on individuals, the team or the organisation;
- that the three badges of leadership are enthusiasm, commitment and perseverance.

A practice should always try to recruit people who are highly motivated. The seven key indicators of high motivation are:

1. energy – not necessarily extrovert but alertness and quiet resolve;
2. commitment – to the common purpose;
3. staying power – in the face of problems/difficulties/set-backs;
4. skill – possession of skills indicates aims and ambitions;
5. single-mindedness – energy applied in a single direction;
6. enjoyment – goes hand in hand with motivation;
7. responsibility – willingness to seek and accept it.

Choosing people well (and if mistakes are made, confronting and remedying them early) means looking at motivation, ability and personality and an interviewer should, when interviewing, look for real evidence behind the interviewee's façade.

Looking for the 'Michelangelo motive' (where the quality of the work itself is a key motivator) can yield good results in selecting highly motivated individuals. The following should be looked for:

- a sense of pride in the individual's own work;
- an attention to detail;
- a willingness to 'walk the extra mile' to get things right;
- a total lack of the 'it's good enough, let it go' mentality;
- an inner direction or responsibility for the work (without the need for supervision);
- an ability to assess and evaluate work, independently from the opinion of others.

It should be stressed that perfectionism is not what is called for – the best can be the enemy of the good. Managers should check whether individuals are in the right job with the right skills and abilities, otherwise motivation techniques will fail. The aim is to select people who are motivated for the most appropriate job.

Each person should be treated as an individual, i.e., what motivates them personally, generalised theories or assumptions should not be relied on. Dialogue should be entered into with each team member to help *them* to clarify what it is that motivates them. The results of this dialogue should be used for mutual benefit.

To ensure that each person is treated as an individual, the team leader should ask of themselves the following questions:

- Do you know the names of people on your team and their teams if they are leaders?
- Can you identify ways in which those who report to you differ from each other?
- Do you accept that an individual's motivation changes from time to time?
- Do you spend time with people to know them, work with them, coach them?
- Does your organisation see you as an individual?

Realistic and challenging targets should be set. This can only be done in the context of understanding the organisation's aims or purpose. It is only then that targets and objectives can be identified and tasks defined.

It can be necessary to remotivate the team by rebuilding self-confidence and by re-establishing:

- aims – and clarifying objectives;
- plans, resources needed;
- leadership;
- overlooked factors;
- the value of the task(s);
- involvement of individuals in key decisions.

15.3 Summary

Implementing the changes needed to ensure a practice can meet longer-term business objectives needs motivated people at all levels. Motivated people are the legacy of effective leaders and managers – and great leaders and managers can be developed, provided they understand the challenges of the job and are prepared to spend the time and energy needed to meet them successfully.

16 The structure of a practice

16.1 Introduction

Organising development and growth is of fundamental importance to every business and is generally a task allocated to the person best suited to deal with it. For the professional partnership, by tradition, the description 'partner' often instils a belief in every partner not only that he has a right to manage the firm but also that management must come a poor second to servicing the clients. In attempting to change this, one has to start from the understanding that practices are just the same as other businesses; there has to be a recognised hierarchy of roles which allows the business owners (the partners) to organise and co-ordinate their activities in such a way that the firm's annual and long-term development aims are successfully met. If this approach is adopted there is every likelihood that the clients' needs will be well serviced and the firm will be profitable (the ideal combination!).

Organisation and management of the practice demands attention to practice structures. Recent developments may have a bearing on how the business is organised in the foreseeable future. It is possible to become an LLP, for example, the consolidators have emerged, and strategic alliances using limited company status are emerging in services such as financial services, IT and consultancy. Operating in a very competitive market place and needing to respond quickly to the pace of change (including what clients demand from their advisers) places even more emphasis on getting the right framework for delivering services and improving profitability. Emphasis on value and building value will (should) allow a clearer perspective on what is best for managing the business.

It is important to re-emphasise that management requires the use of available resources to achieve desired objectives; the role of management is to pull together all resources to achieve identified goals. The professional firm cannot use or pull together resources unless it has a fundamental understanding of its corporate identity, having asked and answered the questions, 'Where are we?', 'Where are we going?' and 'How do we get there?'. Although it is difficult, every partner can answer the questions by identifying the strengths and weaknesses he sees in the organisation, dividing his views between how he sees the other partners (and himself) and how he sees the business and resources.

At the time of writing, the Enron case in the US is a development that affects the way professional firms are run and managed – one that fundamentally impacts the management and structure of the firm. Historically, professional firms were organised as partnerships to give comfort to clients. Partnerships could be relied on to be financially stable because, in case of default, the partners themselves would be entirely liable. But times have changed and the notion of personal liability benefiting clients is now nothing more than an anachronism. Clients have no idea of the financial security provided by the personal assets of the partners. Rather, security for clients is provided by professional indemnity insurance. So what are the other benefits of partnership status to justify the risk of personal liability? The one most frequently cited is that the firm's accounts do not need to be published. A brief reference to the annual Interfirm comparison surveys carried out by the professional trade press will give a pretty accurate breakdown of the take-home pay of the partners in just about any law or accountancy firm worth writing about. Partnership has had its day. Legal and accounting firms and their partners need the security and flexibility that limited liability brings, and to re-examine their operating structure to accommodate them.

16.1.1 Organisation and growth

The organisational structure must be sufficiently flexible for delegation of responsibility. Ultimately, the successful operation and management of the firm depends upon the owners (the partners). The independence of spirit, which ensures that each partner conducts daily activities with the same care as if in business alone, must also be organised and co-ordinate to the needs of the operating plan if the firm is to succeed and grow. Before tackling and changing practice organisation, however, it is advisable to assess 'where are we now' in terms of size and progress. Initially, therefore, we must be clear where we are in the growth cycle. There are several phases of growth commonly acknowledged. The attributes of each are set out in **Table 16.1**.

Table 16.1 Phases of growth

Phase	Principle features
1	– Partner dependent service – New client development predominates – Informal communication – Low overheads, high profits
2	– Managing partner appointed – Standard systems and controls – Service departments – Regular management reporting – Staff hierarchy

	– Formal communication
	– Specialisation
3	– Geographic expansion
	– Executive committee
	– Self accountable divisions/offices
	– Management by exception
	– Growth through acquisition/merger
4	– Centralised support functions
	– Centralised data processing
	– Standardised practice planning
	– One-firm approach
	– One-pot profit sharing
5	– Consensus management
	– 'Team' orientated organisation
	– Project teams of experts
	– Simplified procedures
	– Conferences are the 'glue'

A typical Phase 1 firm is a smaller practice, either a sole practitioner or two or three partners. The distinctive feature is that each partner is involved in servicing all clients, frequently operating as an assignment manager in addition to providing partner-level skills for tax and financial planning. Because of this immediate contact with the client base, there is considerable new-client development activity, and because staffing levels tend to be low there is a predominance of informal communication. Even where there are two or more partners involved there is a tendency to manage the practice without formality. Naturally enough, all this leads to a direct pay-off in terms of profit and partner involvement. That said, the operation of the business must have a definite structure and shape if it is to grow. Most services in the firm are of a general compliance nature (accounts preparation, tax returns, payrolls, management accounts, etc.) and are a volume based activity with fees generally at the lower end of the spectrum. Price pressure is heavily felt. Operating as a collection of sole practitioners who happen to be in partnership is itself a barrier to growth. To generate extra profits and to cope with more business there has to be a 'factory' or production-line approach to work processing.

Problems may arise with success – fee levels, client numbers and staffing levels all increase and the greater the growth in size, the greater the need for more formality in practice management. The pressure of servicing work falls more on to the partners. Control problems surface because staff report to individual partners on all aspects and all types of client and their loyalty tends to vest in the partner, not the firm. Clients require a wider range of skills and services, and one partner is unlikely to be capable of providing these. The informal communication that once was a perceived benefit now becomes a problem because individuals in the firm are unlikely to be fully aware of what is happening elsewhere. Pressure is created, therefore, for more management in terms of structure, common policies and procedures, quality-control methods and an overall sense of direction for the business.

The identification of a plan, imposition of a structure and agreement to overall common policies have to be in place without drawbacks or the need to impose greater levels of bureaucracy. If the problem is ignored, however, the partner is exposed to greater personal, financial and professional risk.

Phase 2 firms are exemplified by growth through leadership, typified by the appointment of a managing partner. His objective is to ensure that the firm's business plan is clearly outlined, is supported by budgets and forecasts, is known to all principal members of the firm and is capable of being applied and monitored on a day-to-day, week-to-week basis. Ideally, the appointment should follow on from, or coincide with, standardised work systems and quality controls, which themselves provide the ongoing benefits of ease of staff training and greater facility for staff to share work. The introduction of stronger management will focus on functional organisation and place more emphasis on service departments for auditing and accounting, accounting services, taxation services and specialised activities. Financial control will be improved by the use of regular financial reports, staff will be given appropriate job titles and be subject to evaluation and review (important hygiene factors) and there will be a greater emphasis on formal meetings, e.g., partners meet once a month with a formal agenda and support papers. The practice development emphasis will be to provide services for existing clients rather than continuously attracting new clients. As a result, profitability levels will be maintained.

If the firm continues to grow, the management administration in place may become too bureaucratic. There is likely to be an escalation in overheads and greater staff turnover (because of the emphasis of maintaining quality standards, maintaining chargeable time targets and job control disciplines). This need not be a problem if a proper sense of perspective is maintained of the firm's growth; the partners must always be in a position to call a halt and redefine the organisation they wish to have in order to go forward. Phases 3, 4 and 5 are an extension of this growth process, but in real terms this is how firms in the top 20 are affected and organise themselves to cope with increased size and client demands.

16.1.2 Organisation and clients

Many partners have an inability to say 'no'. That is, to say 'no' to a prospective client! Partners seem to feel flattered because an individual or business wishes to become a client. What is forgotten in the warm glow of the approach is the overall practice plan and the stated intention to grow through profitable business, rather than through growth for its own sake. Once a critical mass had been reached there is every opportunity for greater selectivity in taking on new businesses, and many firms establish a minimum fee level for different types which can be quoted on the initial interview. Other firms stipulate the business or industries for whom they do not wish to act. The principle is straightforward: the skill of the partner in deciding what is and is not 'quality' business is rather more difficult to identify.

Practices will know from a stratification of the existing client base (the Pareto analysis) where the size and type of work lies in the firm. This can be used to plan the best basis for organisation of the production of the work and how the firm is managed.

Table 16.2 Client Pareto analysis example (12-partner practice, with four offices)

Fee range	No.	%	£'000	%
£0–1,000	3,063	76.2	1,014	29.5
£1,001–2,500	654	16.3	947	27.5
£2,001–5,000	210	5.3	678	19.7
£5,001–10,000	70	1.7	449	13.0
Over £10,001	22	0.5	352	10.3
	4,019	100.0	3,440	100.0

The effort required to service an increasing volume of clients tends to obscure the importance of the qualitative aspects of practicing life. In the typical practice, where the partners are working a 50-hour week:

- the partner may not be aware of the number of clients he acts for;
- the partner may not have a breakdown of the type of work he does or the spread of his fees;
- the partner always answers the telephone and takes all incoming calls;
- the partner tries to see every client (failing to prioritise between the simplest tax return case and the most sophisticated corporate case); and
- the work maintains its own inertia.

The partner may not be aware that the sheer volume of clients involves additional heavy costs where savings might be gained, because there are certain fixed-time costs incurred for every client:

- the client name has to be placed on a control list/database;
- the work needs planning;
- the records need to be requested at least once a year;
- the client will probably need to meet with staff;
- the client believes naturally enough that he is at liberty to telephone at any time about anything (and be dealt with); and
- most clients expect to have a meeting with the partner at least once a year.

The result is continuous pressure. There is more: in addition to time costs, there are overhead costs including the need to process the accounts, a covering letter for every client and tax computations, opening one or more working files and having sufficient space in which to store the files. The message is clear – there must be organisation if there is to be growth, and there must be selectivity and adherence to the practice plan if there is to be profitable growth.

16.1.3 Organisation charts

For the firm to run as a successful business it must, irrespective of size and complexity, determine its present and projected operational structure. This should not be left to chance, individual memory or general understanding but should be put in writing and supported by organisation charts. The underlying secret to success lies in recognising when the individual functions should be delegated or shared and how this helps the partner to distinguish between his positions as a business manager and as an owner.

When preparing the organisation chart there are three steps to observe:

1 set out ownership (partners of the firm);
2 set out who formulates policy. For smaller firms this might be the whole of the partner group. In larger firms a management or executive committee allows flexibility to meet the changing needs of the firm. The established policy and the partners as a group confirm it;
3 set out the firm's management (either a managing partner or a management or executive committee). This leadership role must have clear lines of authority and responsibility and the chief characteristic of the individual(s) selected must be business ability rather than technical ability.

Introduction

Growth imposes an increasing need to delegate responsibility. Delegation should be according to the respective abilities of partners and staff, recognising the differences between those who are more suited technically (hence who should be responsible for technical activities) and those who are more suited to business management. The majority of practices try to ensure that each partner undertakes one or more aspects of practice management, whilst growth leads to a need for further hierarchical changes, in particular where the firm has more than one office; when there is a wide geographical network of offices there will be heavily devolved responsibility.

Figures 16.1–16.4 set out organisation charts for typical practices and differentiate between technical, administration and management areas.

Figure 16.1 Typical Firm A

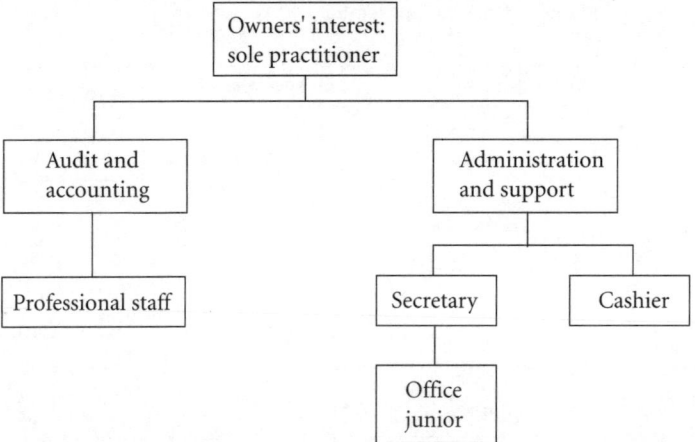

Figure 16.2 Typical firm B

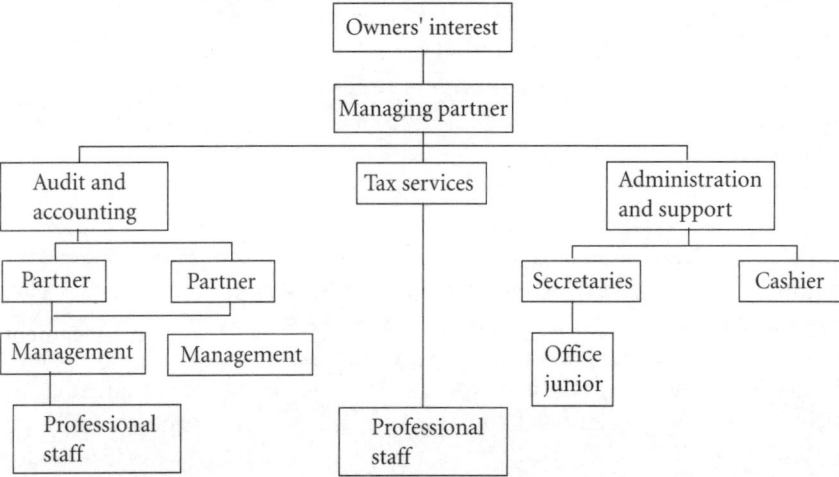

Figure 16.3 Typical firm C

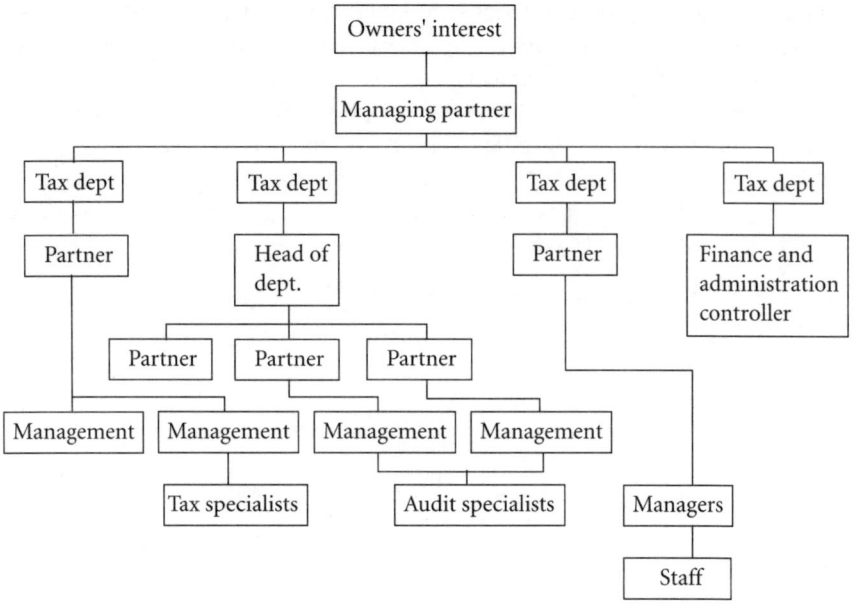

Figure 16.4 Typical firm D

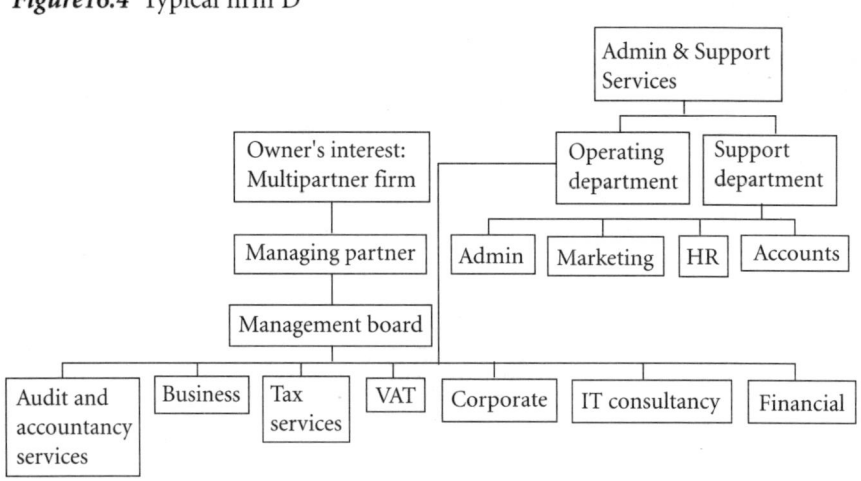

The structural aim must be to produce an optimum level of management and control. The opportunity exists for bringing in specialists who are non-chartered accountants (or professionals) but have the skills required in tax, VAT, corporate finance, etc. For these areas and for these people, the appropriate service line structure could be corporate, not non-corporate. Frequently the sector or service line responsibility may be best based in a corporate body, or could be a strategic alliance in a joint-venture company. Once established this should lead to profit improvement by reducing administration to routine, providing opportunities for effective delegation to the requisite level, improving the effectiveness of the firm's resources, reducing personal work load and pressure, and increasing efficiency. It is surprising how an administration/organisation review leads to improved profitability in most professional firms.

16.1.4 Organisation of operations

The range of services offered by the independent firm will vary but are likely to include some or all of the following:

Core services:

- audit and accountancy;
- accounts preparation;
- management accounts;
- payroll;
- bookkeeping, VAT returns, other bureau services;
- personal tax returns;
- corporate and business tax.

Specialist services:

- tax consultancy;
- VAT consultancy;
- corporate finance;
- M&A;
- corporate recovery;
- personal financial planning;
- financial services.
- Administration including personnel, accounting, time recording, credit control, reception, filing and general duties.
- Management – including practice development, training students, etc.

Core service areas are predominantly compliance based and, almost by definition, are subject to price (fee) constraints. A typical practice will have a lot of this work, very often up to 80 per cent of the work processed falls into this category. The key to ensuring improved profit margins lies in strongly controlling the volume, and utilising appropriate people in the production of the work.

The analogy is with a factory process. The slicker the organisation, the speedier the turn-round and the cheaper the process. So what are the key elements?

- Departmentalising the work.
- Using appropriate software.
- Employing and training staff of the requisite quality and competence for the work.
- Organising the client to produce his records at the time required by the firm.
- Planning the production timetable from receiving the base information to issuing the work and rendering a fee.
- Applying the quality review methodically and central procedures appropriate for the work.
- Constantly delegating the work to the person best suited to perform it.

Departmentalising by splitting work into larger audit and accountancy jobs, incomplete records and small accounts preparation cases, and personal tax allows for control of the department to be concentrated in the hands of the reliable manager. Apart from dealing with their own portfolio, the manager will be (using the factory analogy) the production controller who co-ordinates planning and allocation of work, progress chases, deals with overruns and staffing issues and so on. The partners will filter all work into the department via the manager. Thus each department will be supervised by a senior member of staff. The benefits of this arrangement include the following:

- the supervisory filter assists quality control and job organisation and saves partner time;
- organised production gives cost benefits from improved job control and better client service;
- the partner has more time for planning and overview and client-by-client practice development;
- staff have more of a structure and a career structure to which they can relate.

Systematising the operation leads to improved time utilisation by staff, one of the factors leading to improved profitability. The approach also focuses the partner on his role, releasing valuable time and knowledge for the advisory and development role to which his abilities should be suited, and from which added value fees can be generated. Furthermore, the hierarchy established defines the cost base to which the practitioner must work, and this principle applies the larger the firm becomes and the more partners who are introduced. Partner to staff ratios are extremely important in maintaining practice profitability because of the leverage factor.

Specialist services are the area from which the firm will generate good fees and profits. It is no coincidence that the better-performing practices have at least one (usually more) developed service niche, and the strategy must be to build a more multifaceted firm. Although it would be wrong to say that the days of the general practice are over, nonetheless organising 'the factory' and adding special services is the profitable route to adopt. Typically, the added-value services found are financial services, tax consultancy and corporate finance (an activity which growing SMEs and owner-managed business who form the market for the independent firm increasingly require for business development, succession and retirement issues).

The specialist 'team' may be a partner or a senior member of staff, or may be a mix of partners and senior staff, and other members of the firm will be called on from time to time to help fulfil assignments.

16.1.5 Information technology

In 1981 over 80 per cent of professional practices in the British Isles did not use a computer or word processor. Change over the last 20 years has seen a complete reversal of this statistic, indeed, over 90 per cent of firms how have some form of information technology application in their office. A wide variety of software is available on the market to cover compliance and specialist work. The benefits derived from the use of information technology include standardisation of procedures and presentation, reduction in staff costs and savings in job costs.

16.1.6 Alternative structures

Limited liability partnership is a very recent business vehicle that was introduced following professional pressure to minimise partners' personal liabilities in the event of a professional indemnity claim. In the accountancy profession the first firm to adopt this structure was Ernest & Young, a top four international practice.

Seeking to provide an ideal blend of the 'see-through' tax advantages of partnership with the limitation on personal liability inherent in incorporation,

LLPs were always intended as a hybrid between the two models. The idea is suitable for businesses that might prefer a partnership to a company but do not want all their assets on the line. Under the new scheme you can be actively involved in the business but have liability limited, like shareholders.

The key question is – to what extent are the LLP benefits overshadowed by the complexities and expense of paying professional fees to find a practical way through the legislation to deliver the best of both worlds? In working through the complexities of the legislation in its current form there are some important points that could be all too easily missed by the uninitiated.

First, an LLP structure will not protect individual members from personal liability for their own negligence, even for work done in the LLP's name. Indemnity insurance with run-off cover remains vital for personal security.

Second, be aware of the 'claw back' provisions. LLP members like company directors, may be forced to make repayments if the LLP carried on trading after the members should have known that insolvency was unavoidable.

Third, there is no model constitution for LLPs, unlike ready-made limited companies. In the absence of express wording to the contrary, members fall back on very limited default provisions, which mean sharing profits and losses equally, having equal rights to manage, unanimous approval for membership changes and no right to remuneration. In anything other than a two equal partner deadlock relationship this could be a disastrous position. A 'members' agreement', a private document, should be prepared by a lawyer to cover these and other issues.

The fourth point is that members have no 'shares' in an LLP, but rather an 'interest', subject to obligations, under the members' agreement or the default provisions. Members therefore need to deal with how and when that interest can be transferred and assess the implications in terms of voting and control. This is where value issues can arise, such as buy-backs from members leaving the LLP, and decisions to sell the main business.

There are some tax issues still to be resolved. In addition, as there is no power for an LLP to convert to a limited company: any potential float would require a transfer of the business to a Plc as a first stage. A full cost/benefit analysis would clearly be advisable before a final decision is made, but the discipline of defining objectives in a suitable members' agreement can itself help clarify expectations.

The signs are that LLPs are valuable additions to other business models and there may be substantial benefits for many in the new regime. Flexibility and informality are to be encouraged, but there is still scope for the government to provide some alternative default provisions and to encourage the Inland Revenue not to undermine the new tax regime.

17 The managing partner – how to run a practice

17.1 Leadership

'Leadership is not leading.' Any firm that perceives this statement to be true of their firm will find themselves in difficulty. 'Leadership' is at the basis of managing a successful practice, but what exactly is 'leadership'? Sir John Harvey-Jones is quoted as saying that, 'leadership is encouraging extraordinary performance from ordinary colleagues'. This means the managing partner taking personal responsibility and caring about their staff, coaching them to raise their performance levels so that they take responsibility and really care for the practice's clients, internal customers, other personnel, brand, vision and future.

The managing partner should look at the vision for the firm, i.e., the purpose of the firm, the proposition to the market, reasons why clients stay with the firm to do their business, reasons why colleagues continue to invest their careers in the firm, and the reasons why prospective recruits of both clients and colleagues consider the firm as a part of their future.

On recognising the compelling proposition that the firm has to both internal and external markets, i.e., both for clients and colleagues, the managing partner should share that vision with them. That is, show them how they fit in, how this is important and relevant for them, why they should continue with the firm, why they should join with the firm in playing their part in it. Often, this is referred to as 'getting buy in'. Without it staff will lack the belief and therefore the real commitment that is worth more than the money value of payroll or fees.

So, what has all this to do with managing a professional service practice? Such a practice is about people, i.e., it is a people business, people are employed to provide personal services to other people. If those people do not believe in the firm, they will not buy from it and the firm will have a limited future. The principle remains: leadership first, then management.

17.2 Management

There has, over the years, been a protracted debate about the partnership ethic and views on how this impacts on the management of a professional services firm. Many see this as the partners 'making profit for each other' and this will work with a partnership of a small number of like-minded people (e.g., two or three partners, at a similar stage of their careers, with similar aspirations, in all probability working in a lifestyle business). However, it is less than satisfactory where there is a greater requirement for a more commercial approach to business. For example, where there are a reasonable number of employees investing their careers with the firm, where there area number of clients that the firm wishes to regard as clients of the firm, i.e., rather than clients of a particular partner, or where there is a commercial funding arrangement which depends on decent financial as well as professional performance. In these circumstances how do the partners see that each and every one of the partner group is indeed 'making profit for each other'? This responsibility falls to the managing partner.

In many partnerships, the unsuccessful ones are, by and large, those without a clear definition of roles and responsibilities throughout the partner group. This is true of accountants, solicitors, chartered surveyors, architects, estate agents and many other businesses. What seems to set apart the professional service firm partners, however, is that because, in their own view, the partners are well educated, that entitles each one of them to be involved in the decision making. The result is often indecision at best, and at worst partnership failure, as the firm is overtaken by more incisive and effective competitors.

How, then, should a progressive practice be managed? The partnership should be regarded as, in effect, a corporate entity. The managing partner may decide to formally incorporate the partnership (but this is outside of the scope of this chapter). Indecisive management occurs in limited companies that are effectively 'quasi partnerships' as much as in actual partnerships. The crucial issue is to recognise the separation of management from ownership.

The managing partner should get fellow partners to acknowledge, and agree, that there has to be personal responsibility between the partners, exactly as expected from the employees. It should be agreed which partners have management responsibility for which parts of the firm and how this in actual practice will operate. That is, who reports on what to whom, regardless of title in the organisation. This is all about relevant skills, both hard and soft. It is about playing to people's strengths and avoiding their weaknesses.

In **Chapter 16,** Phil Shohet and Andrew Jenner have set out their thoughts on the structure of a practice. Take their thoughts and adapt them to your own firm's circumstances. Crucially, the managing partner will have the goal of establishing an accepted management structure by: identifying roles and responsibilities; setting out reporting lines; establishing and seeking adherence to reporting deadlines; and seeking to disseminate as fully as possible the details of the performance of the firm to the partners group.

By way of example, many firms, run a corporate governance model which involves the partner group electing a managing partner for a defined term with clearly defined roles and responsibilities. The managing partner, working with a small 'board' of administrators and some other partners, is delegated the job of actually running the firm, and reports to the wider partner group in a formal partners meeting usually quarterly or monthly. This is the partnership equivalent of the corporate management reporting to the shareholders, a model which should be very familiar in the corporate context.

The managing partner will have to design these procedures and set out the respective roles and responsibilities. David H Maister *Managing the Professional Service Firm* is a useful reference on this point.

The 'board' comprises the managing partner, some other partners, as required, and 'administrators'. In a progressive firm 'administrator' includes a director of finance and a director of marketing. Smaller firms should consider outsourcing these tasks to specialist consultants.

The managing partner will have to deal with the inevitable attitude from fellow partners that these specialists helping to run the firm are simply employees and will be reluctant to pay attention to them. As the use of these specialists has been authorised by the managing partner, and the managing partner has been authorised by the partners in full meeting to manage the firm's finances for the best return to the partners in accordance with the firm's business plan, the partners should be expected to follow the lead of the managing partner and respect their specialist colleagues who are doing their best to meet planned performance by the firm.

17.3 Planning

The managing partner may often take the lead with the firm's business plan. Setting out strategy and tactics for the upcoming year, accepting the objectives and the plan, and then delivering on the plan are the main goals. Some of the partners will be very goal focused but some will object to measurable objectives that are actually measured and reported upon. Resistance to establishing measurable objectives should be expected, as should confusion, claims of irrelevance, reference to other measures, or even refusal, when it comes to reporting measured performance.

To avoid this attitude it is realistic to start with the business planning process. The aim should be to get 'buy in' by the partner group to the planning process and, ultimately, to the business plan itself. Participation is the key. For example, the planning process could take place at an annual partners retreat. Preferably, this will take place outside of the office, away from interruptions and distractions (especially client and staff demands). This is the time for working on the firm's most important client – the firm itself.

The firm's performance statistics should have been distributed to the partners throughout the year. However, it is useful to refocus the firm's performance on industry standard benchmarks. These performance benchmarks are available through subscription to the Institute's interfirm comparisons, or through joining an association that focuses on performance comparisons.

Preparations for the partners retreat should include providing the partners with comparisons of actual performance with accepted benchmarks such as:

- production measured as chargeable hours compared with target and industry standard;
- realisation rates achieved by billed production;
- lock-up as expressed in days sales for both work in progress (WIP) and debtors; production achieved as a multiple of direct labour salaries (including a notional salary for partners) both in terms of overall totals, and in terms of individual staff and partner personal performance;
- net profit available to the equity partners expressed as a percentage of billings; partner to staff gearing ratio; balance sheet financial gearing;
- drawings compared with profits; cash flow requirements and from where sourced including Schedule D tax payments, etc.

The partners could do some 'homework' before the retreat. For example, each participant could be asked to produce a SWOT analysis of the firm and its performance from their own viewpoint, in particular with regard to the area of the firm that they have responsibility for. David Maister has a 'Fast Track Strategy' described in his book *Managing the Professional Service Firm*. This can be used as a way of focusing attention on how to improve or develop existing parts of the firm. Delegates set out SMART (specific, measurable, agreed, realistic, timed) goals based on the information that has been provided by the managing partner, and based on the knowledge that each delegate has of the firm. This will form the basis of excellent debate. Careful facilitation of the process will ensure agreement to goals set in this forum and, consequently, 'buy in' to the resulting plan. An outsourced facilitator can be engaged to undertake this task if preferred. As always with consultants, a full briefing is essential.

The involvement of the partner group in the planning process, and paying due attention to the thoughts and ideas of the partners will, with careful facilitation, produce a powerful outcome. Remember the quotation attributed to Sir John Harvey-Jones at **17.1** above.

17.4 Coaching

Once the plan has been produced and the partners have 'bought in' to, the next stage of the process is to achieve the results set out in the plan. Some partners will automatically get on with the tasks in hand, others will lose focus to varying degrees and get distracted by other more immediate problems. The secret to refocusing on agreed goals, praising achievements and encouraging extra effort is coaching based on open questions. This is totally different from the audit based training on man-management that has been encouraged by the accounting profession in the past. It is not about telling someone what to do, it is about asking open questions with patience so that the partner concludes what the action is that should be taken by them personally. This helps to build up the 'buy-in' and commitment of the partner concerned.

A coaching programme should be set out for all partners reporting to the managing partner. For those with a substantial challenge it will be more frequent than for those who are taking matters more in their stride. This helps the managing partner to establish if there is any difficulty and helps him to keep up with progress on the plan before too much time elapses and recovery to planned performance becomes more difficult. Be sure to keep it up. It is important to remember that every point of interaction with a colleague can be a coaching moment. The managing partner can also benefit from coaching and many coaching organisations are now commercially available to help with this if required.

17.5 Anticipation

This is an entrepreneurial age. Everyone is expected to be an entrepreneur, even if it is not a natural persuasion, and the managing partner is no exception to this. The managing partner, as practice leader, will need to get the recognition of colleagues and this will largely depend on his ability to anticipate the decisions that will be required to take the firm forward.

Every business has a life cycle. Within the business, the constituent elements all have their own life cycles. The freshness and vigour that the firm brings to its internal and external market places is related to the stage of the life cycle that the firm is actually at. The secret is to anticipate the life cycle and to keep the firm fresh. The difference between a rising firm and a declining firm is one of timing and anticipation of decisions that are inevitable. Decisions that are taken too early, usually, will be more effective than decisions that are taken too late. Timing is all, yet very few entrepreneurs get the timing exactly right. When, with hindsight, they have done so, it is often, to a great degree, down to luck rather than fine judgement.

So, what does this mean for the managing partner of the professional services firm? The firm's service offerings should be reviewed critically, e.g.,

- How do these compare with the best of the competition?
- How do they compare with offerings in the US, or in Australia?
- What is the future of the markets that the firm is serving?
- Are your clients in growing or shrinking industries?
- Are the services that the firm is offering likely to be replaced by clients becoming more self sufficient and reducing their 'take' from the firm?

The firm's knowledge base should also be reviewed critically.

- Who are the firm's rising stars?
- What knowledge do they have that the firm is not using?
- How far is the human knowledge resource invested in skills relevant to a shrinking market?
- Are too many of the firm's staff, for example, auditors with no knowledge of management problems faced by entrepreneurial clients?

It is no accident that rising stars employed in UK commercial banks are encouraged to study for MBA qualifications at leading university business schools.

Anticipation, therefore, is about timing the decision to change something. The goal is to keep the the firm fresh and attractive by making decisions early.

17.6 Culture

The difference between performance in firms often comes down to culture. The managing partner is highly influential in what form the culture of the firm actually takes. The culture will be there, whether or not any steps are taken to change it, but is it the desired culture? The saying, 'Birds of a feather stick together' is true of professional service firms as for most other types of business. If the firm gives the impression of being tired, unimaginative, old fashioned (traditional), then it will attract personnel who like that image and clients will be attracted that feel comfortable with that approach. However, crucially, the 'go ahead' ambitious recruit who will be the future of the firm, is unlikely to be attracted to the business. The firm is also unlikely to attract the ambitious client in an emerging industry who will be the source of increasing volumes of work and be part of the form's future prosperity.

To avoid this scenario, the managing partner should share his vision of the firm with the partners. It is important to discuss (individually and in a group) what part each has to play in the future of the firm. Most people want to be excited by their work and by their business. It is all about a sense of self belief and self worth. Anticipating the decisions that inevitably will be required and sharing that vision with the partners will make a difference to their perception of the firm.

17.7 Approach to the markets

Why markets plural? The managing partner will be thinking about the markets for prospective clients; existing clients; prospective employees and partners; existing employees and partners; referral sources; and influencers in the business community, who may not directly refer work to the firm, but may be a supportive (or unsupportive) reference point for the firm's prospects.

Specialists in marketing and human resources should be used by the firm to ensure that it is taking the appropriate approach to these markets. So often there is little to distinguish one professional service firm from another. The consequence of this is that buying or investment decisions by your markets will be made on the only discernible difference that your audience can perceive... pricing. For most professional service firms, there is no future in trading on price, i.e., paying the highest salaries, yet charging the lowest fees.

What is your firm's compelling proposition to the market and why would anyone want to spend or invest with you? Some of this will be to do with services and specialisms, some to do with industry experience, some to do with existing personnel and clients, a huge amount will be related to culture and perceived market positioning (which your marketing consultant will advise you is a function of brand awareness. However, there has to be something behind the brand, and that is the culture, as discussed at **17.6** above.

The managing partner's role in this is as follows:

- briefing and managing the consultants;
- having the vision and sharing it with partners, colleagues, referrers, and clients;
- coaching colleagues to help them be more effective in the context of the vision for the firm;
- providing feedback to the team on successes and areas still to be fully developed.

Crucially, in all of this, experts with specialist knowledge should be consulted.

17.8 Partner rewards

Deciding on partner rewards is the most difficult of all tasks that the managing partner is responsible for seeing through. There are many excellent publications on this subject which can provide detailed descriptions of different partner-reward structures suitable for different types of firm, and these should be studied.

The approach taken to manage a small three or four partner firm will be different to that taken when managing a larger firm of, say, 10 to 20 partners. In both cases, however, the goal will be the same, i.e., to see that the firm has an agreed reward structure for partners that is: dependable; regarded as fair and reasonable by the participants; highly visible to the partners; likely to promote behaviour that is congruent with the firm's goals; and has some longevity to its basic design.

In the larger firm, the managing partner is likely to get the best result where the partner group delegates the responsibility to a remuneration committee chaired by the managing partner. In a smaller firm, the remuneration committee is likely to be the entire partner group, again chaired by the managing partner.

The reward structure decided upon by the firm will be much to do with the firm's culture. Some firms, for example, are resolute that partners are all equal and share equally. Some firms take a 'corporate' view where ownership is unequal, often based on buying an investment in the firm, where partners' rewards are separated into rewards for work done, and returns on investment. Some firms take the view that partners are not equal and should therefore receive rewards of different amounts due to different characteristics.

A preferred reward structure would perhaps be the appropriation of profit to take account of:

- 'salary' at a sensible level, so that the partner can deal with household budgeting and against which regular drawings are made;
- interest on capital invested in the firm's capital accounts either by direct injection or by retained profits;
- and a return for ownership to reflect the reward for commercial financial risk.

17.9 Ownership

Old-fashioned views on ownership of professional service firms range from 'come in naked and go out naked' to a partner based ownership geared to a valuation of the firm and payment by annuity or salary sacrifice.

Views have changed significantly in view of the experiences of the 'consolidators' in the US and the UK. Increasingly the view is that the firm should be regarded as a 'corporate' (whatever the legal structure) with ownership and valuation in the corporate way.

The goal of the managing partner is to see that partners have a direct interest in building the commercial viability and therefore the future of the firm. What better way to do this than to engage the partners in ownership and therefore participation in growing the commercial asset in which they have a clearly defined share?

These matters can be properly defined in the partnership agreement, or shareholders' agreement if the firm is corporate. The managing partner will probably need to seek help from the remuneration committee when looking at the 'who and when' of ownership transfers.

17.10 Valuation

Traditional methods of valuation have been variations of the multiple of 'gross recurring fees' (GRF) philosophy. A more realistic approach to the valuation of a modern professional services firm means a move away from the multiple of GRF and a move towards a capitalisation of earnings based on profits after deducting a sensible amount for equity partners' salaries.

There are clear benefits of the earnings approach. For example, the multiple of GRF pays no attention to:

- the quality of the personnel;
- the intellectual property in the firm, including established systems and IT;
- the quality of the clients and what they spend with the firm in a non-recurring way;
- the move away from compliance fees;
- the market positioning of the firm, and its branding; and
- crucially, the profitability and therefore the affordability of the firm from a buyer's point of view.

All of these matters can be better covered in the earnings approach. Furthermore, the earnings approach is more widely understood, not only by buyer and seller, but also by the buyer's bank manager if a fund-raising exercise is called for.

The managing partner will have either inherited an earnings based methodology, or will have to introduce one (unless of course the managing partner is simply buying or selling a block of fees that is no longer required, rather than buying into or selling out of a firm as a going concern).

As with other matters to do with the financial affairs of your partners, the challenge as managing partner is to achieve fairness, visibility and, in this case, a result that shows a good return for the exiting partner and an affordable economic investment for the acquiring partner.

17.11 Succession

The goal, as managing partner, is to secure longevity for the firm for the benefit of its stakeholders. These are the partners, colleagues, clients and suppliers. This will be achieved by a succession policy which can be assured by:

- the firm's vision and culture making it an attractive place in which up and coming employees, prospective employees and partners will be willing to invest their careers;
- the firm's compelling proposition to the market attracting good-quality clients that can be properly serviced;
- the firm's freedom from damaging partner disputes due to the clarity of its partnership agreement dealing with profit-sharing arrangements, and ownership transfers and therefore being goal focused on a clear vision for the future;
- the firm's clear leadership by the managing partner.

18 Taxation aspects of succession and retirement

18.1 Introduction

When contemplating succession, the main taxes that need to be considered are income tax and capital gains tax (CGT). Whilst retiring partners also need to be fully conversant with these provisions and how they are affected by them, they will also need to address pension provision and how to generate an income following retirement as a partner.

Partnership mergers should be addressed in their own right.

18.2 Income tax aspects of retirement/introduction of a partner

In the first instance, new or retiring partners need to understand the mechanics of how partnership profits are taxed.

18.2.1 The current-year basis of assessment

Partners are liable to income tax and Class II and Class IV National Insurance Contributions (NICs) on their share of the partnership income of the accounting period ending in the tax year. Existing partners in a partnership with, say, a 30 April year end would be liable to income tax in 2004/05 on their profit share for the year ending 30 April 2004. If the partnership had a 31 March year end, the taxable income for 2004/05 would be based on the accounts for the year ending 31 March 2005.

Special rules apply in the first, second and final years of appointment or when there is no 12-month period ending in the particular tax year.

The first year of assessment is the profits, apportioned on a daily basis, from the starting date to the next 5 April, and the second year is either the 12 months to the accounting date ending in the tax year following starting; or where there is no such date, the first 12 months of trading.

A partner appointed on 1 May 2003 to a partnership with a 30 April year end would be liable to tax on the profit share as follows:

- 2003/04: 340/365 profits for the year ending 30 April 2004;
- 2004/05: profit share for the year ending 30 April 2004;
- 2005/06: profit share for the year ending 30 April 2005.

It is clear to see that 340/365 of the profits for the year ending 30 April 2004 would be taxed twice. These profits are called 'overlap profits' and the period in which they arise is referred to as the overlap period. These overlap profits are available to reduce the partner's taxable income on retirement (or a change of accounting date/cessation of the business, if earlier). The overlap profits are not indexed-linked and, with the efflux of time, their value reduces simply due to the time value of money.

Incoming partners need to recognise that certain profits may be taxed twice and, if the partnership does not itself reserve for the partners' tax liabilities, the incoming partners must provide for a tax/NIC liability on 31 January following the end of the tax year in which they were appointed to partnership. In the above example this would be 31 January 2005. This is especially the case for those partners who were not previously self-employed or within the income tax payments-on-account cycle because, on their first 31 January payment date, they will be settling the whole of their liability for the previous tax year and also making their first payment on account for the current tax year.

Continuing with the above example, the incoming partner's first income tax/NIC payment would fall due on 31 January 2005.

Table 18.1 Income Tax/NIC calculation

	£
Balance of income tax/NIC due for 2003/04 (plus CGT, if any)	30,000
First payment on account of income tax/NIC for 2004/05*	15,000
Total due 31 January 2005	45,000

* being one half of the preceding year's income tax/NIC liability.

Continuing with the example, if the partner retired on, say, 30 April 2020, he would be liable to tax on his profit share as follows:

- 2019/20: profit share for the year ended 30 April 2019
- 2020/21: profit share for the year ended 30 April 2020
  less: 340/365 profits for the year ended 30 April 2004 (i.e., the overlap profit)*

* assuming no change of accounting date

New partners who have not previously been self-employed must notify that they have commenced self-employment. Failure to do so within three months of the end of the calendar month of commencement renders the partner liable to a penalty, currently up to £100.

18.2.2 Withdrawal of cash basis for professions

With effect from 2000/01, professional partnerships need to report their taxable profits on an earnings basis, using a 'true and fair' basis for calculating those profits. In order to ensure that the opening position for 2000/01 was correct, the additional income which arose on a true and fair basis for the accounts ending in the 1999/2000 tax year had to be calculated.

This calculation on a true and fair basis for 1999/2000 involved including closing work in progress, debtors, etc., in calculating the taxable profits, which inevitably led to additional income becoming taxable compared to calculations on the historic basis. This additional income is commonly referred to as the 'catch up' charge. This catch up charge is taxed over a period of up to 10 years and, in the majority of cases, it related solely to work in progress that had not previously been recognised.

In essence, the additional profits calculated on a true and fair basis is automatically spread over 10 years of assessment, starting in 1999/2000. The maximum amount of the charge assessed each tax year is shown below:

- one tenth of the adjustment charge; and
- one tenth of Schedule D Case II profits of the business before deducting capital allowances or adding any balancing charges.

In the tenth year of assessment the balance of the catch up charge becomes taxable in full.

If the partnership accounting period started on 6 April 1999, the change from the cash basis would have been made on 6 April 2000, in which case the catch up charge arose in 2000/01 and not 1999/2000. The catch up charge for each tax year is calculated at the partnership level and is then allocated between partners in the profit-sharing ratio.

The catch up charge is liable to tax under Schedule D Case VI and will count as net relevant earnings for pension purposes but, under current legislation, does not give rise to a Class IV NIC charge.

For a partnership which has an accounting period of 12 months ending on the same accounting date each year, the catch up charge is allocated in the profit sharing ratio of the accounting period ending in the tax year, provided that the partnership has not elected to accelerate the catch up charge. Partners who retire within the 10-year period will therefore only have part of the catch up charge assessed via their self assessment tax returns. Partners who join during the 10-year period will pick up a share of the adjustment charge going forward despite the fact that they were not partners when the catch up charge arose.

In essence, incoming and outgoing partners need to recognise that the true and fair basis means that income associated with the catch up charge has been recognised in the partnership accounts, but the tax liability associated with the introduction of that income has been deferred over a period.

Once a partnership has moved to a true and fair view basis, it has until the 31 January after the tax year end to make an election to accelerate the tax charge if so desired. This might be desired, for example, on a retirement. If such an election is to be valid, the signature of each partner who shares in the catch up charge is required.

The partnership will also need to decide when to distribute the extra assessed income. Unless a partnership reduces the time between the work done and receipt of cash, the additional income recognised in the accounts will not be matched with additional cash to distribute. Distributions will need to be monitored and it is possible to match the distribution with the tax payment period or to distribute only when partners retire.

A great deal will depend upon the accounting policy for the catch up charge that the partnership has adopted but, to maintain equity, those who share in the income should also bear the tax on that income. The most common way of dealing with this, when the work in progress was first introduced into the partnership accounts, was to allocate the appropriate amount of additional income to the partners' capital accounts or a non-distributable capital reserve. The amount credited, after reserving for tax on the catch up charge, would then be applied to meet the tax on the catch up charge as it fell due over the 10 years of collection.

The partnership deed should have been amended to reflect this change in position and, if the above accounting policy was adopted, only the net amount would be repaid to the retiring partner.

If the partnership pays annuities or provides consultancies to former partners, the partnership may wish to reduce the quantum of the annuities/consultancies (or any form of termination payment) by the amount of extra profits allocated on the change in basis.

Whatever is finally agreed, it is important that it is recorded in the partnership agreement.

18.2.3 Work-in-progress valuation

The main principle of the partnership accounts is that they should seek to match the recognition of costs with related revenues. Work in progress will be valued at the lower of cost or its value and, in determining the appropriate amounts to recognise in the accounts, the normal accounting principles of materiality, etc., are relevant. As Schedule D time costs are not charged in the profit and loss account, such costs will not be included in the valuation of work in progress and the retiring partner may need to seek an adjustment to reflect the underlying work in progress as part of the exit from the business.

18.3 Provision for retirement

Partners, with the exception of salaried partners, cannot participate in occupational pension schemes established for staff. The primary means of providing for retirement is the making of personal pension contributions; the two other most common methods by which partnerships provide an income stream for ex-partners are by:

- the payment of annuities; or
- consultancy or employment contracts post retirement.

18.3.1 Pension provision

The non-salaried partner can contribute a portion of net relevant earnings for each tax year in the form of a contribution to a retirement annuity contract or, post 30 June 1988, in the form of a contribution to a personal pension scheme. Any qualifying premium paid is deducted from the taxable profits of the partner for that year.

The position for personal pension schemes will be addressed but not that for retirement annuity contracts in view of the fact that it is only long-standing contributors to such policies that are eligible for tax relief.

The maximum contribution that a partner may make to a personal pension scheme for any year is based upon the partner's net relevant earnings, to which the appropriate percentage is applied (by reference to the age of the partner at the beginning of the tax year). This percentage is applied to the lower of the partner's net relevant earnings and the earnings cap.

The earnings cap was introduced in 1989/90 and the cap for recent years has been detailed below:

- 2000/2001   £91,800
- 2001/2002   £95,400

With effect from 6 April 2001 all contributions to personal pension schemes are made net of basic rate income tax. The pension provider recovers the basic rate income tax direct from the Inland Revenue and higher rate tax relief is, if appropriate, claimed on the partner's individual self-assessment.

In addition since 2001/02 individuals have been able to elect to nominate any of the previous five tax years as their 'basis' year, and it is the elected basis year's net relevant earnings that determines the maximum contribution payable as opposed to the actual year's relevant earnings.

As mentioned above, the contributions which a partner can make into a personal pension scheme are based on the partner's age at the start of the tax year and **Table 18.2** shows the percentage that should be applied to either the net relevant earnings of the year in question or the basis year (if so elected) or, if lower, the earnings cap:

Table 18.2 Pension contributions

Age	Percentage
Less than 36	17.5%
36–45	20%
46–50	25%
51–55	30%
56–60	35%
61–74	40%

The historic basis whereby a partner could pay a pension premium in one tax year and, at a later date, elect for the premium to be offset against net relevant earnings for the preceding tax year (together with any unused pension relief for the preceding six years) has now been abolished.

Currently, partners may only carry back those pension contributions that are paid by 31 January following the end of the tax year to utilise unused relief for the preceding year only. If a partner wishes to carry back pension contributions it is necessary to elect, at the time (or before) the contribution is being made, that the contribution is to be carried back. It is not possible to make an election retrospectively.

For new partners, the pension provider will need some contemporaneous evidence as to the level of the partner's earnings where the contribution being paid exceeds £3,600 (gross).

There a number of requirements in relation to the funds within the personal pension scheme, including that the funds must be used to purchase an annuity which:

- should commence by the age of 75; and
- cannot commence before the age of 50 unless the partner is incapable of carrying on his occupation by reason of infirmity, or early retirement is customary in the particular partner's occupation.

The funds provided may be used, in part, to pay a lump sum to the retiring partner at the time a pension is first payable, and the partner consequently draws a reduced annuity. The lump sum itself cannot exceed 25 per cent of the total value of the funds available from the personal pension scheme.

There are a number of conditions that apply in the event that a separate annuity is to be paid to the surviving spouse or dependant, but these are outside the scope of this chapter.

The low annuity rates that may be available at the time when the annuity is to be purchased has received much press coverage together with the fact that, currently, an annuity has to be purchased by age 75. The member can enter into an income withdrawal arrangement until aged 75 provided that the scheme rules permit this and appropriate Inland Revenue approval has been obtained.

A tax-free lump sum, if to be taken, has to be taken at the time that income withdrawal starts and not when the annuity is purchased. Income withdrawal merely delays the requirement to actually purchase the annuity. The balance in the pension scheme fund is used as a basis for determining what minimum and maximum withdrawal figures can be taken without purchasing an annuity, which is an actuarial calculation and issued in tables published by the Government Actuary Department. The minimum and maximum figures remain in place for a triennial cycle after which revised figures have to be calculated. The income withdrawal may vary from year to year as circumstances dictate and can continue up until the date an annuity is purchased, which currently must be prior to the member's 75th birthday.

The income withdrawals are liable to income tax under Schedule E as earned income, with the insurance company deducting income tax under PAYE.

In the event that a member dies during income withdrawal, there are a number of options available and these depend upon the origin of the funds and the status of the spouse/dependants. This is a complex area and qualified independent professional advice should be sought.

18.3.2 Annuities to retired partners

It is often the situation that a partnership agreement provides for the payment of an annuity by the continuing partners to retired partners. Such an annuity would be paid under deduction of basic rate income tax.

The annuity is treated as earned income for the former partner provided that:

- the outgoing partner has retired due to age or ill health or on death;
- the annuity is payable under a partnership agreement, supplementary partnership agreement or under an agreement with an individual who acquires the whole or part of the partnership business;
- the annuity is paid to the outgoing partner, his widow or dependants; and
- the sum payable is less than one half of the average of the former partner's share of the best three of the last seven years' taxable profits (when substantially the whole of the partner's time was devoted to the partnership business).

Such annuities are sometimes paid instead of purchasing goodwill. Caution should be advocated in associating an annuity with goodwill in the partnership agreement as CGT may become payable. This will not be the case provided the annuity is no more than reasonable recognition of past work and effort by that partner.

18.3.3 Consultancy arrangement

If a partner retires and enters into a consultancy arrangement with the partnership, it will be necessary to ensure that the payments are commensurate with the service provided to ensure that the payments are tax deductible, having been incurred wholly and exclusively for the purpose of the trade.

The service provided under the consultancy agreement may be written or oral advice, or attendance at meetings with the partners, staff, clients or suppliers. The key point is that some service should be provided to meet the trade deduction test.

The nature of any consultancy arrangement would need to be examined to determine the employment status of the former partner, in line with general principles. Whether such a payment is taxable under Schedule D or E would have PAYE, NIC and VAT consequences.

In the event that a consultancy arrangement is being entered into then it would be appropriate to reclassify a partner, on stationery, etc., as a consultant as opposed to a partner.

18.4 Capital gains tax (CGT)

18.4.1 The basics

The legislation for the taxation of capital gains of partnerships has evolved via a number of statements of practice and these provide a useful basis for assessing partners for capital gains, albeit that it should be noted that the statements of practice are not statutory and do not therefore carry the force of the law.

The Taxation of Chargeable Gains Act 1992 does not allow for the possibility of a gain or a loss being made by the partnership. Instead, each partner is regarded as owning a fractional share of each partnership asset. Individual partners must therefore compute their own gains or losses by reference to their partnership interest in assets and, once calculated, these are aggregated with the personal gains and losses of that partner and reported on the partner's own tax return.

The partnership tax return merely requires the partnership to provide details of each partner's share of the disposal proceeds of partnership assets, whilst the detailed CGT calculation should be reported on the individual partners' returns.

In determining partners' capital gains it is the partnership capital-sharing ratio that is relevant, which is normally the same as the income sharing ratio. If the ratio is different then this will usually be specified in the partnership agreement.

Most adjustments to capital entitlements in a partnership involving partners are on a no gain/no loss basis and there are four main occasions when a CGT charge may arise on a partner in relation to partnership assets:

- the disposal of a partnership asset;
- when a partner leaves the partnership;

- when a partner's share in a partnership asset that has been revalued in the accounts decreases (e.g., on the admission of a new partner); and
- the distribution, in specie, of a partnership asset.

18.4.2 Taper relief

Taper relief from CGT was introduced in 1998. This relief exempts a proportion of the capital gain that is chargeable to CGT, according to the number of complete years of ownership, or from 6 April 1998, if later.

There are two rates of taper relief: a more generous business rate of taper is available in respect of business assets with a less generous rate available in respect of non-business assets. There is guidance published by the Inland Revenue as to what constitutes a business asset but, in relation to unincorporated businesses, essentially it is an asset used wholly for the purposes of a trading activity.

18.4.3 Disposal of a partnership asset

When a partnership asset is disposed of, partners will have disposed of their fractional interest in that asset for their (fractional) share of the disposal proceeds.

The position is best illustrated by an example.

Example 18.1 Disposal of a partnership asset

A and B commenced trading in partnership in April 2001, with A introducing £50,000 of capital and B introducing £25,000 of capital. It was, however, agreed that they would share capital profits and losses equally, notwithstanding having an income profit-sharing ratio of 2:1.

The partnership subsequently purchased premises for use in the trade at a cost of £60,000 and goodwill for £10,000.

The respective base costs of the two chargeable assets are as follows.

	A £	B £
Premises	30,000	30,000
Goodwill	5,000	5,000

The fact that A contributed more capital than B is academic, it is the capital-sharing ratio that is relevant.

Capital gains tax (CGT)

> In April 2005 the partners dispose of the property, that has always been used wholly for trading purposes, for £150,000.
>
> The CGT calculations would be as follows:
>
> | | A | B |
> |---|---|---|
> | | £ | £ |
> | Proceeds | 75,000 | 75,000 |
> | Cost | (30,000) | (30,000) |
> | Gain | 45,000 | 45,000 |
> | Taper relief* | (33,750) | (33,750) |
> | Chargeable gain | 11,250 | 11,250 |
>
> * Maximum rate of business asset taper relief available
>
> It may be possible to roll over this gain.

18.4.4 Retirement and goodwill

When a partner retires there is a connected persons transaction between the partners. It follows that the Inland Revenue have the power to substitute market value where an asset is acquired otherwise than by way of a bargain at arm's length, or for a consideration which cannot be valued.

In practice the Inland Revenue tend not to invoke the connected persons rules unless the partners are connected other than as partners (for example father and son), and a transaction between partners will not normally be attacked on the grounds that the transaction is not at arm's length unless family members are involved. If, therefore, there is a transaction in relation to a bonafide partnership arrangement, the Inland Revenue accept that they will not seek to invoke the market value rule.

It is common for the partnership accounts not to include goodwill, but on retirement, the retired partner may receive a sum for goodwill. The partnership deed may specify the position re goodwill (for example, two times the average annual profits over the last three years), but if no mention is made then there will be no goodwill payable on retirement.

Where goodwill is payable to a retiring partner, a CGT computation will be required and, for the purposes of calculating the gain (or loss), it would be necessary to trace the capial gains base cost, taking into account partnership changes in capital-sharing ratios throughout the partner's time with the business.

The availability of business asset taper relief may make a capital sum attractive to a retiring partner but the remaining partners are more likely to wish to put an annuity/consultancy in place such that tax relief could be obtained for the amounts paid to the retired partner.

18.4.5 Payments for goodwill by incoming partner

Any payments made directly between partners outside the framework of the partnership accounts are treated as acquisitions and disposals in the normal way. Therefore, if an incoming partner in return for an interest in the goodwill pays a partner £20,000, the first partner would have a capital gain based on the difference between the £20,000 received and the appropriate part of the original cost (or market value as appropriate).

18.4.6 Change in the capital-sharing ratio

A partner who reduces/surrenders a share in an asset surplus is treated as making a CGT disposal, whilst an incoming partner or one who increases their fractional interest will be treated as making a similar acquisition.

Incoming partners to partnerships where there are partnership assets held since 31 March 1982 will still benefit from rebasing, notwithstanding that their interest in the assets arose post 31 March 1982.

If C was introduced to the partnership on 1 May 2003 and the capital-sharing ratio became 40:40:20, both A and B will be deemed to have disposed of a 10 per cent interest, but these are no gain/no loss disposals.

Whilst a revaluation of partnership assets would not crystallise a CGT charge per se, a subsequent alteration in the capital-sharing ratio may well do so, notwithstanding that no cash actually changes hands.

Example 18.2 Property revaluation

For example, D and E are equal partners and acquired a property for £80,000. The property was revalued in later accounts to £150,000. F is introduced as an equal partner, introducing his own capital into the partnership.

D and E are deemed to have each disposed of a one-sixth interest (50 per cent less 33.33 per cent) in the partnership property on the date of F's introduction as a partner.

		£
Property value pre introduction	(150,000 × 50%)	75,000
Value post introduction	(150,000 × 33.33%)	(50,000)

Deemed proceeds	25,000
Attributable cost of interest disposed (say [50%–33.33%] × 40,000)	(13,000)
Capital gain (pre taper and indexation)	12,000

The respective base costs carried forward of D and E are £27,000 (80,000/2 – 13,000), whilst F's base cost would be £50,000.

If, in **Example 18.2**, prior to admission of F, the value of the property in the original accounts was reduced, such that there would be no revaluation surplus in the accounts, then the capital gains charge could be avoided. This could be achieved by the partners agreeing to share any profit on the sale of the asset in the old capital-sharing ratio up to its value at the date of the partnership change, with any further increase in the value being divided in the new capital-sharing ratio. The final outcome would be that CGT could be avoided.

18.4.7 Distribution of assets in specie

If partnership assets are distributed in specie to a partner, the partner receiving the asset will not be deemed to have made a CGT disposal. CGT computations will, however, be required in respect of the disposal of the other partners' fractional shares in the asset.

If the property referred to in **Example 18.1** above had been transferred to A in part satisfaction of his capital account, B would have an identical CGT computation to that above but the cost for CGT purposes for A would be calculated as follows:

Table 18.3 CGT computation

	£
Market value	150,000
Gain not charged	(45,000)
CGT base cost	105,000

18.5 Inheritance tax

A partner in a professional business will, under current legislation, be able to utilise Business Property Relief ('BPR') to exempt his share in the business from inheritance tax. Following retirement, a partner whose estate may have previously been totally covered by BPR and other exemptions could well have a fully chargeable estate due to the loss of BPR.

In view of the difficulties surrounding inheritance tax and BPR, it is not uncommon in family partnerships for elderly partners to reduce activities but still remain as partners in the partnership. This should not only protect the availability of BPR but also retain eligibility for CGT roll-over relief.

Where an estate is sufficiently large to allow assets which qualify for BPR to pass down to the next generation, without depriving the surviving spouse of sufficient funds, then inheritance tax efficiency can be achieved by ensuring that assets qualifying for BPR do not form part of an exempt residue.

18.6 Value Added Tax (VAT)

It is important when partners retire and take no active role in the business that the partnership stationery and other material is amended appropriately and Customs and Excise are notified, on form VAT 2, that the membership of the partnership has changed. Similarly, form VAT 2 should be filed with Customs and Excise notifying of any new partner appointments. Form VAT 2 should be filed within 30 days of appointment/retirement.

The point to note is that the incoming partners will only be responsible for VAT liabilities incurred after the date of their appointment, and retiring partners will no longer be responsible for VAT liabilities arising after the date on which Customs were notified of their retirement.

18.7 Partnership mergers

A partnership merger provides a serious alternative to the introduction of new partners and is a way of consolidating and expanding the business by allowing the trade to continue and grow.

The change to the 'true and fair' basis for 2000/01 et seq. should have solved the majority of practical problems of differing accounting treatment for work in progress and debtors. The partners do, however, still need to address the income tax and CGT implications of the merger, the effect on the individual partners' income tax position as well as the VAT position.

18.7.1 Income tax

The income tax position of partners in relation to a merger is governed by SP9/86. There are three possible scenarios in the merger of partnership A and B:

- both partnership businesses cease;
- the partnership business of one of the parties ceases whilst the other continues; or
- both partnership businesses continue in the merged firm.

It will largely be a question of fact whether or not the same type of businesses are being carried on and, if one or both of A and B are deemed to cease at the date of the merger, the profits from the old partnership will be charged from the first day of the current accounting period, with the partners' overlap relief crystallising. The partners' shares of the merged firm will, in such circumstances, be taxable as the new partner rules as described above.

If one or both businesses are deemed to continue, the partners will not be treated as having a new source of income and the partners' share of profits for the old and merged firm for the accounting period ending in the tax year will be taxable. Where non coterminus year ends are involved, a measure of overlap relief would be available.

Example 18.3 Taxing income

Partnerships A and B merge on 1 October 2005, with business A ceasing and business B continuing. Both partnerships have two partners, sharing profits equally, with each partner's profits for the year to 30 April 2005 being £80,000 and £40,000 for the period from 1 May 2005 to the date of the merger. The partners in A both have overlap relief of £60,000 and their share of profits in the merged firm in the period from 1 October 2005 to 30 September 2006 is £120,000.

Taxable income	2005/06	2006/07
	£	£
Profits from A		
12 months to 30 April 2005	80,000	
5 months to 30 September 2005	40,000	
Overlap relief	(60,000)	
Profits from AB	60,000	
6/12 of year ending 30 September 2006	60,000	
Year ending 30/9/06		120,000
	120,000	120,000

If partnership A were treated as not ceasing, the position would be as follows:		
Taxable income	2005/06	2006/07
	£	£
Profits from A		
12 months to 30 April 2005	80,000	
5 months to 30 September 2005		40,000
Profits from AB		
12 months to 30 September 2006		120,000
less overlap relief (5/11 of £60,000)		(27,273)
	80,000	137,727

18.7.2 CGT

The CGT implications of mergers are covered by the Statement of Practice D12 which states that when the members of two or more existing partnerships come together to form a new one, the CGT treatment will follow the same rules as for changes in capital-sharing ratios for existing partnerships.

Each partner in each firm will, in practice, exchange a part of the interest in the original firm for an interest in the new, combined, firm.

If four, equal capital-sharing partners in firm A merge with firm B, which has two equal capital sharing partners, then the partners in firm A (assuming there are no changes in the capital sharing ratio and that the agreed ratio of firm A:B is 80:20) would receive 25% × 80% = 20% of the capital profits of the merged firm.

This actually is an exchange of assets and technically the market value of each chargeable asset in each partnership should be determined in order to calculate gains and losses on the proportions disposed of. The Inland Revenue is, however, prepared to regard the route to the merged firm as no more than a series of capital-sharing ratio adjustments, and the CGT treatment follows the same principles as that for a change in partnership capital-share ratios.

Roll-over relief may also be available.

A CGT liability could, however, arise in relation to non-business assets such as shares in a service company where roll-over relief would not be available.

18.7.3 VAT

Following a merger it is usual for the bigger practice to retain the VAT registration number of the larger of the two preceding firms and a revised form VAT 2 should be sent to Customs and Excise notifying them of the introduction of new partners.

The form VAT 2 notifying Customs of the change of constitution (or indeed the name of the merged partnership) should be submitted within 30 days of the merger.

The VAT registration number will be unaffected by this, but, as referred to earlier, it is in the retiring partners' interest to ensure Customs and Excise are notified as soon as possible to ensure that they are not liable for future VAT liabilities.

The old partnership should, strictly, cancel its registration on form VAT 5, but Customs and Excise in practice, accept a letter. The cancellation of the registration must be made in writing within 30 days of the date of the merger. A final VAT return covering the period from the last VAT accounting period to the date of merger will be issued and must be completed and sent to Customs with any payment due by the due date.

19 HR strategy

19.1 Background

In a practice, people are the engine room and without them nothing happens – no profit, no value. As a consequence, HR strategy needs to be at the centre of the total business planning process. The current value of a practice and its ability to be profitable will be based on how successful the management of the 'people element' of the practice has been in the past. Future profitability and value can be significantly improved by developing and refining an integrated HR strategy.

In overall terms the HR strategy needs to be flexible and be able to deal with issues affecting the short term (the next 12 months), the medium term (years two to three) and the longer term (four years).

In the short term the key issues will be to resource the immediate workflow and balance the work demands against the resources available. In times of economic slow down there will be difficult decisions to make about potential redundancies. During such periods, resignations drop and this will need to be factored in to the forward plan.

In the medium term the business plan and manpower plan will need to identify projected work flows and manpower needs. The underlying assumptions should be written down as this will help future evaluation of changes and facilitate an accurate review of requirements.

Longer term issues will involve the future strategic direction of the business, its ownership and structure. Whatever the objectives, a sound HR strategy will assist in achieving them.

A practice's HR strategy should be dynamic and iterative and capable of adjustment as actual events unfold. Crucial to any strategy is knowing where a practice has come from and the position it wants to get to.

19.2 Identifying the requirements

At the centre of an HR strategy is the manpower plan. This document should draw on past experience and staff utilisation and also on the business plan and objectives for the future. It may be useful to develop the plan in four dimensions:

1. current clients – projected recurring work;
2. current clients – projected non-recurring work;
3. business development – targeted recurring work;
4. business development – targeted non-recurring work.

The process should be broken down in sufficient detail to enable a specific comparison to be made against the manpower plan as time progresses, thus enabling a practice to revise and remodel the plan based on the actual out turn of events. For current client work there should be an individual manpower plan broken down as follows:

- by work type;
- by grade level;
- by timing;
- by hours.

The value of the hours should be automatically linked to the financial plan and capable of being modelled. Specific staff/partners should be allocated against the plan and after the first comparison the overall surplus or deficit and the impact of timing differences assessed.

The process then moves to the planning stage in an attempt to balance resources against needs. Crucial gaps or surpluses in skills and resources can be identified early and action plans implemented to provide a solution.

19.3 Impact of technology

In the current climate of dramatic changes in IT, the impact of new technology on the business plan and the manpower plan is critical. The rationale for introducing a particular system may be to reduce manpower levels and improve efficiency. This needs to be factored in.

In a business that relies on revenue generated through hours charged by professional staff, the impact of technology and the benefits need to be carefully evaluated to ensure that the benefit accrues to the firm and that revenue is not lost. It is likely that the skills required by staff may need to be upgraded. The training and familiarisation time will need to be factored in to the manpower plan. Additional resources may be required to manage the IT support.

Whatever the scenario, a major change to IT or the introduction of any major new systems will have a dramatic impact on the manpower plan.

19.4 Staff planning and succession planning

As a parallel exercise, individual staff plans for each member of chargeable staff should be prepared anticipating known events, e.g., study leave, holidays, retirements. Promotions and grade changes should also be factored in to create a forward staff profile.

It is very difficult to factor in to the forward staff profile potential leavers from the practice. Some firms prepare the plan without incorporating this data, knowing that their profile is the optimum and any unforeseen leavers will have an immediate impact on the manpower plan. In some cases it may be desirable to actively plan for people reaching a certain grade as a maximum. Active planning to improve the quality mix of staff should also be considered and the cost of this should be built into financial budgets.

For this reason, the supply of potential recruits should never be 'turned off'. A dialogue should be maintained with recruitment agencies on a regular basis. All that should change is the specification of the type of person the practice would be prepared to recruit.

When the staff profile plan is compared to the manpower plan this will identify a number of issues including:

- wrong mix of staff;
- seasonal peaks and troughs;
- wrong skill sets for short, medium or longer term needs of the practice;
- future gaps at certain grades, particularly partner level.

All of these could have a damaging impact on the profitability and value of a practice and HR strategies should be designed to minimise their financial impact.

19.5 HR strategies and solutions

HR strategies are required for a wide range of issues and should be committed to writing and where necessary approved by an employment lawyer. This is particularly important where a practice is proposing to change the terms and conditions of employment of existing staff or where it is the intention to introduce terms and conditions for new staff that are significantly different from those applicable to current staff.

19.5.1 Hours of work

Many of the following have contractual implications and if a practice is proposing to make changes to existing contracts then advice should be sought from an employment lawyer.

- Increasing the length of the working day can deliver additional chargeable hours beyond the equivalent salary cost.
- Flexing the working year by increasing the hours at busy times of the year and reducing the hours at quieter times.
- Employing part-time or flexible working resources.
- Hiring contract staff to cover peak work flows.
- Structuring a clear policy on overtime and reward.
- Restricting the incidence of holidays during peak working times.

19.5.2 Appraisal and development

Structured assessment and feedback after each major assignment will improve value and also assist in setting the budget and manpower planning for the future. The subject of motivation is covered elsewhere in this book but needs to be emphasised in this context. There are a number of advantages in setting realistic goals and targets for staff. These should be a part of the overall business development plan and should be closely monitored and assessed.

Ideally staff appraisals should involve the participation of the immediate line manager and the member of staff and also someone senior in the organisation with overall responsibility for the business unit, to give an overview and deal with any issues that arise.

Appraisal of individuals should be balanced and not place too much emphasis on recent performance. The process should also identify their skills shortages and the training needs, and agree a course of action to be completed before the next review.

A positive proactive appraisal process run well is a strong motivator and supports the overall retention strategy. Poorly run it creates apathy and distrust of the organisation and has a disproportionately negative effect.

19.5.3 Training

Care should be taken to avoid training for training's sake, as this is expensive and counterproductive. The principal driver for training should be the needs of the practice, not just the needs of the individual. There is a possibility that a person will be trained out of their role with a firm and the only outcome is that they leave to achieve their career objectives elsewhere.

Particular care should be taken over the decision to take on staff without any expertise and provide them with training towards a particular qualification. Whilst undoubtedly there are advantages in employing trainees under a training contract, there are wider issues of utilisation and also the work experience they will obtain during their training contract and immediately after qualification.

Future staff profiling and planning that aims to project development and retention of individuals beyond five years is highly vulnerable. For this reason the recruitment of a student to train as a chartered accountant should not be treated as a solution to a projected need no more than two years after qualification.

19.5.4 Coaching and mentoring

One of the more recent developments in HR is the introduction of specific coaching and mentoring programmes. This involves the specific tailoring of personal development plans for individuals that are closely aligned to business objectives. Experience has shown that such programmes have a high level of return for organisations and individuals.

Depending upon the size of the organisation, the programmes can either be developed and facilitated in house or through the use of external executive coaching consultants.

19.5.5 Communication

Communication at various levels and on a wide range of subjects is essential to the building of a high-quality team. This is particularly important as a means of communicating succession information about a practice and what has been achieved.

There are a number of mediums by which communication can be delivered, and a clear matrix of what is to be communicated, when, by what method and to whom, should be set out:

- regular news letter;
- notice board;
- press releases;
- social events;
- team briefings;
- annual conferences.

19.6 Reward and performance payments

19.6.1 Basic salaries

Basic salary levels should accurately reflect market levels and the relative experience of the member of staff. Ideally a practice should build in a premium against market for key people to discourage them from moving for purely financial reasons. Market level salaries should be kept under regular review by screening the press, speaking to local recruitment agencies and through networks of similar businesses operating in the geographical area. Salaries should be kept up to date and, if necessary, due to market pressures the practice should have the flexibility to adjust salary levels more than once per annum.

Basic salary levels and structures should be committed to a written document that is part of the business plan. Each of the partners in the practice should know and understand the salary policy issues for their department and also understand the salary levels and grading structure that is in operation. Managers should be encouraged to be aware of the financial implications of running a successful team. They are a key resource in supporting the retention strategy.

Undoubtedly, there will be areas of pressure within a practice and certain partners, either through force of personality, or based on the particular performance levels of their practice area, will seek to work outside the agreed levels and try and force through different salary levels for staff they consider key. The implications of this need to be worked out carefully.

It is well known that staff discuss salary levels and it should be assumed that nothing will remain confidential. It is important that hiring decisions are made by the appropriate level of person within the firm and that only one person has the delegated authority to agree salary levels for new recruits and to issue offer letters.

19.6.2 Overtime payments

A clear policy needs to be drawn up that sets out the firm's policy on the treatment of overtime. It is recommended that all overtime is recorded as this ensures that the true costs of providing a service to clients is available. For this reason some form of financial reward is recommended as this encourages staff to record all time spent. There should also be some form of pre-authorisation of overtime to prevent overruns on jobs and unfocused and wasted time.

Alternative overtime reward strategies include:

- payment in full for hours worked at standard salary rate;
- overtime is partly compensated by taking time off in lieu and partly paid. This is particularly useful where there are significant seasonal peaks and troughs in the work flow;
- payment at variable rates depending on when the overtime was worked;
- overtime hours logged and payment made by way of a discretionary bonus.

There may well be a benefit in developing different strategies at each grade level.

19.6.3 Performance payments

'Performance related pay' has become a much used phrase and indeed has generated a culture of belief that where someone performs satisfactorily this warrants a bonus. The reality is that bonuses should be used to reward performance that is clearly above average and where the effort has been of significant advantage to the firm.

In a competitive environment where packages on offer in industry can include share options and other performance related bonuses, firms need to be able to compete.

There is also the issue of whether bonuses should be objectively set or be entirely discretionary. If an organisation is to include bonuses as part of its HR strategy and overall employment costs, then generally accepted practise is to include bonus structures that allow for objectively set schemes and also discretionary schemes that reward after the event.

Bonus types can include the following:

- specific event based bonuses;
- overall bonuses based on team performance;
- bonuses based on the overall performance of the firm.

It is recommended that bonus structures are developed for each grade of staff and that their format and relevance are aligned to the firm's expectations as regards performance and also the ability of the individual to specifically deliver measurable performance to justify a bonus payment. Bonuses should not be used as substitute for lower base salaries. As mentioned above bonuses can be paid for overtime worked.

Timing of bonus payments needs to be established as part of the overall HR strategy. A timing delay on certain annual bonuses can help with retention, as can a process of part payment of bonuses on a deferral basis. Where staff are always due payment for a bonus earned then it can make them think twice about leaving where their reasons are primarily financial.

19.7 Other benefits

A firm should decide as part of their HR strategy what benefits are important, either to enable them to compete in the market place, or to assist the firm in the delivery of its overall business objectives. Whatever the policy adopted it is important to communicate the real value to staff so that they are aware of the true value of their emolument package.

The biggest problem with benefits is that employees tend to view their package in terms of base salary and do not take account of benefits provided by and paid for by the firm. Other benefits can include:

- provision of a car or a car allowance – the practicalities of this need to be evaluated against the tax position of the individuals and the firm. Firms should be able to evaluate this easily;
- pension contribution – this can be on a matched contribution basis up to a maximum level, or entirely non-contributory by the employee. Increasingly the schemes adopted are individual pension plans rather than corporate schemes. Specialist advice should be sought about the range of options available;
- private medical insurance – this can be grade related and can include a range of benefits commensurate with seniority. As staff are promoted, this benefit can increase in value. Of all benefits this one can be positively advantageous for the firm as it can ensure prompt treatment for non-life threatening illnesses or conditions;
- club or society membership – where a senior employee is expected to play a major role in business development then membership of a club can support this.

- professional subscriptions are normally paid by firms on behalf of their employees;
- in certain cases fully supported training and study leave packages are paid;
- additional holidays – where the work is seasonal then a firm can gain from a policy of increasing holiday entitlement but specifying when the additional holidays can be taken.

19.7.1 Recruitment

There should be a clearly defined HR strategy as regards recruitment covering the following:

- responsibility for recruitment;
- advertising and use of media;
- use of web sites and the internet;
- use of recruitment agencies;
- networking;
- staff introductions;
- interview and assessment procedures;
- offer procedures and approval;
- referencing procedures;
- initial review of performance.

19.7.2 Responsibility

The partnership should clearly specify an individual with key responsibility for recruitment. This is a key appointment and the person selected should have the necessary seniority and ambassadorial qualities to represent the firm to potential recruits.

Invariably the qualities demanded of this role are such that the person selected is likely to be in demand elsewhere in the practice. Nevertheless, the individual should be given the necessary time to enable them to carry out this important role.

It is also important that this person has an understanding of the various aspects of legislation relating to recruitment. This includes equal opportunities, race relations and discrimination legislation, as well as data protection legislation.

19.7.3 Advertising and media

Detailed media information should be maintained on the likely advertising media that the firm might use for recruitment advertising. As an alternative, and depending upon the likely volume of advertising, the firm may wish to retain the services of an advertising agency to support them with advice, media selection, copy writing and (if required) response handling. Normally charges for this service are covered from the commission earned by the agency from placing the advertisements in the media.

There should be tight control over who can commit the firm to advertising costs and all advertising should be processed through the individual referred to above.

It is also essential that there is tight control over advertising copy to ensure accurate representation of the firm and also of the roles being advertised. It is important that appropriate response mechanisms are set up and that those nominated are fully briefed and set up to handle the response arising.

19.7.4 Use of websites and the internet

The firm should have a clear strategy about the use of their own website for recruitment and ideally have developed a response to the proliferation of job websites that exist in the market place.

In arriving at a strategy for the use of the internet, consideration should be given to the following issues:

- potential for saving significant costs against recruitment fees;
- potential for a wider reach to candidates;
- ability to communicate a consistent message;
- ability to improve recruitment efficiency by having all responses by e-mail;
- advertising 'free' on an agencies' website is not free as they will still charge a fee for any subsequent candidate placed by them with the practice irrespective of the fact that the candidate responded to the practice advertisement;
- some sites are completely unfocused and unlikely to appeal to experienced professionals seeking a change of career.

19.7.5 Use of recruitment agencies

The quality of service provided by recruitment agencies and the fees charged are extremely variable. It is therefore advisable to research the local market place for the sector leaders build relationships with them and identify contacts who can be a useful source of market information.

Having identified the key recruitment agencies, firms should develop a concept of becoming a 'preferred client' and building a relationship that ensures that the practice sees the best candidates first and that information on changing market conditions is received quickly.

Ideally it is a good idea to set up these relationships when the practice is not actively recruiting. At that time the practice has an opportunity to discuss their fee levels. Where some form of 'exclusivity' or 'volume' recruitment can be offered then there should be potential for getting the fees reduced. It is also possible to negotiate refund terms and payment terms provided this is carried out before the event rather than at the time an issue arises.

It is likely that the practice will need more than one agency to handle the different staff types and levels that will be recruited. A programme of regular reviews with preferred agency suppliers should be implemented and detailed statistics of the agencies' performance maintained. The practice should endeavour to make the agencies aware that their continued status as a 'preferred supplier' is dependent upon their quality of performance.

Accurate information on which agency candidates have been sourced from should also be maintained. This avoids the issue of CVs on the same candidate being received from different agencies and causing subsequent fee problems regarding the introduction.

Individual consultants also move around the market a great deal and it is therefore a good idea to have some form of relationship at a senior level in the recruitment consultancy to ensure continuity.

19.7.6 Networking

One of the most effective ways of developing a cost-effective recruitment channel is to encourage staff and partners to network within their social and business groups to identify people who might be of interest to the firm in the future. Rewarding staff for introductions is covered in more detail below.

An active alumni programme should also be established, with nominated partners responsible for maintaining contact with key individuals who have left the firm. This is an ideal way of recruiting future partners.

Networking should happen automatically as part of business development, but the trigger and monitoring of the alumni programme should be through HR or the partner in charge of recruitment.

19.7.7 Staff introductions

Staff should be made aware if the firm has an active policy of introducing potential recruits to the firm and the criteria that are to be applied. A clear strategy should be set as regards reward for this and the process requires sensitive handling.

Reward is normally financial and depends upon the level of seniority, usually determined by salary level. In some firms the level of bonus can be as high as 10 per cent. Normally there is a qualifying period during which the new employee and also the current employee have to remain with the firm before payment is made. This can be up to six months.

Ideally staff should discuss prospective employees with the appropriate recruitment partner and obtain a CV prior to any meeting.

The relationship between the firm's employee and the prospective applicant needs to be clearly established.

19.7.8 Interview and assessment procedures

A firm should have clearly documented interview and assessment procedures that are designed to ensure that all relevant information is received and that the interview process comprehensively covers the identification of skills and achievements of the applicant.

Areas that should be covered within the HR policy on recruitment include:

- a requirement that all applicants complete a standard application form and attach a copy of their own CV;
- all interviews should be supported by detailed interview notes clearly addressing the facts identified during the interview that support the skills and experience being recruited;

- standard offer letters and terms and conditions of employment should be created (these should be reviewed periodically by an employment lawyer to ensure compliance with current legislation).

It is important for a practice to review their professional indemnity insurance cover as this may require specific notification of the practice's recruitment and referencing policies to support hiring decisions.

19.7.9 Offer procedures and approval

As mentioned previously, there should be a clear policy stating who is responsible for issuing an offer letter. This offer process can have as many independent checks as a firm considers appropriate to ensure that all the HR recruitment policy procedures have been followed, but it should be finally signed off by the person responsibile for recruitment. Policy guidelines should also set out what documentation should accompany the formal letter.

An outline offer letter with the key elements of the offer can be sent. Subject to acceptance, a full employment contract can be produced and sent. This can avoid the circulation of the practice's detailed package and terms to potential employees who might not accept the offer of employment from the practice. Reference in the offer letter to automatic salary increases or reviews to contractual terms, i.e., notice period after a qualifying period, should be avoided.

19.7.10 Referencing procedures

As part of the offer process clear instructions should be set down as regards the firm's referencing procedure. Where offers are made subject to references then the wording for the contract should be cleared with an employment lawyer.

The practice needs to set down clearly who references are to be sought from and how they are to be obtained. Where verbal references are obtained these should be confirmed back to the referee in writing. This provides a written record of the reference. Where previous employers decline to provide a reference on technical ability they should, as a minimum, provide a character reference.

In cases where references are unsatisfactory and where the conditional clause in the offer documentation is properly constructed, a withdrawal of the offer is possible. Where satisfactory references are obtained then the employment should be confirmed in writing thereby removing the conditional reference clause.

19.7.11 Initial review of performance

A firm should set down clearly the assessment procedures in place and the probationary period, if appropriate, during which the actual experience and skills of a new recruit will be validated.

At interview stage, or certainly when they join, clear objectives for new employees should be set and measured as part of the appraisal process. The timing of this will depend on the level of appointment and the complexity of the role.

Where performance is well below the expected level then decisive action should be taken to rectify the problem or dismiss the employee and recover the relevant proportion of any agency fee paid.

19.7.12 Retention

As part of the overall manpower plan, key individuals should be identified and an active retention strategy should be developed for each person. Ideally, a specific partner should be given responsibility for key individuals.

It is generally accepted that some staff will leave, and in any organisation where the management structure is pyramid shaped it is necessary to have people leave. The more generally accepted shape of an organisation delivering professional services is a vertical-sided pyramid with a smaller pyramid at the top. This structure allows for greater retention and deployment of managers and experienced professional staff.

There remains the problem of limited opportunity for 'promotion' to partner. Firms are approaching this issue in a number of different ways and it is important to develop a clear HR strategy to define senior staff grades and where practical to establish senior grades that are rewarding and carry sufficient status and job satisfaction to retain key senior staff. Active policies of 'placing' key staff with larger firms or clients to broaden their experience can also be developed as part of their retention planning.

Increasingly firms are using Director grades for non 'chartered' qualified staff, and salaried partner status for key people either on route to equity partnership or as a final grade level.

Many retention strategies cover issues such as motivation, recognition and other non-financial factors. It is generally accepted that although money in itself is not perceived as high on the chart of motivation, it is equally true that if someone feels underpaid this will have an immediate and ongoing negative impact.

It is relatively easy to develop a range of strategies for HR in relation to retention, but it is not the writing down of what has to be done that is important, the key is implementation. This is a function of the culture within the organisation and everyone's commitment to the concept and team values.

The other key issue is that the implementation of retention policies needs to be continuous and needs to be supported by everyone in the firm all of the time. Any single lapse can undo all of the previous efforts.

19.8 Support staff

A great deal of time is spent on planning chargeable staff utilisation. As part of the process a clear plan of support staff requirements needs to be developed. As with chargeable staff, new technology or revisions to working practices can require changes to support-staff working practices. Where these are envisaged then careful planning is necessary to avoid disruption.

HR strategies and policies should be developed for all levels of staff and a team culture should be established.

19.9 Summary

A clearly established HR Strategy is crucial to the future success of a practice. There are four phases:

(1) phase 1 – development of the policies and strategy;

(2) phase 2 – implementation;

(3) phase 3 – evaluation of the impact and outcomes;

(4) phase 4 – redefining the policies and strategies.

This process can happen as fast as the market and circumstances dictate. It should not be treated as a once a year job that is completed, dusted down and put in a drawer.

Unless the practice's HR strategy is truly dynamic and reactive to the needs of the business as determined by the external influences on the firm, the business will underachieve and may even fail. HR strategy is not an important part of the jigsaw, it is the jigsaw!

Index

References are to paragraph numbers

ABBA (National Association of Business to Business Advertisers) 14.3.1, 14.3.4
account books
   partnership agreement 1.16
accountants
   defined 1.5
acquisitions *see* **fee acquisition and disposal**
Acrobat Reader files 10.8
Act! (database) 6.13
added-value services
   mergers, partnerships 7.1
advertising
   HR strategy 19.7.3
   marketing communications 14.3.4
agencies, recruitment 19.7.5
American Association for Humanistic Psychology 15.2.3
annual accounts procedures
   partnership agreement 1.16
annuities, retiring partners
   payment out 2.4.5
   taxation 18.3.2
appraisal of staff 19.5.2
arbitration
   dispute resolution methods 2.7.2
assessment
   HR strategy 19.7.8
   performance, of *see* **performance reviews**
asset finance 3.2.3, 3.6.1
assets
   CGT
      disposal 18.4.3
      distribution in specie 18.4.7
   partnership as asset-accruing vehicle 2.4.7
   tangible, measurement of (FRS 15) 9.3.1
assignment of leases 9.2.2
association
   defined 1.5
audit documents
   quality control 13.4.8
audited accountants
   defined 1.5
auditors, firm as
   complying with quality-control requirements 13.5.1
Authorised Guarantee Agreement
   leasehold property 9.4.3
Authoritative Literature
   XBRL 10.10
authority, limits of
   partnership agreement 1.11

B2B (business to business) 10.8
Baker Tilly
   as national firm 4.6.1
balance sheet preparation
   termination of partnership 1.21
banking issues
   partnership agreement 1.16
banks, finance sources
   capital accounts 3.4.1
   current accounts 3.5.2
   generally 3.2.2
   loan finance 3.4.1, 3.5.3

Index

banks, finance sources—*cont.*
   true and fair accounting
      principles 3.5.1
belonging, need for 15.2.3
benchmarks, industry standard
   17.3
Blanchard, Ken 10.5
bonuses 19.6.3
Boomer, Gary (Boomer
   Consulting) 10.6
Boomer's Technology Physical
   10.6
borrowing capacity
   freehold tenure 9.2.1
BPR (Business Property Relief)
   inheritance tax 18.5
brand development 14.3.1
brand strategy
   marketing communications
      14.3.4
Brand Values
   marketing 14.3.3
Branson, Richard 15.1.3
broadband, impact in UK 10.8
budgets 12.3
business brand 14.3.1
   planning 14.3.3
business development
   HR strategy 19.2
business planning process 17.3
Business Property Relief (BPR)
   inheritance tax 18.5
'buying in'
   coaching 17.4
   planning 17.3

Caesar, Julius 15.1.3
Capital Gains Tax (CGT)
   assets
      disposal of 18.4.3
      distribution of in specie 18.4.7
   capital-sharing ratio, change in
      18.4.6
   determining of partners' gains
      18.4.1
   goodwill
      payments by incoming
         partner 18.4.5
      retirement and 18.4.4
   legislation 18.4.1
   mergers, partnerships 18.7.2
   partnership tax return 18.4.1
   roll-over relief 18.5, 18.7.2
   taper relief 18.4.2
capital provision
   finance sources 3.2.1, 3.4.1
   partnership agreement 1.14
capital-sharing ratio
   CGT 18.4.6
car provision
   HR strategy 19.7
cash management 12.8
   current accounts 3.4.2
Chartered Accountancy
   marketing strategy 14.3.3
CharterGroup
   networking 4.6.2
civil litigation proceedings,
   changes in 3.6.4
clients
   changing attitudes of 4.3
   changing kinds of work
      Type 1 4.2.1
      Type 2 4.2.2
   changing practice structure 4.3
   changing requirements 4.1
   existing
      HR planning 19.2
      retaining 13.4.2
   gaining 13.4.3
   mergers, value for 7.5
   practice structures and 4.3,
      16.1.2
   quality control 13.4.12
   service matters App 1
closed questions 5.2.3

club/society membership
  HR strategy 19.7
coaching
  HR strategy 19.5.4
  managing partners 17.4
Codes of Practice
  leasehold tenure 9.2.2
communication
  HR strategy 19.5.5
communications
  marketing and promotion 14.3.4
compliance work
  competition for 4.3
consolidation
  advantages perceived
    central support functions 8.4.8
    cross-selling opportunities 8.4.4
    integration 8.4.1
    lateral hiring 8.4.5
    legal services 8.4.5
    local knowledge with national support 8.4.3
    motivated staff 8.4.7
    national coverage 8.4.2
    outsourcing 8.4.5
    recruitment 8.4.5
    single brand and structure 8.4.6
  concept 8.3
  correct climate, creating 8.1
  disadvantages
    initial income reductions 8.5.4
    market fluctuations 8.5.2
    targets, failure to achieve 8.5.3
    undercapitalisation 8.5.1
  medium-sized practices, issues facing
    capital growth 8.2.5
    investment, lack of 8.2.1
    management structure 8.2.2
    recruitment 8.2.4
    retention 8.2.4
    succession 8.2.6
    unlimited liability 8.2.3
consultancy arrangements
  retired partners 18.3.3
contact disciplines
  marketing communications 14.3.4
contact strategy
  marketing communications 14.3.4
continuing partners
  defined 1.5
  termination of partnership, consequences 1.21
corporate literature
  marketing communications 14.3.4
Cox, George 10.8
creative strategy
  marketing communications 14.3.4
CRM (customer/client relationship management) 6.13, 10.3
culture of firm 17.6
  partner rewards 17.8
current accounts
  finance sources 3.2.1, 3.4.2, 3.5.2
Customs and Excise
  VAT 18.6
  partnership mergers 18.7.3
'cyber era' 14.3.2

databases
  networking 6.13
death of partners 1.19, 2.1.12
  timing of payments in event of 2.1.11

debt factoring 3.6.2
debt management
  criteria 12.10.6
  invoicing and collection
    12.10.4
  monitoring 12.10.5
  overall policy and control,
    responsibility for 12.10.1
  risks and 12.10.2
  terms of business 12.10.3
deed of partnership *see*
  partnership agreement
deficiency needs 15.2.3
definitions 1.5, App 1
design
  websites 14.3.2
development issues
  appraisal of staff 19.5.2
  assessment of performance
    5.1.1
  new partners, appointing
    5.2.12
  new skills, identifying need for
    5.1
  performance reviews *see*
    performance reviews
  responsibility for own
    development 5.1.1
  'think learning' philosophy
    5.1
dilapidations
  leasehold property 9.2.2,
    9.4.1
direct mail
  marketing communications
    14.3.4
dispute resolution methods
  arbitration 2.7.2
  civil justice reforms (1990s)
    2.7.2
  expert determination 2.7.3
  importance of provisions 2.7.1
  mediation 2.7.4

drawings
  mergers, potential problem
    areas 7.6.6
  partnership agreement 1.16
du Plessis, Erik (Impact
  International, head of) 14.3.4
duration of partnership
  partnership agreement 1.6

e-business strategy 14.3.2
earnings basis
  taxable profits 18.2.2
earnings cap
  pension provisions 18.3.1
'eat what you kill'
  meaning 1.15
equity cleansing
  dispute resolution methods
    arbitration 2.7.2
    civil justice provisions
      (1990s) 2.7.2
    expert determination 2.7.3
    importance of provision
      2.7.1
    mediation 2.7.4
  exit routes, setting by agreement
    see **Exit routes**
  expulsion
    'all bar one' policy 2.3.2
    provisions, need for 2.3.1
    without cause 2.3.2
  payment out
    amount 2.4.1–2.4.2
    annuities 2.4.5
    goodwill 2.4.3
    interest 2.5.2
    LLPs 2.5.3
    mechanics 2.5.1–2.5.3
    partnership as asset-accruing
      vehicle 2.4.7
    partnership as 'trust' 2.4.4
    security 2.5.3
    timing 2.5.1

equity cleansing—*cont.*
    work-in-progress 2.4.6
    post-retirement obligations
        outgoing partners, indemnity given for continuing partnership debts 2.6.1
        professional indemnity insurance 2.6.2
        tax payments 2.6.3
    underperforming partners
        encouraging improvement 2.2.3
        practical improvement steps 2.2.4
        roles of partners, differing 2.2.1
        suitable metrics, selecting 2.2.2
esteem needs 15.2.3
exit routes
    death 2.1.12
        timing of payments in event of 2.1.13
    deed, importance of 2.1.1
    illness 2.1.9
        timing of payments in event of 2.1.11
    mental illness 2.1.9
    PA 1890 provisions 2.1.2
    retirement *see* **retirement of partners**
    winding up a partnership 2.1.3
expert determination
    dispute resolution methods 2.7.3
expulsion of partners
    'all bar one' policy 2.3.2
    partnership agreement 1.20
    provisions, need for 2.3.1
    without cause 2.3.2
extensible business reporting language (XBRL) 10.10
external marketing planning 14.3.3

external quality controllers
    advantages of using 13.6.1
Eysenck, Hans 15.2.2

'Fast Track Strategy'
    planning 17.3
FDM (frequency division multiplexing) 10.8
fee acquisitions and disposals
    buying and selling considerations 7.4.1
    fee levels 7.4.1
    GRF (gross recurring fees)
        buying and selling considerations 7.4.1
        valuation 7.4.2
    information 7.4.1
    location of firm 7.4.1
    market place 7.3
    payout arrangements 7.4.3
    sale agreement 7.4.4
    size of firm 7.4.1
    staff continuity 7.4.1
    valuation 7.4.2
    see also **mergers, partnership**
fee disposal
    market place 7.3
fee negotiations
    quality control 13.4.4
feedback (performance reviews)
    constructive, rules for 5.2.9
    giving 5.2.9
        to partners/colleagues 5.2.10
    negative 5.2.9
    receiving 5.2.7
fees
    financial management 12.4
finance sources
    asset finance 3.2.3, 3.6.1
    banks 3.2.2, 3.5.1–3.5.3
    capital, fixed 3.2.1, 3.4.1
    choice of business medium 3.1

Index

finance sources—*cont.*
  civil litigation proceedings 3.6.4
  current accounts of partners 3.2.1, 3.4.2, 3.5.2
  debt factoring 3.6.2
  freehold, disadvantages and 9.2.1
  growth management 3.7
  joint ventures 3.6.3
  overview, relative proportions 3.3
  partnership bankers 3.2.2
  service stream finance 3.6.4
  size of business 3.3
financial management
  cash management 12.8
  debt management
    criteria 12.10.6
    invoicing and collection 12.10.4
    monitoring 12.10.5
    overall policy and control 12.10.1
    recovery 12.10.5
    risk management 12.10.2
    terms of business 12.10.3
  fees 12.4
  forecasting 12.8
  objectives of business/partners 12.1, 12.2
  operating costs 12.6
  performance data 12.11
  profitability, scope for improvement and 12.3
  property costs 12.6
  strategic planning 12.2
  support staff 12.6
  time management 12.5
  value, adding of 12.1
  work-in-progress, managing
    analysing 12.9.2
    booking time 12.9.1
    fees, converting into 12.9.4
    fixed-fee tasks 12.9.1
    monitoring 12.9.2
    unbillable time, recognising 12.9.3
  working capital control 12.7
financial services
  professional indemnity insurance 11.3
financial statements
  XBRL 10.10
financial year
  defined 1.5
  pensions and 1.17
firm
  defined 1.5
firm name
  defined 1.5
Forbidden Technology 10.8
forecasting
  financial management 12.8
former partnership
  defined 1.5
freehold property
  advantages and disadvantages 9.2.1
  mortgage, subject to 9.3.1

garden leave 1.20
Gartner Group research
  information technology 10.5, 10.8
Goldmine (database) 6.13
good faith
  duty of partners 1.3
goodwill
  covenants to protect 1.23
  mergers, potential problems 7.6.1
  payment out 2.4.3
  payments by incoming partner 18.4.5
  retirement and 18.4.4

Grant Thornton
   as national firm   4.6.1
Great Plains Software   10.10
GRF (gross recurring fees)
   fee acquisitions/disposals   7.4.1
   valuation methods   17.10

HA&W (Habif, Arogeti and Wynne)   10.2, 10.7
Harvey-Jones, Sir John   17.1
Hazelhurst, Tim
   brand development (positioning)   14.3.1
   marketing communications   14.3.4
Herrmann, Ned   15.2
Herzberg, Frederick   15.2.5
hierarchy of needs   15.2.3
holidays
   partnership agreement   1.13.1
Horwath Clark Whitehill
   as national firm   4.6.1
HR strategy
   advertising   19.7.3
   appraisal and development   19.5.2
   background   19.1
   benefits, general   19.7
   coaching   19.5.4
   communication   19.5.5
   general matters App 1
   hours of work   19.5.1
   initial performance review   19.7.11
   internet use   19.7.4
   interview/assessment procedures   19.7.8
   manpower plan   19.2
   media   19.7.3
   networking   19.7.6
   offer procedures/approval   19.7.9
   payments, reward and performance
   overtime payments   19.6.2
   performance payments   19.6.3
   salaries, basic   19.6.1
   phases   19.9
   planning   19.2
     staff and succession   19.4
   recruitment   19.7.1
     agencies, use of   19.7.5
   referencing procedures   19.7.10
   requirements, identifying   19.2
   responsibility   19.7.2
   retention of staff   19.7.12
   staff introductions   19.7.7
   support staff   19.8
   technology, impact of   19.3
   training   19.5.3, 19.7
   website use   19.7.4
Hurst, Simon   10.4, 10.9

ICAEW (Institute of Chartered Accountants for England and Wales)
   definition   1.5
   handling of clients' money   1.16
   IT survey   10.2
   professional indemnity insurance   11.1
   Profitable and Sustainable Practice task force   10.10
   XBRL use   10.10
ICTA (Income and Corporation Taxes Act) 1988
   definitions   1.5
   pensions   1.17
IDC (Intrusion Detection Systems)   10.9
illness
   partnership agreement   1.13.2
income tax
   cash basis, withdrawal of (for professions)   18.2.2

305

income tax—*cont.*
    current-year basis of assessment
        18.2.1
    mergers, partnerships 18.7.1
    work-in-progress valuation
        18.2.3
incoming partners
    goodwill payments by 18.4.5
    income tax liabilities
        18.2.1–18.2.3
indemnity clauses
    partnership agreement 1.16,
        1.24
inefficient practices
    quality control 13.4.13
information
    defined App 1
information technology *see* **IT
    (information technology)**
inheritance tax 18.5
**Institute of Chartered
    Accountants for England and
    Wales)** *see* **ICAEW (Institute of
    Chartered Accountants for
    England and Wales)**
Institute of Director's Guide
    IT security 10.9
insurance requirements
    partnership agreement 1.12
intelligent dialogue
    websites 14.3.2
internal marketing planning
    14.3.3
internet use
    HR strategy 19.7.4
interviews
    HR strategy 19.7.8
introductions, staff 19.7.7
**Intrusion Detection Systems
    (IDC)** 10.9
IT (information technology)
    applications for practices 10.3
    assessment of technology 10.6

benchmarking criteria 10.6
broadband, impact in UK 10.8
business jargon 10.1
document management 10.4
financial management and
    12.6
fulfilment of expectations 10.1
internet use 19.7.4
knowledge management
    systems 10.4
learning 10.5
meaning App 1
mergers, potential problem
    areas 7.6.8
practice staff 10.7
practice survey (ICAEW) 10.2
security 10.9
terminology 10.1
websites 14.3.2, 19.7.4

Jenner, Andrew 17.2
Johari window
    feedback 5.2.8
joint ventures
    finance sources 3.6.3
Julius Caesar 15.1.3

Kaplan, Professor Robert 12.11
Klein, Robin (MD of Singleview)
    10.4
Kouzes, James 15.1.3

large firms
    finance sources 3.3
    networking 4.6.5
**Law Commission Consultation
    Paper (Partnership Law)** 2.1.3
leadership
    defined 17.1
    motivational
        authority of leaders 15.1.3
        best-performing companies,
            study 15.1

leadership—*cont.*
   'Business Excellence' 15.1
   changes and 15.1
   characteristics of effective
      leaders 15.1.3
   choices 15.1.2
   decision-making 15.1.3
   functions 15.1.3
   human resources 15.1.1
   leaders made, not born
      15.1.3
   needs 15.1.3
   responsibilities of leaders
      15.1.3
   role of leaders 15.1.3
   see also **motivation**
leasehold property
  advantages and disadvantages
    9.2.2
    flexible leases 9.2.3
    occupier management 9.2.3
    sale and leaseback
      transactions 9.3.1
    strategies
  Authorised Guarantee
    Agreement 9.4.3
  declining market 9.4.7
  dilapidations 9.4.1
  disposals 9.4.3
  growth/contraction, planning
    for 9.4.2
  Licence to Assign 9.4.3
  old fashioned building 9.4.6
  over-rented premises 9.4.4
  repair 9.4.1
  short lease term 9.4.5
Licence to Assign
  leasehold property 9.4.3
life cycle of business 17.5
Limited Liability Partnerships *see*
  LLPs (Limited Liability
  Partnerships)
liquidation of partnerships 2.1.3

listening skills
  clarifying of questions 5.2.6
  importance of 6.7
  impressions, giving 6.7.1
  neutral responses 5.2.6
  performance reviews 5.2.4,
    5.2.6
  reflecting meanings 5.2.6
  reinstatement 5.2.6
  small talk 6.7.2
  summarising 5.2.6
LLPs (Limited Liability
  Partnerships)
  bank finance 3.5.1
  'claw back' provisions 16.1.5
  finance sources 3.4.1
  payment out 2.5.3
  practice structures 16.1.5
  retirement, notice period
    2.1.7
  tax advantages 16.1.5
loans, bank 3.4.1, 3.5.3
'lock-step'
  meaning 1.15
lockups
  current accounts 3.4.2

Macgregor, Douglas 15.2.3
Maister, David H 17.2, 17.3
majorities
  simple 1.18.3
  special 1.18.2
  see also **voting**
management of practice
  managing partners, role of
    coaching 17.4
    corporate governance model
      17.2
    culture 17.6
    leadership 17.1
  managing partners, anticipation
    17.5
  markets, approach to 17.7

management of practice—*cont.*
   ownership of professional
      service firms   17.9
   planning   17.3
   rewards, partner   17.8
   succession   17.11
   valuation   17.10
  partnership agreement
   meetings of partners   1.18.3
   simple majorities   1.18.3
   special majorities   1.18.2
   unanimous voting   1.18.1
management structure, mergers
  potential problem areas
   7.6.2
Managing the Professional Service Firm (David Maister)   17.2, 17.3
marketing committees   14.3.3
marketing personnel
  networking   6.13
marketing and promotion
  action plans   14.3.3
  communications   14.3.4
  current situation   14.3.3
  e-business   14.3.2
  internal and external planning   14.3.3
  key tasks   14.1
  managing partner, role of   17.7
  objectives   14.3.3
  planning   14.3.3
  services marketing   14.3.3
  strategy   14.3.3
   brand development tools   14.3.1
   strategic business plan   14.2
  SWOT analysis   14.3.3
  websites   14.3.2
Maslow, Abraham   15.2.3
maternity leave
  partnership agreement   1.13.2

media
  HR strategy   19.7.3
mediation
  dispute resolution methods   2.7.4
medical insurance, private
  HR strategy   19.7
medium-sized companies, issues facing
  capital growth   8.2.5
  investment, lack of   8.2.1
  management structure   8.2.2
  recruitment   8.2.4
  retention   8.2.4
  succession   8.2.6
  unlimited liability   8.2.3
meetings of partners
  partnership agreement   1.18.3
mentoring
  HR strategy   19.5.4
Mercia organisation
  professional standards   11.1
mergers, partnerships
  added-value services   7.1
  advantages   7.5
  agreement   7.8
  capital contributions   7.6.5
  Capital Gains Tax (CGT)   18.7.2
  client review   7.9.1
  clients, value for   7.5
  drawings   7.6.6
  geographical spread   7.5.1
  goodwill   7.6.1
  income tax   18.7.1
  information technology   7.6.8
  initial steps   7.5.2
  management structure   7.6.2
  market advantage   7.5.1
  market place   7.3
  meetings, initial   7.7.1
  merger candidates, objectives   7.5

mergers, partnerships—*cont.*
  objectives of firm 7.2
  partner personal solvency
    7.6.11
  pension arrangements 7.6.6
  post-agreement follow-up
    client review 7.9.1
    partners and staff 7.9.2
  potential problem areas
    capital contributions 7.6.5
    drawings 7.6.6
    goodwill 7.6.1
    information technology
      7.6.8
    management structure
      7.6.2
    partner personal solvency
      7.6.11
    pension arrangements
      7.6.6
    premises 7.6.3
  professional indemnity
    insurance 7.6.9, 11.1
  professional standards 7.6.10
  profit-sharing arrangements
    7.6.4
    working structures 7.6.7
  problem solving 7.5.1
  procedures, technical 7.7.4
    level of cover 11.2
    potential problem areas
      7.6.9
  profit-sharing and 7.6.4
  purpose 7.1
  stages
    concluding 7.7.5
    exploratory 7.7.2
    investigative 7.7.3
    synergy 7.5.1
  technical procedures 7.7.4
  types of merger 7.5.1
  VAT 18.7.3
  volume of business 7.5.1
  working structures 7.6.7
  see also **fee acquisitions and
    disposals**
Microsoft Access (database) 6.13
**Modalen, experimental town
  (Norway)** 10.8
motivation
  demotivated people,
    characteristics 15.2.1
  'generic commonalties' 15.2.1
  getting best from people
    15.2.7
  'Michelangelo motive' 15.2.7
  motivated people,
    characteristics 15.2.1
  people, understanding 15.2.2
  performance reviews 15.2.6
  strengthening 15.2.7
  team building 15.2.7
  unmotivated people,
    characteristics 15.2.1
  see also **leadership,
    motivational**

**National Insurance
  Contributions** *see* **NICs
  (National Insurance
  Contributions)**
nature of business
  partnership agreement 1.6
needs, hierarchy of 15.2.3
net relevant earnings
  definitions 1.5
  pensions 1.17
networking
  active 6.3
  assistance (giving and receiving)
    6.11
  attitudes 6.1
  cold calling, no need for 6.3
  fears of 6.4
  first move 6.5
  follow-up process 5.10

networking—*cont.*
  group 6.9
  HR strategy 19.7.6
  impressions, giving 6.7.1
  individual approach 4.6.4
  larger firms, non-accountant partners 4.6.5
  listening, importance of 6.7
  see also **listening skills**
  local organisations 4.6.3
  marketing activity of firm 6.2
  marketing personnel, critical role 6.13
  names, remembering 6.6
  national firm 'almost a merger' situation 4.6.1
  procedures 6.12
  small practice as specialist 4.6.4
  SMEs 4.6.5
  systems 6.12
  umbrella groups 4.6.2
  working the room 6.8
new partners
  partnership agreement 1.7
NICs (National Insurance Contributions)
  current-year assessment basis 18.2.1

occupier management
  property issues 9.2.3
offer procedures/approval
  HR strategy 19.7.9
OMBs (owner managed businesses) 4.1
open questions 5.2.3
organisation charts 16.1.3
organisational structures *see* **practice structures**
outgoing partners
  definitions 1.5
  indemnities for continuing debts of partnership 2.6.1

  termination of partnership, consequences 1.21
'overlap profits' 18.2.1
ownership of professional service firms 17.9
ownership structures
  property strategies 9.3.1

PA (Partnership Act) 1890 *see* **Partnership Act (1890)**
Pareto analysis 16.1.2
partners
  appointing 5.3
  authority, limits of 1.11
  death 1.19, 2.1.12
    timing of payments in event of 2.1.13
    defined 1.5
    duties 1.10
    expulsion
    'all bar one' policy 2.3.2
    partnership agreement 1.20
    provisions, need for 2.3.1
    without cause 2.3.2
  illness 2.1.9
    mental 2.1.10
    timing of payments in event of 2.1.11
  meetings of 1.18.3
  mental illness 2.1.10
  new, partnership agreement 1.7
  retirement 1.19
  reward structure 17.8
  salaried 1.24
  selection of 11.1
  solvency, personal 7.6.11
  suspension 1.20
  underperforming
    improvement 2.2.3–2.2.4
    roles of partners, differing 2.2.1
    suitable metrics, selecting 2.2.2

310

partners—*cont.*
  see also **continuing partners; exit routes; incoming partners; management of practice**: managing partner, role of; **outgoing partners; retirement of partners**
partnership
  asset-accruing vehicle, as 2.4.7
  defined 1.5
    statutory definition 1.1
    dissolution of 1.19, 1.22
  termination, consequences of 1.21
  trust, as 2.4.4
  see also **partnerships**
Partnership Act (1890)
  authority, limits of 1.11
  death or retirement of partners 1.19, 2.1.12
  dissolution of partnership 1.22
  holidays 1.13.1
  management of business 1.18
  partnership, statutory definition 1.1
  variations to partnership agreement 1.2
  winding up of partnership 2.1.3
partnership agreement
  absence
    holidays 1.13.1
    illness 1.13.2
    maternity leave/pregnancy 1.13.2
  account books 1.16
  banking 1.16
  capital provision 1.14
  clauses commonly included 1.4
  death of partners 1.19
  dissolution of partnership 1.19, 1.22
  drawings 1.16
  duration of partnership 1.6
  duties of partners 1.10
  expulsion of partners 1.20
  firm name, requirements 1.8
  formal,
    advantages/disadvantages 1.1
  good faith duty 1.3
  goodwill, covenants to protect 1.23
  indemnity clauses 1.16, 1.24
  informal,
    advantages/disadvantages 1.1
  insurance 1.12
  limits of authority 1.11
  management of business 1.18
  nature of business 1.6
  new partners, change in firm members 1.7
  payment out 2.4.1
  pensions 1.17
  place of business 1.9
  profits and losses 1.15
  purpose 1.3
  retirement of partners 1.19
  salaried partners 1.24
  suspension of partners 1.20
  termination of partnership, consequences 1.21
  third party insurance 1.12
  variations 1.2
partnership bank
  defined 1.5
partnership ethic 17.2
Partnership Law (Law Commission Consultation Paper) 2.1.3
partnership mergers
  CGT 18.7.2
  income tax 18.7.1
  VAT 18.7.3

Index

partnerships
  corporate entities, regarded as 17.2
  unsuccessful 17.2
  see also **LLPs (Limited Liability Partnerships)**; **partnership**
payment out
  amount
    calculating 2.4.2
    partnership agreement 2.4.1
      annuities 2.4.5
      goodwill 2.4.3
      interest 2.5.2
      LLPs 2.5.3
    partnership as asset-accruing vehicle 2.4.7
    partnership as 'trust' 2.4.4
    security 2.5.3
    timing 2.5.1
    work-in-progress 2.4.6
pension provisions
  HR strategy 19.7
  mergers, potential problem areas 7.6.6
  partnership agreement 1.17
  property issues 9.3.1
  SIPP Funds 9.2.3
  SSAS (small self-administered scheme) 9.2.3
  taxation 18.3.1
performance related pay 19.6.3
performance reviews
  areas of performance 5.1.2
  bonuses 19.6.3
  carrying out, responsibility for 5.2.1
  development, own, responsibility for 5.1.1
  feedback
    constructive 5.2.9
    giving 5.2.9, 5.2.10
    negative 5.2.9
    receiving 5.2.7
    initial 19.7.11
  Johari window 5.2.8
  listening skills 5.2.4, 5.2.6
  mental preparation 5.2.2
  monitoring of progress 5.2.12
  motivation 15.2.6
  note taking 5.2.5
  organisational structure 5.2.1
  paperwork 5.2.2
  place 5.2.2
  praise 5.2.11
  preparation 5.2.2
  quality control 13.4.10
  questioning skills 5.2.3
  recognition 5.2.11
  senior management 5.1
  'strokes' 5.2.11
  time 5.2.2
  written preparation 5.2.2
performance-related profit sharing 1.15
physiological needs 15.2.3
place of business
  partnership agreement 1.9
planning
  HR strategy 19.2
  management of practice, managing partners, role of and 17.3
  marketing 14.3.3
  strategic business plan 14.2
  pensions 9.2.3
positioning
  brand development 14.3.1
  markets, approach to 17.7
Posner, Barry 15.1.3
practice structures
  bureaucracy 16.1.1
  clients and 4.3, 16.1.2
  control problems 16.1.1
  core service areas 16.1.4
  departmentalisation 16.1.4
  Enron case (US) 16.1

practice structures—*cont.*
  growth phases 16.1.1
  information technology 16.1.5
  LLPs 16.1.5
  management, role of 16.1
  operations, organisation of 16.1.4
  organisation charts 16.1.3
  performance reviews 5.2.1
  quality control 13.4.14
  specialist services 16.1.4
pregnancy
  partnership agreement 1.13.2
premises
  defined 1.5
  mergers, potential problem areas 7.6.3
  old-fashioned building 9.4.6
  over-rented (leasehold property) 9.4.4
PROcost Control Desk (IT application) 10.3
professional indemnity insurance
  accountancy profession, education area 11.1
  acquisitions 11.1
    claims examples
      advice, non-specialist subjects 11.6.3
      bad habits 11.6.1
      blind eye, turning 11.6.2
      complacency 11.6.1
        loss of document cover 11.6.5
        misappropriation of funds 11.6.4
        stock relief draw-back 11.6.3
        subject, failure to understand 11.6.4
  financial services 11.3
  'housekeeping' 11.1
  ICAEA 11.1

Joint Monitoring Unit, introduction of 11.1
  level of cover 11.2
  mergers 11.1
    potential problem areas 7.6.9
  post-retirement obligations 2.6.2
  run-off 11.4
  sale of practice 11.4
  selection of partners 11.1
  succession planning 11.5
  top-up 11.2
profit and loss account preparation
  termination of partnership 1.21
profit sharing
  mergers, potential problem areas 7.6.4
  salaried partners 1.24
profitability
  financial management 12.3
  quality control 13.4.1, 13.5.2
  recoveries and App 1
profits
  current-year assessment basis 18.2.1
  defined 1.5
  leakage of, operating processes 12.3
  overlap 18.2.1
profits and losses
  partnership agreement 1.15
promotion policies
  quality control 13.4.11
  websites 14.3.2
  see also **marketing and promotion**
property issues
  financial management 12.6
  occupier management 9.2.3
  owning/leasing debate 9.1
  partnership agreement 1.14

property issues—*cont.*
  partnership business plans, aims 9.1
  sale and leaseback 9.3.1
  strategies, ownership structures 9.3.1
  tenure, forms of *see* **freehold property; leasehold property**
PSA (Professional Services Applications) 10.3
public relations (PR)
  marketing communications 14.3.4

quality control
  assistance offered by 13.4–13.4.14
  audit documents, standard 13.4.8
  client relations 13.4.12
  clients
    gaining 13.4.3
    retaining 13.4.2
  compliance, beyond 13.5.3
  complying with requirements where firm registered auditor 13.5.1
  effective procedures, establishing and maintaining 13.5–13.5.3
  existing clients, retaining 13.4.2
  external controllers, using, advantages 13.6.1
  fee negotiations 13.4.4
  inefficient practices by partners/managers 13.4.13
  job planning 13.4.9
  letters, responses to 13.4.12
  maintaining 13.7.1
  new clients, gaining 13.4.3
  options covered 13.2
  performance appraisal 13.4.10

  profitability 13.4.1
  promotion policies 13.4.11
  purpose 13.1
  qualities of effective controllers App 2
  questions and answers App 1
  reasons for 13.1
    competent partners and staff 13.3
  recruiting 13.4.5
  staff planning 13.4.9
  standards and profitability, striking balance between 13.5.2
  structure of firm 13.4.14
  succession planning and 13.8
  technical skills and competence 13.4.7
  training 13.4.6
questioning skills
  performance reviews 5.2.3
    clarification of questions 5.2.6

Rankin, David (MD of Tenon Technology) 10.10

recruitment
  HR strategy 19.7.1
    agencies, use of 19.7.5
  quality control 13.4.5
references
  HR strategy 19.7.10
Regulatory Filings
  XBRL 10.10
relevance and value
  websites 14.3.2
rent reviews 9.2.2
repairs and renewals
  leasehold tenure 9.2.2
reports, accounting and business
  XBRL 10.10

retirement of partners
  age, by 2.1.4
    selecting retirement age 2.1.5
  early, on notice 2.1.6
  effective date 2.1.8
  goodwill and 18.4.4
  income tax aspects
    cash basis for professions, withdrawal 18.2.2
    current-year assessment basis 18.2.1
      work-in-progress valuation 18.2.3
  notice period 2.1.7
  partnership agreement 1.19
  post-retirement obligations
    indemnities for continuing partnership debts 2.6.1
  professional indemnity insurance 2.6.2
  tax payments 2.6.3
Reuters
  XBRL 10.10
reviews of performance *see* **performance reviews**
reward structure
  partners 17.8
  staff
    basic salaries 19.6.1
    overtime payments 19.6.2
    performance payments 19.6.3
Rogers, Carl 15.2.3
roll-over relief
  Capital Gains Tax (CGT) 18.5, 18.7.2
run-off
  professional indemnity insurance 11.4
Ryan, Mark 10.4

safety needs 15.2.3

sale and leaseback transactions 9.3.1
  benefits and drawbacks 9.3.2
sale of practice
  professional indemnity insurance 11.4
sales promotion
  marketing communications 14.3.4
SAS 240
  quality control 13.5.1
Schedule D profits
  cash basis, withdrawal of, for professions 18.2.2
  consultancy arrangements and 18.3.3
  work-in-progress valuation 18.2.3
Schedule of Dilapidations
  leasehold strategy 9.4.1
Schedule E
  consultancy arrangements and 18.3.3
  pension provision 18.3.1
self-actualisation, need for 15.2.3
self-invested pension plan (SIPP) 9.2.3
service stream finance 3.6.4
services
  charging for 4.3
services marketing 14.3.3
Shohet, Phil 17.2
Simms, Dan 10.2
SIPP (self-invested pension plan) Fund 9.2.3
SMART (specific, measurable, agreed, realistic and timed) goals 17.3
SMEs (small and medium-sized enterprises)
  client requirements 4.1
  consolidation
    correct climate, creating 8.1

SMEs (small and medium-sized enterprises)—*cont.*
  medium-sized practices, issues facing 8.2.1–8.2.6
  finance sources 3.3
  networking 4.6.5, 4.6.4
  specialists, as 4.6.4
software packages 10.3
SSAS (small self-administered scheme) 9.2.3
staff appraisal 19.5.2

staff introductions
  HR strategy 19.7.7
staff planning
  HR strategy 19.4
  quality control 13.4.9
Star Internet Group 10.9
start ups
  finance sources 3.3
Statements of Practice, mergers
  VAT implications 18.7.2
strategic business plan
  marketing and promotion 14.2
strategic planning
  financial management 12.2
strategies
  brand 14.3.4
  brand development tools 14.3.1
  business plan, strategic 14.2
  contact 14.3.4
  creative 14.3.4
  e-business 14.3.2
  HR *see* **HR strategy**
  leasehold
    Authorised Guarantee Agreement 9.4.3
    declining market 9.4.7
    disposals 9.4.3
    growth/contraction, planning for 9.4.2
    Licence to Assign 9.4.3

    old fashioned building 9.4.6
    over-rented premises 9.4.4
    repair/dilapidations 9.4.1
    short term 9.4.5
  mergers and acquisitions 7.2
  property issues
    leasehold strategies 9.4.1–9.4.7
    ownership structures 9.3.1
structures of practices *see* **practice structures**
subletting
  freehold tenure 9.2.1
  leasehold tenure 9.2.2
succession date
  defined 1.5
succession planning
  freehold tenure and 9.2.1
  HR strategy 19.4
  leasehold tenure 9.2.2
  management 17.11
  professional indemnity insurance 11.5
  quality control 13.8
suspension of partners
  partnership agreement 1.20
SWOT analysis
  marketing and promotion 14.3.3
  planning 17.3
Symantec security package 10.9

taper relief
  Capital Gains Tax (CGT) 18.4.2
targets, financial 12.3
taxation issues
  annuities to retired partners 18.3.2
  bank loans, relief on interest paid 3.4.1
  Capital Gains Tax (CGT)

taxation issues—*cont.*
   basics 18.4.1
   capital-sharing ratio, changes in 18.4.6
     disposal of partnership assets 18.4.3
     distribution of assets in specie 18.4.7
     goodwill 18.4.4
     retirement 18.4.4
     roll-over relief 18.5, 18.7.2
     taper relief 18.4.2
   cash basis, withdrawal of for professions 18.2.2
   consultancy 18.3.3
   current-year assessment basis 18.2.1
   goodwill
     payments by incoming partner 18.4.5
     retirement and 18.4.4
   income tax
     cash basis, withdrawal for professions 18.2.2
     current-year assessment basis 18.2.1
     partnership mergers 18.7.1
     work-in-progress valuation 18.2.3
   inheritance tax 18.5
   meaning of taxation 1.5
   partnership agreement 1.16
   partnership mergers
     CGT 18.7.2
     income tax 18.7.1
     VAT 18.7.3
   pensions 18.3.1
   post-retirement obligations 2.6.3
   retirement provision
     annuities to retired partners 18.3.2
     CGT, and 18.4.4
     consultancy arrangement 18.3.3
     pensions 18.3.1
   stock relief claw-back, liability for 11.6.3
   Value Added Tax (VAT) 18.6
   work-in-progress valuation 18.2.3
   XBRL applications, tax returns 10.10
technical skills
   quality control 13.4.7, App 1
technology
   defined App 1
   impact, HR strategy 19.3
   internet use 19.7.4
Technology Leadership Scorecard 10.6, App 2
test market
   marketing and promotion 14.3.2
third party assurance
   partnership agreement 1.12
this deed
   defined 1.5
time management
   financial management 12.5

training
   HR strategy 19.5.3, 19.7
   quality control 13.4.6
transparency
   leasehold tenure 9.2.2
travel
   websites 14.3.2
'true and fair' basis
   tax calculation 18.2.2, 18.7
trust, partnership as 2.4.4
Turnbull Guidelines
   corporate governance issues 10.9

Value Added Tax (VAT) 18.6

mergers 18.7.3
values
  brand development 14.3.1
voting
  unanimous 1.18.1

websites
  HR strategy 19.7.4
  marketing and promotion 14.3.2
Whole Brain Business Book **(Ned Herrmann)** 15.2
William the Conqueror 15.1.3
work-in-progress (WIP)
  analysing 12.9.2
  booking time 12.9.1
  converting into fees 12.9.4
  fixed-fee tasks 12.9.1
  income tax 18.2.3
  monitoring 12.9.2
  payment out 2.4.6
  unbillable time, recognising 12.9.3
working capital control 12.6

X-Y theory
  Douglas Macgregor 15.2.3
XBRL (extensible business reporting language) 10.10